Edward A. Filene
1860–1937

SPEAKING OF CHANGE

A Selection of Speeches and Articles

by

EDWARD A. FILENE

Published by Former Associates of Edward A. Filene

NEW YORK

1939

Printed in the United States of America by
Kingsport Press, Inc. Kingsport, Tennessee

Edward A. Filene was generally recognized, even by those who disagreed with him, as an important influence not only in the economic but in the political, social and spiritual thought of the period of human history in which he lived.

It must be many years, however, before the real contribution of his long and useful life of public service can be adequately appraised.

For Mr. Filene was always looking ahead—discussing events of the day and attitudes of the day not in terms of any hypothetical "existing situation," but with a profound conviction that "nothing is situated," and all things must be judged, therefore, not according to any absolute formulas, but in their relation to the ever changing times.

Mr. Filene himself chose the title of this book, when its publication was first projected in 1937. He also selected its contents from his more recent speeches and articles. The publication of the book, however, was suspended upon Mr. Filene's death in Paris in September 1937, in the course of one of his summer study tours of European conditions.

In the fall of 1938 Mr. Filene's friends and former associates decided to publish the manuscript as one of the living memorials of his unique mind. It appears now, in form, title and content, exactly as Mr. Filene planned it, except for the foreword and biographical material which have been added.

FOREWORD*

My first ambition as a boy was the usual one—I wanted to keep a candy store. When I became older and found that there was a stomach-ache in too much candy I changed my ambition, and an engineer operating a railroad engine seemed a god worthy of imitation. Next I wanted to be a conqueror—to ride on a big black horse with nodding plumes and go out into battle with a sharp flashing sword, cut off four heads at one time and come back riding through streets with the assembled multitudes waving flags and acclaiming me as a hero and strewing roses in my path.

But there came a day when I realized that to ride back from battle on a big black horse along a rose-strewn road, having killed men and left their families to suffer from want and starvation, also had an ache in it.

So childish days went, and with my adolescence came an ambition to be useful, to study and make myself a learned man, and although I was working in a store until nine o'clock every night (and Saturday was the only night I did not work until nine, because I worked then until one o'clock on Sunday morning), I managed to prepare myself to enter Harvard. And then after all I couldn't go because my father was sick with heart trouble, and I had to look after things. I remember my disappointment and how ill-used I felt myself to be when I could not go to Harvard. I thought that I should never now be a learned man, never be a very useful one, without this Harvard education.

Instead I began to study subjects with which my work brought me into contact in a practical way—that is, subjects that would correct or amplify the theories I was applying to the problems of my business. But this was not done in schools, nor was it con-

* A statement found among some old papers, after Mr. Filene's death.

fined to nights, Sundays and holidays. I found myself studying daily and hourly in my store, where I considered in turn as they arose industrial and banking questions, labor relations and other similar business and economic subjects. I found that those investigations were all helping me to see the road I was travelling and the direction I ought to go. I gradually came to understand that the intelligent running of a store was a very good substitute for a college. After a while I became reconciled to my lot.

I think shopkeeping is like sin—first you endure and then you embrace it. I found out that although one may not become as learned in shopkeeping as by going through Harvard University, one may become wiser than some of the men who go through Harvard, if wisdom means having the things you know or have learned permeated with love and sympathy and understanding for your fellow men.

And so I have not achieved my boyhood ambitions. I have grown-up ambitions now and although I have not yet achieved those either, I have gotten into a work which is a daily post-graduate course and which makes me study as hard as or harder than ever before, and which gives me the hope that even if I do not become learned before I die, I shall at least from year to year be likely to know more and perhaps be more useful. And that, I think, is an ambition which it is worth while to try to satisfy. I would not change this, even if I could, for the engine cab or the big black horse.

Table of Contents

PAGE

FOREWORD v

INTRODUCTION—"THERE AIN'T NO SUCH PERSON" xi

RELIGION AND DISTRIBUTION 1
Address at dinner of The Synod of New York of the Presbyterian Church in the United States of America, Towers Hotel, Brooklyn, N. Y.—October 21, 1936.

THE CONTRIBUTION OF OUR SECONDARY SCHOOLS TO BETTER BUSINESS AND INDUSTRIAL CONDITIONS 15
Address at Convocation of The University of the State of New York Celebrating the Tercentenary of Secondary Education in America, State Education Building, Albany, N. Y.—October 17, 1935.

UNLEARNING BUSINESS 32
Address before the School of Business Administration of The University of Buffalo, Buffalo, N. Y.—December 9, 1936.

ON THE EVE OF THE ELECTION 45
Address delivered at 11:30 P.M., Monday, November 2, 1936, over a nation-wide hookup of both the National Broadcasting and Columbia Broadcasting Systems, as part of the final rally of the campaign to re-elect President Franklin D. Roosevelt.

CAPITALISM AND THE CONSUMER CO-OPERATIVES 51
Address at conference of the International Association of Sales Executives, Hotel Biltmore, New York, N. Y.—April 3, 1936.

OUR PRESIDENT AND OUR NEWSPAPERS 60
Address over a national hookup of the Columbia Broadcasting System—December 21, 1935.

YOUTH AND OUR ECONOMIC SUPERSTITIONS 66
Address before Tenth Annual Congress of the National Student Federation of America, Parker House, Boston, Mass.—December 29, 1934.

WHAT'S NEXT IN ADVERTISING? 77
Address at Annual Convention of the First District of The Advertising Federation of America, Hotel Garde, New Haven, Conn.—November 9, 1934.

THE NEW RELATIONS BETWEEN BUSINESS AND GOVERNMENT . 88
Address before The American Academy of Political and Social Science, Bellevue-Stratford Hotel, Philadelphia, Pa.—January 5, 1934.

PAGE

BUSINESS AND THE WAGE PROBLEM 100
Address before the Commonwealth Club, Fairmont Hotel, San Francisco, Cal.—February 6, 1935.

THE A. B. C. OF THE NEW DEAL 110
Address before the Providence Chamber of Commerce and Brown University, at Brown University, Providence, R. I.—May 23, 1934.

LEADERSHIP IN THESE NEW TIMES 125
Address before Graduate Students of the Massachusetts Institute of Technology, Cambridge, Mass.—April 14, 1937.

THE AMERICAN WAY OF RECOVERY 137
Address before the Pittsburgh Community Forum, Carnegie Institute, Pittsburgh, Pa.—November 21, 1934.

GEORGE WASHINGTON AND FINANCIAL LIBERTY 151
Address before the California Credit Union League, Hotel Sacramento, Sacramento, Cal.—February 22, 1936.

STREAMLINING BUSINESS 161
Radio address from Station KEX, Portland, Ore.—August 24, 1934.

EDUCATION FOR THIS NEW TIME 167
Radio address from Station W1XAL, University Club, Boston, Mass.—April 18, 1935.

PROTECTING THE TAXPAYER 173
A broadcast in a series on YOU AND YOUR GOVERNMENT, presented by the Committee on Civic Education by Radio of the National Advisory Council on Radio in Education and the American Political Science Association, in co-operation with the National Municipal League, over a nation-wide network of the National Broadcasting Company from Station WEEI, Boston, Mass.—January 8, 1935.

MORALS IN BUSINESS 178
A Weinstock Lecture at the University of California, Berkeley, Cal.—February 7, 1934.

BUSINESS AND RELIGION 197
Address delivered to a gathering of ministers and laymen from various churches invited by the Laymen's Committee (non-sectarian) for the Federal Council of Churches, at the Harvard Club, New York, N. Y.—November 15, 1929.

DO WE NEED A LEADER? 217
Campaign talk delivered over a nation-wide hookup of the Columbia Broadcasting System from Station WABC, New York, N. Y.—October 2, 1936.

EPOCH-MARKING CHANGES IN BUSINESS TODAY 223
Address before the College of Commerce and Business Administration of Tulane University, New Orleans, La.—June 11, 1935.

A MERCHANT SURVEYS THE NEW DEAL 234
Radio address over N. B. C. Network—June 22, 1934.

THE CONSTITUTION AND ECONOMIC CHANGE 246
Address before the National Conference for Clarifying the Constitution by Amendment, held under the auspices of the Michigan Committee, Hotel Statler, Detroit, Mich.—February 1, 1937.

PAGE

WHOSE SUPREME COURT? 253
Broadcast over a nation-wide hookup of the Columbia Broadcasting System—April 28, 1937.

AN OPEN LETTER TO THE PRESIDENT AND DIRECTORS OF THE UNITED STATES CHAMBER OF COMMERCE 259
May 23, 1936.

THE NEW DEAL AND THE NEW TIMES 264
Address at the Roosevelt Rally held under the auspices of the Progressive National Committee, Carnegie Hall, New York, N. Y.—October 28, 1936.

WHY WE MUST MAKE HIGHER WAGES COMPULSORY. . . . 275
Statement issued during the 1936 campaign to re-elect President Franklin D. Roosevelt.

EDUCATION IN THIS NEW AGE 281
Address before the Department of Superintendence of the National Education Association, Cleveland, O.—February 28, 1934.

MASS PROSPERITY AND MEDICAL CARE—A BUSINESS MAN'S VIEWPOINT 294
A broadcast in a series on DOCTORS, DOLLARS, and DISEASE, presented by the National Advisory Council on Radio in Education, over a nation-wide network of the Columbia Broadcasting System—December 3, 1934.

THE NEW DEAL AND AMERICAN DEMOCRACY 300
Address before the Board of Trade and Rotary Club at a joint meeting in Vancouver, B. C.—August 28, 1934.

HOW TO MAKE THE MOST OF LIFE 315
Address over a nation-wide hookup of the National Broadcasting Company in co-operation with the Office of Education of the United States Department of the Interior on the occasion of the First National School Assembly Program—May 14, 1937.

WHAT RELIGION MEANS TO ME 320
Contribution to widely-syndicated symposium on "Religion—Today and Tomorrow," published May 26, 1934.

EDWARD A. FILENE 324
Facsimile from "Who's Who in America."

"There Ain't No Such Person" *

An Inquiry into the Meaning of Edward A. Filene

Someone has observed that it takes all kinds of persons to make a world. I am convinced that that isn't the whole truth. In the making of this modern world, at least, it also takes Edward A. Filene.

I have worked with Edward A. Filene, off and on, for many years; and I rise to state that he is not a kind of a person. He is ever so many kinds, all mutually exclusive. I have heard on supposedly unimpeachable authority that Lincoln Steffens is supervising the writing of his biography. I don't believe it. It can't be done. I've tried it and I know. Filene is a cosmic force. He is an influence in social evolution. One cannot write a biography of radioactivity or of permutation, even if they do remind one at times of somebody one has met.

The Filene influence was never greater in America than it is today; but few yet realize the extent of that influence or, in fact, just what the influence is. It is not the kind of influence exerted by a Roosevelt, for under no conditions would he ever accept any public office. Nor is it the kind exerted by Henry Ford who succeeded in abolishing the America he loved and is now preserving in a museum. Filene is, to be sure, president of a large and successful business; but the Filene store is not now radically dif-

* This article, hitherto unpublished, was written early in 1934, while Mr. Filene was still actively in the midst of his career, by an associate who worked with him for a number of years. Its inclusion was not contemplated in plans which were made for publication of this book before Mr. Filene's death. Afterwards, it seemed that its brief picture of the author of the speeches might be of interest to readers, and it has therefore been added to the volume in the form in which it was originally written, in spite of the passage of time and the changes that have taken place since 1934. (See also NOTE on page xxv.)

ferent from many other great American department stores, and Edward A. Filene does not at present admire it overmuch.

For want of a better characterization, the newspapers frequently refer to him as "the well-known merchant and philanthropist." But there is a catch in that. Possibly Steffens knows him, because Steffens knows everybody; but otherwise, as all who have been most closely associated with him will testify, Edward A. Filene is *x*. And he is not a philanthropist. There is even a question as to whether he is as much a merchant as he is an extraordinary merchandising genius.

It will not be questioned, however, that it was his genius which built up the store known as Wm. Filene's Sons Company. While William Filene is a name of honored memory, it was not until this dynamic son took charge that those sensational innovations were adopted by which the store fairly rocketed to fame and fortune, becoming *the* largest store of its kind in the world. But these innovations, while some of them are still intact, are no longer innovations. They are features, rather, which have been adopted in time by many other most successful stores.

Those who now control Filene's may be able enough merchants; but there is a vast difference between an able merchant and a merchandising genius. Able merchants who are good executives are much easier to work with. Geniuses are likely to be geniuses at finding things which must be done. They never rest. They do not grow old and retire from activity. Incidentally, they do not allow others to rest, although the others do sometimes age very rapidly.

Edward A. Filene is often hailed as a seer. He is. He probably sees more things that are hidden to the rest of us than any other business leader of our time—especially things which require immediate action. It is this quality which captivates thousands of people when they meet him first—especially serious young people who long to do great things instead of burying themselves in the world's routine. Others may counsel caution and urge them not to attempt too much; but Filene, although he is a great stickler for following facts instead of feelings, discloses facts which encourage them to even greater hope and daring.

Although not a polished speaker, and not even a good speaker by any accepted standards, this little "shopkeeper," without any background of academic education, has frequently set great audiences, especially of university undergraduates, on fire. Yet he doesn't preach or exhort. He does it by talking business, in terms of changes now in progress, and unveiling for them the "better world" which must inevitably arrive when those in control of business once act upon the business facts.

And it is this same quality—this ability to see the things that need to be done—which accounts for almost all the things which Edward A. Filene is *not*.

It is not only in the Filene store that the founder and inspirer is seemingly shelved. The same interesting phenomenon can be noted in connection with a great number of enterprises launched by Edward A. Filene.

Boston has a large and thriving Chamber of Commerce. Edward A. Filene is a member, but inquiry will disclose that he is neither a prominent nor a very popular member. He was merely responsible for its reorganization along progressive lines—the man whose vision, and whose ability to goad people into action in line with his vision, made it a more successful enterprise.

The United States Chamber of Commerce is surely an impressive body. Edward A. Filene is a member of that, too, but not the most popular member. In the 1934 annual session of the Chamber, Filene, who had something special on his mind, was not given time to speak. There was nothing personal in this ban. It was simply that he had a proposal to make, with which almost no one wanted to be bothered. It was his contention that the structure of business in America had undergone a number of almost revolutionary changes, and that the form of organization of the Chamber of Commerce was perhaps not well adapted to cope with the new conditions; so he wanted a committee appointed to study the present conditions, and, if it seemed advisable, to propose changes in the form of organization, to be submitted for discussion at some future meeting.

Not a very radical proposal, to be sure, but nevertheless troublesome. For things were running smoothly in the United

States Chamber of Commerce, even if they were running none too smoothly in American business generally. Everybody in charge, at least, was perfectly satisfied with the existing form of organization. It had taken years of hard work to start the Chamber in the first place—back in 1912. Two previous efforts had failed; but on the insistence of somebody, who not only gave his own time, energy and money to the task, but goaded all concerned to do the same, the job had finally been completed and the United States Chamber of Commerce became a great success. It might be admitted, to be sure, that that *somebody* was Edward A. Filene, and the Chamber, if asked, would probably erect a tablet to his memory. But Filene doesn't want tablets. He wants big jobs done; and when a big job is done, instead of sitting down and enjoying the results, he wants all hands to get busy on some bigger job. Like other cosmic forces, Edward A. Filene never knows when to stop.

People, on the other hand, like to stop occasionally—even ambitious, inspired, enthusiastic young people who are eager as can be to get things done. They may not wear out. They may not entirely lose their enthusiasms, and they may remain earnest and forward looking persons. But after they have completed a job, they do want time to stretch; and they want to congratulate themselves, and be congratulated, for the job they did. If they look to Edward A. Filene, however, for such congratulations, they will look in vain. Not that he isn't appreciative. He is so appreciative of hard workers that he always finds still harder work for them to do; and his mind is so busy with things that need doing that it simply cannot dwell on past performances.

It isn't true that Edward A. Filene frequently quarrels with his associates. Such impersonal forces do not quarrel, and quarreling with him is like quarreling with the weather. People may get very angry at the weather, but the weather doesn't get angry. It only seems to. It has, to be sure, many different phases, which are miscalled moods. Sometimes we find it pleasing and we call it kind. Often we find it highly stimulating. But heat burns and frost bites; and so, at times, does he. As for being satisfied, and deciding not to inaugurate any further changes—

if one can succeed in selling the weather on such a policy, he might then try it on Edward A. Filene.

Filene, I have said, is not a philanthropist, at least not in the sense in which he is supposed to be. In a way, he seems to love humanity. At least, he sits up nights thinking out plans by which humanity may be benefited. But generally speaking, this love for humanity does not extend to concrete specimens of *genus homo*. He has given millions, all told, to prevent human suffering; but let the hat be passed in behalf of any organized charity and his response cannot always be counted upon, although "off the record" there are many stories of thoughtful gifts and timely helps both to friends and to entire strangers.

In his work for humanity, apparently, he cannot stop to consider people. It is doubtful if any prominent American has more ex-secretaries. After they have quit their jobs, they frequently become friendly—for no one can work with "E. A." and not get loads and loads of experience; but on the job, no matter what the pay and how inspiring the contacts, there is not a moment's ease. He goads others as he goads himself; which, one ex-secretary observed, is his idea of the *goadin' rule*. Even in the matter of pay, although Edward A. Filene is one of the world's outstanding exponents of the theory of high wages, he never voluntarily raises any subordinate's salary for the purpose of effecting a more friendly attitude toward himself. To him, that would look like bribery and special consideration; and he doesn't want that—he wants general betterment. In case after case, he has raised the salaries of subordinates, but only after he has irritated them to a point that the raise, while still acceptable, does not inspire pleasant thoughts.

Filene himself makes no pretense of generosity. His reason, he insists, for doing everything he does, is purely selfish. He believes in business for profit; and he is called a social idealist, he thinks, only because he is misunderstood by both social idealists and business men. If the social idealists had their way, he thinks, they would not only ruin business but ruin human society; whereas if business would only act upon the facts of business, and seek its profits in a truly scientific way, business would be more profitable than ever and all the things which the social idealists long for would be more than realized.

Filene activities, however, while they may seem to him to be purely business activities, seem anything but that to millions of Americans. The labor unions, for instance, have found in him a "staunch and loyal friend"; but Filene has not promoted labor unionism out of sympathy for the downtrodden worker (at least, this is what he says), but because the high wages and more leisure which the unions fight for are business necessities in a country which is so increasing its production that, in the absence of more mass buying power and more leisure in which the masses may consume these products, business will surely find itself without a profitable market.

Recently, he has been broadcasting by radio, to the extreme irritation of many business leaders, that labor must be organized nationally and that the company union will not do. Much as this pleases the average labor unionist, however, he has not been doing it for their pleasure at all. To provide adequate mass buying power, he says, and to keep business from perishing, business must be co-ordinated under business codes and *wages must be removed from competition.* That means that the chiseler must go. If the New Deal is to be successful, every business must live up to the code; and the best guarantee that business can have that every business *is* living up to its code is a labor union organized on national lines, which cannot be owned and controlled by the man who owns the business.

In many American cities, in recent years, medical clinics have been organized to meet the needs of masses of people of small income who were too self-respecting to accept charity and yet to whom the cost of adequate medical care had become an almost unbearable burden. This movement has been so pronounced that the whole medical profession is now in the throes of an acute controversy between the advocates of social medicine and the champions of the old-style family doctor. Whatever one thinks of this, all will admit that it is a movement of vital importance to the whole nation. It was an idea Edward A. Filene approved and pushed with unremitting energy. He spent a small fortune in fighting for it. But not at all in the interest of the poor sufferers who could not afford adequate medical attention. He did it, he insists, in the interest of business and in the glorious cause of greater total profits.

Money spent for one thing, he observed, cannot be spent for another; and the family of limited means which has to pay more than necessary for medical care will almost certainly pay less than otherwise for other services and for goods offered for sale by merchants. So he studied the cost of medical care, and, through the Twentieth Century Fund, which disposes of the greater part of his annual income, co-operated in organizing the first Committee on the Cost of Medical Care. It is on the findings of this Committee that the new movement is based. It is not claimed that the family doctor's fees are too high, or that his income is too large. Filene insists that the average doctor's income is altogether too small; and he wants to see it doubled or trebled—so that physicians generally will be able to buy more goods. The whole trouble, as Filene sees it, is that, because of the high charges, the masses do not purchase medical care until they have to; and while the care which is given to those who are seriously ill is necessarily expensive, it doesn't do as much good as a little inexpensive attention would have done before they got so sick. He wants the doctors to organize, then, not merely to attend the sick but to keep the masses from getting sick. The family doctor, he says, working independently, cannot do this; so he sends his rich patients to specialists and does the best he can for the others. But if diagnosticians and specialists are organized in one social clinic, charging regular monthly fees for sick and well alike, the fees could be small, the service could be as good as the wealthiest now receive and the income of the average doctor would be far greater than it is.

Few doctors could follow such reasoning. The few who did follow it, however, succeeded, and the organization of low-cost health clinics is now making real progress.

Filene never thinks of himself as a success. Evolution, doubtless, has an inferiority complex too—there are so many things to be done which haven't been half done yet. From another standpoint, however, both have been mighty successful.

More than a quarter of a century ago, for instance, Edward A. Filene reached the conclusion that American finance must be democratized, but nobody but he knew what he meant. People either had money or they didn't; and if they had more than they cared to spend they loaned it out at interest, on well-recognized security, thus accumulating still more money. That, as everybody understood, was finance. One might feel sorry for those who had no money, but what could anybody do about it? And how could such cruel facts be democratized?

Filene didn't feel sorry. Nevertheless, he founded the Credit Union movement in the United States; and in the credit unions, people who had almost no money and needed loans desperately, began to save their small sums collectively and to borrow from their collective selves and to pay interest to themselves on all the sums they borrowed. They had no security which the banks would recognize as security, and the laws of the various states did not recognize their unions as banks. But the experiment worked. All that was necessary, it seemed, was to change the banking laws of all the states and of the nation, and make the masses of the people acquainted with this type of co-operative credit, and then we would have a real object lesson in the democratization of finance. This has cost Edward A. Filene, all told, something over a million dollars, for which he has never either sought or received a penny in return. But don't imagine that there was anything philanthropic about it; for Filene is a selfish business man, who just happened to notice sooner than most that the prosperity of every business depended upon the prosperity of all legitimate business, and that the prosperity of all business depended upon adequate financing of the masses who directly or indirectly make its markets.

In the winter of 1932-33, before the nation had got over its first thrill of the New Deal, Filene made an extensive tour of America. In city after city, to his utter amazement, he was given the sort of ovation usually reserved for presidents or presidential candidates. It was a spontaneous ovation on the part of thousands of adoring credit unionists. For the laws of thirty-eight states and the District of Columbia had now recognized the credit unions as legitimate banks; and although thousands of banks all over America had closed their doors, the credit unions had uniformly weathered the depression, and credit unionism was experiencing its greatest era of expansion. Since then, thanks largely to the devoted work of Roy F. Bergengren, Congress has likewise passed a national credit union bill, President Roosevelt signed it, and new credit unions are now being organized as rapidly as the organizers of the Credit Union National Extension Bureau, financed by Filene, can answer the calls upon their time. But Edward A. Filene, instead of pausing for congratulations, is goading all concerned to renewed efforts to meet the rapidly changing economic conditions, and warning the credit unions of the necessity of the "next step forward."

Leading bankers, incidentally, have long since withdrawn their opposition to credit unionism. It isn't Filene's idea that the credit unions shall supplant the banks, but that finance generally shall operate according to the principles which the credit unions have proved to be most successful. Particularly that the borrower and lender have a common interest, that loans find their just rights in the financial betterment of the people to whom the loans are made, and that money loaned for purposes which do not actually tend to enrich the borrower, or upon terms which the borrower cannot successfully meet, must eventually be lost.

These are but a few of the Filene projects which have given this admittedly selfish millionaire a national and international reputation as a philanthropist. One might ask why, if he is selfish, does he give his money away. But Filene has an answer for that. He believes in following the facts, he says, and the facts indicate that he cannot take it with him. He never married. He says it is because he is superstitious and he asked her twelve times and she said "No." To one observer, at least, it seems more likely that he could never get his mind fixed on anything quite so special and personal as marriage. So he, like other cosmic forces, remains universal. He has no heirs or any special friends to whom he would care to leave his fortune. He would rather use it, while he is alive, in doing things which simply must be done; and if there is any left over, he expects to leave most of it to the Twentieth Century Fund.

He refused to call it the Filene Fund. That struck him as altogether too personal. He refused, even, to direct the Fund, which he created in 1919 to make possible the wisest use of his fortune for the common good. It was his way, rather, to assemble a body of seven directors, each of whom, including himself, should have but one vote as to how his money shall be spent; but they do say that he goads the others considerably as to the necessity for doing this and that. By common consent, however, this money is not spent for charity. There are many funds which can be tapped for such projects, but little money anywhere available for the prevention of economic distress. So the Twentieth Century Fund, to date, has mostly gone in for fact-finding, and making these facts work for the greater prosperity and happiness of all our people. Its study of our internal debts, and its careful distinction between those which were economically payable and those which were actually dead, although not yet written off the books, is one example. Then there was the study of stock exchanges which made its timely appearance just as Congress was beginning to grapple with the problem; also its study of "How to Budget Health," which reviewed the work done and to be done in lowering the cost of medical care. A list of the Fund's activities would constitute an article in itself.

The Filene influence, however, is by no means confined to the Fund, nor to other financial contributions. Many private fortunes have been made because of a tip given by Edward A. Filene. Not once has he speculated in stocks or advised others so to speculate. His business tips are invariably of a different kind. He has tipped business men, rather, as to how some great service can be done, particularly through reorganizing their businesses on a low-price, high-wage, mass production basis. I do not feel free to cite any particular case; but millions of Americans have contributed to some of these fortunes, not by paying higher prices for what they buy, but through getting better values for their money than they were ever able to get before.

The postwar period was noted, among other things, as a period of foreign travel on the part of Americans. Before the war, if an American went abroad, he had to pay out a lot of money for first or second-class passage or else go steerage; and few could do one and not many cared to do the other. Suddenly, however, "Tourist Third" appeared, and hundreds of thousands took advantage of it. They didn't thank Edward A. Filene, and they needn't, for he didn't do it in their interest at all. He did it in the interest of American prosperity.

No, he didn't own or control a single boat. But he saw Europe in distress, without money to pay for American goods. If we were to sell to Europeans to any advantage, some arrangements would have to be made by which Europeans could sell to Americans; and if they could sell to hundreds of thousands of American tourists annually, that would help. The restriction of immigration meanwhile had ruined the once profitable steerage business. The answer, as Filene saw it, was a really good passage both ways at something approaching steerage rates. So he took the proposal to the steamship companies, with figures indicating the profits they might make. Then he kept after them and goaded them into trying the experiment. That's Edward A. Filene.

His money, however, does count. It counts directly, and it gives him prestige. If he hadn't been successful, he would surely be looked upon as just another dreamer. He might suggest things, but he could hardly get much action. It is worth noting, then, just where his money comes from. A substantial part of it comes from the Automatic Bargain Basement.

That Basement is the great feature of Wm. Filene's Sons Company. It is thronged daily, in good times and bad, and it is not only profitable, but so profitable that it often makes the whole store profitable even when great losses show up on other floors. Although Edward A. Filene does not control the store, no one in control would think of discontinuing that Automatic Bargain Basement, and it was distinctly an Edward A. Filene idea.

There was a time, not many years ago, when no one but Edward A. Filene had any idea that it would work. He was in control when he had the idea, but he was not autocratic in putting it across. He just goaded his associates until they did give it a trial.

Many big stores had bargain basements; but this was different. In the first place, it would contain nothing but bargains. It would not be organized to deal in left-overs from the floors above. It would ransack the world for stocks which could be sold at bargain figures, and there would be no large mark-up from which to retreat if the goods didn't happen to sell. Nevertheless, if they didn't sell within twelve days, prices would automatically be cut twenty-five per cent; if they didn't sell in eighteen days, prices would be reduced fifty per cent; and if they didn't sell in twenty-four days, prices would automatically be cut seventy-five per cent; and if they didn't sell in thirty days, they would be given to charity—not because Edward A. Filene believed in charity, but because he had begun to conceive of a store as a place in which to sell goods, not as a place in which to carry goods which would not sell.

It didn't sound reasonable; and it wouldn't be practical even now, if it weren't for the crowds—the masses of people, rich, poor and average—who keep thronging the Basement. But this dealing with the masses and counting on the masses is, as Edward A. Filene sees it, the basic principle of modern business; and it is the business of business to organize business so that the masses can and will buy.

Mass production, he says, *is* production for the masses. He doesn't say it *ought* to be. He is just a calm, detached, unfeeling fact-finder, who has discovered that it can't be anything else. If the masses do not get the products of mass production, no matter how high a standard of living will be necessary if they do get it, this most economical form of production must be discontinued; and not only the masses but business must suffer depression. It is the business of business, then, in its own selfish interest, to serve the masses as abundantly as the masses can possibly be served.

That Automatic Bargain Basement, then, however successful

it may seem to be, is just one little detail to Edward A. Filene. He does insist that a natural law which works in a cellar will in all probability work on higher floors; hence any store which he controlled would be a high-value-for-the-masses Bargain Store. But it would be more than that. It would be a store of "Parent Service"—a store in which every salesperson would be asked not to use any arts to induce people to buy the things which happen to be in stock, but to treat every customer as one would treat his or her own parents if they came to buy, and to point out not only the selling points, but the less desirable qualities of everything offered for sale.

In this way, he knows, a store may fail to get rid of certain goods, but it will also not get rid of certain customers. Better give away the goods to charity, he says, than to give away one's customers to some competitor. Customers who always get what they want at the lowest possible prices will be regular customers. As for goods left on the shelves, he says, the store's buyer will then know enough not to restock with that grade of goods; whereas if the goods are palmed off on the public by smooth salesmanship, he will have nothing to guide him and he will "reload the store with more ammunition with which to drive more customers away."

It is rumored that Edward A. Filene, not content with being president of a store over which he does not preside, is about to launch the most sensational merchandising innovation of his career. No one knows—for we know little more about him yet than we do about the sun spots; but he has been pointing out, for some time now, that a certain kind of store must be launched. Not a mere department store, for a department store's market is limited to one locality; and not a mere chain store, for chain stores do not permit their customers to do all their shopping under one roof. This store which has to be started, then, would be both. It would be a chain of department stores, and each store would be not merely a store of many departments but of many units of different but co-ordinated chains. It would be a store, however, not a storehouse. It would not exist for the purpose of keeping things in stock, but for getting rid of them as rapidly as they can be carried in. It will be run strictly for profit; nevertheless, it will be run strictly for the service of the masses, because only the masses can furnish a market adequate for mass production, and only mass distribution can guarantee the greatest total profits.

Many a social idealist is now agitating for the elimination, or at least the curbing, of the profit motive, and the substitution of the motive of social service. Strangely, such people seem drawn to Edward A. Filene, but Filene doesn't live in their world at all. It is human nature, as he sees it, to want profits, and we might as well try to amend the laws of gravitation as to try to change human nature. All he aims at is the harnessing of the profit motive, so that more profits will roll in, and that these "more profits" will be better distributed to the masses. This means, he has discovered, that every business individually and all businesses collectively, to be most profitable, must be organized to provide the greatest possible service to the masses of the population.

Perhaps that is why *all* the Filene projects succeed. That is a strange statement, but it is true. If Edward A. Filene starts anything, it invariably goes through, and all concerned seem to be satisfied with the results excepting Edward A. Filene. He, to be sure, is never satisfied; for by the time any necessary steps have actually been taken, it becomes urgently necessary to take still further steps, which leaves him in about the same uncomfortable position that he was in to start with.

Edward A. Filene sees what has to be done; and if anything has to be done, there is reason to believe that it will be done. Filene is strongly supporting the Administration. He has been pointing out the necessity of going much further than intended in the directions which have caused the most criticism. We may just about bank upon it, then, that the New Deal will go through, plus nation-wide unemployment insurance, health insurance, old-age insurance, and a lot of other necessary features; and everybody will be economically more secure and more amply supplied with buying power. It will be a better world, finer than anyone has yet dreamed of living in; but it will contain one lonely, discontented pioneer. Edward A. Filene will be disagreeably pointing to the things that still need to be done, and he won't even be invited to the celebration.

NOTE

The foregoing makes no pretense of including all of Mr. Filene's interests and accomplishments. It omits his work as one of the organizers of the Public Franchise League of Boston, which rendered valuable services in bettering local transportation and securing cheaper gas and electric rates in Massachusetts. His success, with James J. Storrow, in founding the Boston City Club as a center to give men of all types, races, creeds and opinions a meeting ground for the exchange of their points of view on important current questions is not touched on. His work with the Metropolitan Planning Commission of Boston and for the "Boston-1915" movement—a movement which Mr. Filene originated and which was a pioneer of its kind in scientific city planning—are further unincluded examples of his deep interest in his city.

Nor does the article make mention of Mr. Filene's services for the N.R.A. as Chairman of the Massachusetts State Recovery Board, nor of the help either in personal effort or money or both which he gave to such organizations as the American Association for Labor Legislation, the American Academy of Political and Social Science, the National Council of Commerce, the Stable Money Association, the National Economic League, the National Student Federation, the National League of Women Voters, and many others.

Internationally, Mr. Filene was for many years actively identified with the work of the International Congress of the Chambers of Commerce, and as Vice-President of the Congress was personally responsible for bringing the organization to the United States for its meeting in Boston in 1912. In 1919 it was again his leadership and persistence which played so large and important a part in the founding of the present International Chamber of Commerce. Mr. Filene's interest in international matters further led to what was perhaps the most unique of his many accomplishments—his invention and development of his "Simultaneous Translator," by means of which it is now possible to make available the translations of a speech or conversation to listeners in any desired language simultaneously with the delivery of the original speech or conversation. (See illustration, opposite page 250.) During the World War, Mr. Filene not only acted in important nonofficial capacities at home and abroad in the interests of world peace, but he was Chairman of the War Shipping Committee of the United States Chamber of Commerce, and Chairman of its Committee for Financing the War. He was a member of Ambassador Herrick's War Advisory Committee in Paris, and a member of the Finance Committee for the Relief of Americans in Paris at the time war was declared. He served on the Executive Board and was Chairman of the Finance Committee and a generous contributor to the work of the League to Enforce Peace. To further world peace and understanding, Mr. Filene also organized and heavily financed in Great Britain, France, Germany and Italy extensive European Peace Prize contests, which had as their object getting the average "man on the street" to think constructively about peace problems.

A list of the books Mr. Filene wrote, the degrees and decorations bestowed upon him by universities and foreign governments, and further details of his varied activities will be found in the facsimile of his "Who's Who" reproduced on page 324.

Mr. Filene's local, national and international work continued actively and unremittingly until the week of his death in his 78th year.

THE EDITORS.

SPEAKING OF CHANGE

Religion and Distribution *

I am a shopkeeper, not a theologian; and it was my intention in coming here, not to talk religion but to talk shop: that is, to discuss certain developments in the realm of distribution which are bound to affect the welfare of the people generally.

But I am embarrassed. For the time has come when we can't keep religion out of the problems of distribution; and incompetent as I may be to discuss the subject, I must do the best I can.

I wonder if any of you religious leaders have ever suffered a somewhat similar embarrassment.

Has it ever occurred to you, as you have observed poverty in the midst of plenty, that you must cry out against the injustice of it all?

And then, I wonder, has one of us business men reminded you that it was not your place, as a spiritual leader, to meddle in business problems?

Have we told you to confine yourself to the dispensation of spiritual comforts and leave the distribution of material things to us?

Well—that formula, if it ever was any good, is good no longer. We distributors may know nothing about religion, and you religious leaders may know nothing about distribution. But ignorance of the law is no defense against its penalties. Religion can no longer go one way while distribution goes another. For religion, as it is usually taught, is service to God, and distribution is service to mankind; and every effort to keep these services separate must result in failure.

I do not mean to charge organized religion with failure. I

* Address at dinner of The Synod of New York of the Presbyterian Church in the United States of America, Towers Hotel, Brooklyn, New York—October 21, 1936.

don't think I need to express any opinion as to its achievements or its lack of achievement. I think I can safely leave the decision on that point to you.

But organized business obviously has failed. We have failed in a way which does not permit us to shift the responsibility upon anybody else. For we at least have had things very much our own way. We have told the church to keep out of our affairs; and the church, in the main, has kept out. We have also given orders to the schools and colleges not to teach doctrines upsetting to our business customs; and they, in the main, have obeyed. Finally, we have told the Government to keep its hands off; and it was something very new and shocking to our business minds that the Government at last developed signs of insubordination.

But what came out of all this business domination? The answer is: Failure—blind, stupid failure—material and spiritual failure.

There were, to be sure, periods of prosperity. We grew the largest crop of millionaires in human history—and the largest crop of gangsters, cutthroats and murderers in any modern civilization. Eventually we became so dizzy with corruption, graft and greed that many sincere churchmen actually welcomed what they called the sobering influences of the depression, although it meant millions threatened with starvation in the midst of plenty.

And now, apparently, we are on our way back to prosperity once more. But what kind of prosperity? That is the biggest problem which any of us has to face today; and one of the questions which we cannot dodge is this: Shall it be a prosperity in which the forces struggling for spiritual development shall continue to keep their hands off the problem of our material development?

I confess that I do not know how to draw the line between the material and the spiritual. Houses, I know, are material, whereas home is a thing of the spirit; and we are all familiar with the observation that a family may have a house but not, in the truest sense, a home.

But can there be homes unless there are decent houses? In our spiritual calculations, will slums do just as well? That, it seems to me, is a basic spiritual problem. But also, we must admit, it is a problem of distribution. It is not a problem of production. To provide adequate housing for every family in America would be almost no task at all, if it were not for our theories of distribution. We have plenty of land, plenty of lumber, brick, stone, steel and cement. We also have plenty of willing and competent workmen who are not engaged in any other urgent work just now. Incidentally, we have plenty of money and credit to finance such nation-wide building, if we could only organize to give people enough earning power to provide money and credit for such a purpose.

Organized business, however, toward which organized religion has so largely pursued a hands-off policy, has so far failed to do this. Business men would generally be delighted, to be sure, to see all that building going on. Such a project would practically abolish unemployment; for with the millions of carpenters and masons and plumbers and electricians who would then be getting and spending real wages, there would be such a demand for goods in every line that our industries could hardly fill their orders.

Why, then, don't we go to it? Why do we leave business at such a low ebb, why do we leave millions of workers unemployed and why do we leave millions of children under the physical and spiritual handicaps of crowded slums and shacks, when it would be better for business that they should have adequate modern housing?

It is not because we have no business ability, nor is it because we have no religious convictions or humanitarian ideals. We have all those things, but it has been our custom to keep them separate.

There are few if any American business leaders who do not believe in God. Almost uniformly, also, they believe in being good, and they contribute generously to all sorts of worthy charities. But that, to them, is religion. It isn't business. Business, as they understand it, is something else again. And one result of this separation of religious thinking from business thinking is that there are always plenty of worthy charities to contribute to.

Another result was the depression. Because business failed to abolish poverty when the machines had become so productive that poverty could have been abolished, the people became so poor that they could not buy the products of our industries and business itself became impoverished.

It wasn't that business was opposed to the abolition of poverty. It was simply that the abolition of poverty seemed to be a humanitarian, not a business, goal. It was a Sunday job; or a job, at least, to be undertaken after business hours. In business, it was supposed, people concentrated on getting what they could. On Sunday, or after business hours, one might give thought to giving what he could.

In such a conflict between Sunday and the rest of the week, is it any wonder that Sunday got the worst of it?

People often ask what happened to the American Sabbath. One answer is that it was greatly outnumbered.

Six days for acquisitiveness. One day for unselfish meditation.

Six days for exploitation. One day for listening to the church's teaching concerning the will of Almighty God.

Six days for an individual, competitive, dog-eat-dog struggle for survival. One day for remembering that we are all brethren, and that the only true principles upon which human life can be effectively organized are the principles of human brotherhood and sympathetic helpfulness.

Is it any wonder, under the circumstances, that organized business did not tackle the problem of employing the unemployed in providing themselves with the things they need?

Is it any wonder that we did not see the business need for using all available money and credit to provide that employment?

If we had considered the problem in terms of what we had learned on Sunday, we would of course have done that very thing. But we didn't and we couldn't approach it from that angle. We approached it instead from the six-day angle—from the standpoint of our individual, competitive struggle for survival.

To what extent organized religion was responsible for this, it is not for me to say. It cannot be denied, however, that although we business men did not object to the gospel of human brotherhood, providing the preachers confined themselves to spiritual generalities, we did object to any insistence that business, in its six-day operations, be organized upon such principles.

And our religious institutions, for some reason or other, generally complied with our demands.

I do not say that this was a conspiracy on the part of capitalists. And I will not even charge that the churches were timid and that they compromised some principle for fear of alienating wealthy supporters. Such explanations are too simple. I think it more probable that there was confusion all around; and just as business failed to see that its great business opportunity now lay in organizing unreservedly for the common good, the religious leaders failed to see and to show how their gospel of love and brotherhood *could* be practically applied. But we can't deny the fact. The best and most profitable business course we could have taken was in line with our Sunday, not our weekday, thinking; and the worst thing that ever happened to organized business was its effort to continue on its customary course.

This course, so in line with business tradition, and so generally unchallenged by our religious institutions, eventually led us into such depths of depression that business leaders were on the verge of despair and the nation generally on the verge of chaos.

But what was the course? It was not a course of dishonesty or of inhuman greed. It was simply the course of getting in business what one honestly could get, and of giving in work and wages what one felt that he could afford to give without endangering his individual survival. In an emergency, to be sure, or in time of special uncertainty, this meant not only getting what one could but hanging on to what one got. Faced by depression, then, our businesses almost uniformly retrenched.

They cut wages and they laid off employees. And with every cut in wages and with every case of unemployment, some family bought less than it had been buying before. Less food. Less clothes. Less medical and dental service. Less household furniture. Less travel. They even moved by the millions out of poor houses into poorer ones. Comfortable homes were vacated, and shanty villages sprang up in our richest cities.

Distributors, of course, sold less, and therefore bought less from manufacturers in every line. So the factories had to close down, or run on part time; and more employees were laid off and wages cut again.

Were we short of money? No. But those who had it were hanging on to it, in the way it was supposed that all thrifty, prudent, practical people should. They would rather have invested it, to be sure, if there had been any opportunities for profitable investment; but under the circumstances, there couldn't be. Money is a medium of exchange. Because those who wanted things no longer had the necessary money, the exchange of work and goods was so interrupted that those who had money couldn't use it profitably.

And one reason for all this was that our religious institutions hadn't meddled in economics. They had the right formula—the only formula which could have got us out of our dilemma—but they themselves didn't know how practical that formula was.

We were all one family—on Sunday. On Monday, and the rest of the week, however, we were rugged individualists. Not actually, of course, but theoretically. Actually, we were one family seven days a week; but we seldom thought of it excepting on the one day when our business offices were closed.

I am not speaking, and I do not feel qualified to speak, specifically of any religious creed. I simply note that in his religious life, man learned that man cannot live unto himself alone. Nevertheless we went on assuming—and nowhere more than in Christian America—that we could make some fine distinction between a spiritual and a natural truth. And so we dedicated one day in every week to this spiritual truth, and six days to the notion that man not only *could* live unto himself but that, if he were really practical, he would.

Well, the formula is either true or it isn't. If it isn't true in the natural world, if it isn't as true in business and banking as it is in church and Sunday school, then it isn't true at all. If man *can* live unto himself alone, the sooner we find it out the better. If he can't, the whole theory of rugged individualism is visionary and impractical, and those who hold to it are the real "crackpots."

Well, can man live unto himself alone? I am not asking whether he should or not: I want to know whether or not he *can*. Fortunately, we no longer have to guess. For modern science has proved, not only that the human animal could not survive without the co-operation of other human animals, but that only in his group life could man develop any of the characteristics which are peculiarly human.

Take language, for instance. Imagine a language so ruggedly individualistic that no one could partake of it excepting its proprietor. Man could not be human without some means of communication. In the beginning—of human life, at any rate—was the Word. Man has to have words; and yet if they remain his own private property on a "No Trespass" principle, they are not words and cannot serve as words. Only as words are distributed do they have any human value.

Art, science, industry, law, religion—all the things that distinguish man from the brute—are social in character. None of them could be developed by an individual without the co-operation not only of his contemporaries but of the generations that have passed away. WE HUMAN BEINGS ARE ONE; AND WE CAN TRULY EXPRESS OURSELVES ONLY AS WE EXPRESS OUR UNITY.

We have found expression in the past, to be sure, in little-group co-operation. The institution of the family, based upon the principle of all for each and each for all, was probably our outstanding human achievement; but the moment that families could not live unto themselves without the co-operation of other families, larger human groupings became necessary. Eventually we developed clans, kingdoms and states; and in the interest of a more abundant human life, we had to learn loyalty to these larger groupings, even giving our lives if need be for their defense.

We did not know what we were doing, doubtless, when we went to war; but we went because, at that stage of our evolution, it was the human thing to do. We were, first of all, not individuals but a group; and we could live as individuals only as we lived in groups. But aliens and outsiders were forever menacing our group life, just as we were always menacing theirs.

War, then, was inevitable; and war will always be inevitable so long as we have aliens, or so long as we believe that other human groups are alien. The basic cure for war is the discovery, if it is true, that there are no aliens; and that, whatever may have been the case at former stages of our human evolution, all human life has now become one family and the time has arrived to give passionate expression of our unity.

We can't cure war by mere negation—by merely refusing to fight. War, whatever else it is, is passionate; and if human beings are to express themselves adequately against war, at this stage of our civilization, they must express themselves passionately. No mere treaties, therefore, will do, and no mere coldly calculated agreements by which men and nations seek to avoid resort to arms—although, of course, these have their place.

You have the answer to war, if you only knew how practical it is. For the alternative to war is not an armistice. The alternative, and the only alternative, is understanding and sympathetic co-operation. It must be co-operation, however, on a scale which will leave nobody out.

There must be no forgotten man. There must be no discrimination against race, creed or color. There must be no special privilege. There must be no recognition of property rights which will carry with it the domination or exploitation of other human beings. If we entertain any of these notions, we cannot engage in wise—that is, understanding and sympathetic—co-operation on the scale that is needed now—needed for the very preservation of our human social order.

I am perfectly aware that the term "understanding and sympathetic co-operation" is a strange one in the business world. Business men use it commonly enough, but they do not use it when they are talking shop. But that's the whole trouble. It is our efforts to run business on the opposite principle which got us, as well as the rest of the country, into such a mess; and now, unprepared as we may be to undertake it, we've got to give first consideration to the common good in *all* our business dealings, if we are ever again to achieve any lasting business success.

So it isn't even a case of selfishness or unselfishness. It is now a case of concentration on the prosperity of all in all our business dealings, or a case of unprofitable business, and serious business depressions, and the possible sudden end of our whole capitalistic business system. A mother isn't necessarily unselfish because she sacrifices her own interests for those of her child. She does it because she is a mother and because such sacrifice, when it is needed, is the highest expression of her motherhood.

If motherhood could be successful by giving first attention to the welfare of the mother and secondary, if any, attention to the child, the case would be very different. And if banking directed in the interest of bankers, or business directed mainly in the interest of business men, could again achieve any lasting success, the case would be very different. But that simply is not possible. Modern machinery has made it impossible. Bankers and business men now depend for their personal success upon the successful operation of our modern machines; and these machines can be successfully operated only if their products are fully distributed.

But who is to fully consume their products? Bankers and business men surely cannot. These products must be distributed to the masses if they are to be distributed adequately; and if they are not adequately distributed, the machines cannot be kept in operation and the masses cannot be kept employed. On the other hand, if they are adequately distributed, poverty is thereby abolished, and human life, for the first time in human history, is liberated to turn its attention to something beyond the mere struggle for survival.

But that isn't all. By this next and necessary forward step in human evolution, the struggle of man against man largely comes to an end. We are already one in fact, but then of necessity comes the consciousness of our unity. Then we shall know that we are one family. Then we shall be liberated to really co-operate one with another. And this, let us remember, is not "crack-pot" idealism. It is plain economics and simple arithmetic. But when a business man gets out his pencil and adds up these facts, do you see why he will be unable to keep religion out of distribution?

But what are our religious institutions going to do? Are they going to preach a rugged individual salvation, refusing to meddle in social and economic problems, or are they going to take the lead in the organization of a more abundant life for all?

Are they going to glorify the past, and content themselves with exalting the traditional family virtues, developed in the days when the family was an economic unit? Or are they going to co-operate in the effort which our nation is more or less consciously making to apply the co-operative principle which made the family what it was, to the economic setup of this machine age?

Are they going to sanction banking primarily in the interest of bankers, and business primarily in the interest of business men, in the very face of the demonstration that such banking and such business can now result only in poverty in the midst of plenty? Or will they join with the masses of the victims of rugged individualism in their effort, often as yet groping and confused, to find their way out of all this distress, and their way into a more co-operative, more human, social order?

I am making no class appeal. Quite the contrary. I am appealing rather against the theory that those who have, no matter how honestly, come into great possessions, are thereby endowed with some divine right to control the economic and spiritual destinies of their fellow men. To pay wages, for instance, which do not permit a decent home environment; to take profits which do not permit adequate distribution to the masses; and to count among their American liberties the liberty to continue business in a way which can have no other result than nation-wide depression.

Such a theory of our rights, unfortunately, is not confined to the possessors of special privilege. This unsocial theory is so ingrained in our social tradition that we often think of it as selfishness or as human nature. But human nature, as I see it, is basically the will to survive, and I don't know how we could ever do without it. If people think they can survive best by getting ahead of one another, I shall expect them to go on trying, as a general rule, to get ahead of one another. When they come to see, however, that their best chance of survival is through getting ahead *with* one another, they will inaugurate co-operation.

In a sense, I myself am a beneficiary of special privilege, and many of my fellow business men are not only mystified but irritated that I should be seeking the way out of a system which gives me, through my wealth, such power over others. I can command their services. I can even threaten them with unemployment, if they don't do what I tell them to do. I could, if I wished, employ a large retinue of personal servants—not in doing anything which needs to be done but in ministering to my personal whims; and these servants, graduates possibly of American schools and American Sunday schools, instead of being shocked at such a misuse of their power to serve, would probably thank me for giving them work. That is what we need to correct. We have passed out of the master-and-servant age into the machine age; and the machine age makes it necessary that the masses be employed, not in serving any favored group but in serving one another—in serving everyone.

I am surely not unselfish. It is simply that my business studies have made me see certain things which are not as yet generally apparent.

"For the greatest good of the greatest number" will scarcely do as a motto now; for we might then figure, for instance, that the whites outnumber the negroes, and try to arrange an economic system in which the whites would have special privileges denied to others. But that would be as bad for business as it would be for the cause of true religion. It would mean that we couldn't sell much to our colored brethren; and if we are going to make this modern business system work, we've got to sell abundantly to all. God and mass production have decreed that.

There is a great new system of distribution developing in America—a system which, if it works, will help business tremendously, by enabling millions in our lowest-income groups to buy, and therefore to have, far more than was ever possible before. I am speaking of the consumer co-operative system. It is interesting to note how some of our American business men are viewing it.

Do they say it won't work? No. They are alarmed, rather,

lest it put them out of business; which is an admission, on their part, that they consider it a more efficient system of distribution than is the one in which they are engaged.

Now, that's a most interesting point of view—both from the standpoint of religion and of business. As a student of business, I can assure them that the consumer co-operative movement, if it succeeds in serving the masses better than they have been served, will help instead of injuring all legitimate business. They need not be alarmed, then, for fear it will succeed. If they were guided by the business facts, instead of by this quaint attitude of theirs, they would be alarmed, rather, lest the new movement might fail; and they would co-operate with the co-operatives in an effort to see that they secured the best possible business management.

But just suppose that this were not so. Suppose the consumer co-operatives, through enabling the lower-income groups to buy more shoes and clothes for the children, better furniture for the home, better medical care for the sick and some of the comforts and luxuries which have hitherto been reserved for the more fortunate classes—well, just suppose that it did put these alarmed profit-seekers out of business. From the standpoint of true religion, what of it? Should their privileges be sacrificed for the common good? Or should the interests of the masses be sacrificed, so that these mere profit-seekers may continue to make profits?

Begrudging the masses a higher standard of living surely does not square with our Sunday thinking any more than it squares with the actual business facts. From the standpoint of human idealism and of economic analysis, such an attitude is wholly indefensible. Whether such complaints come from the intrenched interests of Wall Street or from the struggling little corner grocer, those who make them need not only a business but a spiritual awakening.

But what are the churches going to do about it?

There is no issue between true religion and true business; nor is there any conflict between the true interests of the business man and the true interests of all concerned. But there is an issue between truth and lies; and this still widespread notion that business today can be successfully operated on any other prin-

Edward A. Filene and His Friend Lincoln Steffens

Carmel, California—February 1934

ciple than co-operation with the mass consumer, is a lie which can serve no other purpose than to check progress and conserve poverty and disunity.

So-called business leaders, whose minds are blighted by this lie, may still insist that you ignore the problems of distribution. But consumers are going into business now, not in anybody's special interest but in the interest of everybody; and they, you must have noticed, are taking a very different attitude. So far from asking you to keep out of these specific problems of distribution, they are urging you to come in.

The American masses are waiting. They need your leadership. They want to know how they can dwell together in unity and security. The machinery for such unity and security has already been developed. The business and the spiritual need is obvious. Only the technique remains to be discovered, and millions who have joined or are now joining the co-operative movement are already discovering this technique. Can we look to our churches for leadership in this practical expression of the principles for which they stand?

I am glad to say that the answer seems to be: *we can.* The co-operative movement, to be sure, is basically economic, as was the family and other institutions which have made it possible for man to realize so many of his spiritual ideals. But it is more than economic. It is charged with aspiration and with idealism. It is warmly, humanly passionate; and it is demonstrating day by day that there is more real satisfaction and more business success in working together for the common good than there ever could be in a free-for-all struggle on the part of everybody to get ahead of everybody else. And many churches, I am glad to say, of many faiths and creeds, are already helping to organize such co-operation.

For the co-operative movement belongs to all faiths and creeds. It is a protest against injustice and special privilege, and a protest against everything which keeps man working and thinking against his fellow man. In that very sense, however, it is all-embracing. It leaves nobody out. In its very constitution, it must accept anybody's application, regardless of race, creed, color or property ownership; and it must give to each member, no matter how meager his holdings, as large a voice and vote as it gives to any other.

The co-operative development, having nothing to do with religious creeds, is essentially religious. It cannot help being; for both its theory and its daily practice are definitely designed to achieve a more abundant life for each *by the process of achieving a more abundant life for all.*

The Contribution of Our Secondary Schools to Better Business and Industrial Conditions *

MR. PRESIDENT—LADIES AND GENTLEMEN:

"Fools rush in where angels fear to tread." Sometimes, I think, that is very fortunate. Education, like almost everything else today, is facing a crisis. The great educators themselves seem to be in a quandary. But somebody has got to start something; and under the circumstances, it may have to be some intrepid ignoramus. I make no further apology for being here.

I think it is quite possible that you educators know what to do, but that you may be afraid to do it. And I have a theory, moreover, as to what you are afraid of. I think you are afraid of the fools.

Suppose you were to do the things which should be done—the fools might see to it that you would lose your jobs.

That problem, at least, isn't entirely new. It came up dramatically, some years ago, in the State of Tennessee. The question was: Who are the rightful directors of education—the educated or the uneducated? And the answer was: the uneducated.

Politically, that answer is incontrovertible. The educators must educate in the way the boss tells them to educate—whether the boss be an ignorant dictator or an ignorant public.

If the will of the people is supreme—and there was a time in America when the will of the people was well-nigh supreme—then the schoolteacher must obey the orders of the people, no matter how ignorant the people may be.

---

* Address at Convocation of The University of the State of New York Celebrating the Tercentenary of Secondary Education in America, State Education Building, Albany, New York—October 17, 1935.

He must not, for instance, teach the children anything which the parents do not want the children to know.

Today we are hearing many arguments in behalf of academic freedom. I believe in academic freedom, but I do not think we are likely to get it by ignoring the academic facts. In the public schools, at least, the educator is the employee of the public; and if he goes counter to the prejudices of the public, and the public finds it out, he is *not likely to remain* an employee of the public.

In our higher institutions of learning, usually endowed by private capital, the educator is an employee of—but why bring that up?

Yet we must bring it up. It's a fact. There is little sense in blaming anybody for it. The capitalist who endows an educational institution may not do it because he is consciously interested in special propaganda. He may have excellent or not so excellent motives. He may be vain and simply want his name associated with some such eminently respectable enterprise as a university; or he may be a great and modest philanthropist and idealist, who wants to bring to others those cultural advantages which he himself may lack. Big or small, however, people do not willingly give their money to enterprises which are antagonistic to *their* ideals, *their* convictions and even *their prejudices.*

The believer in academic freedom may cry out against this. He may say it is a shame that our American colleges and universities are so influenced by business interests that the professor teaching the social sciences is not free to tell what he believes to be the truth, the whole truth and nothing but the truth. But that is all the good it will do. Until those who hire the teacher are willing to pay for his kind of teaching, the teacher who asserts his freedom to teach as he wants to teach must accept the consequences; and the consequences are likely to be that he will be freed from his job.

It may seem that I am painting rather a dark picture—one at least in which there is little outlook for academic freedom. But I am not. I am simply calling attention to facts. Education is a war on ignorance. Let ignorance hold the purse strings and ignorance gets a certain definite advantage. But ignorance doesn't win the war. We *do* make progress against prejudice and bigotry, even in educational institutions which seem, at least to some critics, to have been designed to support that prejudice and bigotry.

Many of our great educational institutions in America, for instance, seemed to be designed by their founders primarily for the propaganda of certain theological dogmas. Few, if any, Americans, however, hold such theological concepts now. Those dogmas have vanished; and they vanished largely by virtue of the education received in these institutions.

People may believe so profoundly in witchcraft that they will organize a school of witchcraft for the definite purpose of studying witchcraft so profoundly that its graduates may successfully defend it against its mightiest detractors. But when witchcraft is studied profoundly, it disappears.

In America, our schools—and particularly our secondary schools—have to a great extent been schools of rugged individualism; but the more we study rugged individualism, the harder it is to find it. Its disappearance is nothing new. There simply never was such a thing as pure individualism in human life; for man cannot live unto himself. Of course, everything that is distinctly human—language, art, science, industry or education—is social.

We had something here in America—something very precious—and something which we called individualism. What we actually had was a very interesting and peculiar social setup. But we didn't study the setup. We just took it for granted. We didn't try to analyze it. We didn't compare this setup with previous setups, to discover wherein it was different, what had brought about the difference, and what further changes could logically be expected. Our attitude, rather, was that Americans were free to do as they individually wanted to do; that each American was master of his own fate; that any boy, if he only worked hard enough, could become President; or, if he preferred to go into business, could eventually have everybody else working for him.

There were plenty of things to cause this state of mind. There was an economic setup here which *did* provide opportunities such as no other civilization had ever known; and there was a situation which permitted personal liberty, along certain lines, which the older civilizations could not permit. All wage earners here did not have to remain wage earners; and their children, given an adequate education, could all hope to become capitalists. In fact, thousands and thousands of them did rise to power, especially to money power.

A country where such things could happen was surely a great country. Most Americans, observers all agreed, were peculiarly ambitious—not noticeably ambitious for a better social order, not noticeably ambitious to achieve honest and efficient government of their cities, not noticeably ambitious to suppress crime, to abolish poverty, to clean up the slums or to achieve any particular social goal, but ambitious for personal wealth and power over the lives of other Americans.

I am not ridiculing this. I am not even criticizing it. It seems to me that it was almost inevitable, under the circumstances, and that our educators could not, if they had wished, go very far in pointing out the absurdities and inconsistencies of such a view of life. In such a country, most parents did not want their children to be educated to an understanding of socially applicable truths. They wanted their children fitted, rather, to get ahead—the mere fact that everybody couldn't get ahead of everybody else being considered rather irrelevant.

The parents might be poor and unemployed, but this did not necessarily lead them to become interested in the abolition of poverty and unemployment. If their children could become rich and powerful, that would seem to solve their problem perfectly; and in America, by all the evidence, it was possible for poor children to become rich. The mass American mind, then, was not merely antagonistic to socialism: it was antagonistic to *any social approach* to the problems of business, industry and employment. It insisted on the individual approach—on the approach which would kindle personal ambition for wealth and fame and power.

It is only a partial truth, at most, to say that our schools could not under the circumstances antagonize the aims of the rich and powerful. What they certainly could not do was to antagonize the hopes and dreams and lifelong yearnings of the masses of Americans who wanted their children to become personally rich and powerful.

Nor is there any sense in condemning such an attitude as selfish, greedy and immoral. The great majority, at least, of those who were striving for personal power were very good people. They didn't want to hurt others. They wanted to become rich and powerful so that they could help others. They wanted to build colleges and hospitals. It is possibly significant, of course, that this age of individualistic and anarchistic struggle for power was an age of violence and crime, when America became notorious among the civilizations of the world by putting murder on a mass production basis. We must remember, nevertheless, that it was an age of such large-scale philanthropy as the world had never known before; and even if we produced criminals by the carload, we also contributed magnificently to home and foreign missions.

In such a civilization, what could the high schools do?

The answer is that they could do just about what they did.

They could add fuel to the flames of personal ambition, and they could glorify the civilization which offered so many prizes to its youth that there seemed to be no good excuse for anyone's not becoming much bigger than the average.

They could also teach civics and economics—not actual civics and economics, but the kind which was in the textbooks of rugged individualism.

In the textbooks, cities were governed by mayors and boards of aldermen, and the high school student was supposed to go on believing that. If the teacher happened to be a practical man and discovered who the real boss of the city was, and how he managed to hold his position, he was doubtless also sufficiently practical so that he did not tell his class. That would have been teaching real civics; and the gas company and the trolley company, and other leading citizens who had been successful in the struggle for power, might not like it. They would probably have managed somehow to remind the Board of Education that the high school is "no place for radical agitators to be poisoning the minds of youth under the guise of education."

In economics, also, teachers had to be careful. If they followed the textbooks, they were safe; for textbook economics were flat and static and gave no hint of problems which would arise in the course of economic evolution. If events were pressing toward economic collapse, the teacher, if he knew it, could not point it out. If the situation was bound to bring nation-wide unemployment, with little opportunity for the masses to earn even a bare living, to say nothing of their each achieving unlimited wealth and power, the teacher, unless he wanted to join the unemployed, would do well under the circumstances to keep his mouth shut and to go on explaining the "economic man."

If there were labor troubles in town—strikes and riots and social war—the teacher had to be particularly wary. If he was convinced, to be sure, that the sole fault of the strike lay with the strikers, he was allowed considerable academic freedom; but to analyze the strike, to discover its causes and, if there was violence, to discover what forces had really led to this violence—that was not considered legitimate economics.

Remember, I am not blaming the teachers. They were hired employees. Their salaries were paid by the taxpayers; and the strikers, as a rule, were not very important taxpayers. Nor was it merely a case of their being hired by a public which had an erroneous social viewpoint. They were hired by a public which had *no* social viewpoint and did not want their children to get a social viewpoint. What they wanted—what even the strikers themselves might want—was that *their* children should become successful—successful especially as employers, in which case only those who did not count in this scheme of life would then be doing the striking.

What the educators did, then, was under the circumstances sensible. Since everybody, practically, wanted to become successful, they took counsel of the successful—especially of successful business men—as to what course education should pursue.

And all in all, it didn't turn out very badly.

These successful business men, to be sure, might not know

anything about education; and they surely knew little, if anything, about what was actually brewing in America as a result of this lawless struggle for personal power. But they did know a good deal. They knew, for instance, that to be successful, they had to introduce more efficient methods, and they knew that these methods were constantly being discovered by fact-finding research. So they needed employees, they knew, with scientific training. They needed chemists and physicists and engineers. They wanted practical people, too, not dreamers. They didn't want those who would take the old formulas for granted, as the last word on the subjects concerned. They wanted live, alert, analytical, objective thinkers who could discover things which had never been understood before.

The result was that teachers who could teach chemistry, physics, mechanics or engineering in such a practical, objective way were given almost complete academic freedom; providing, of course, that they stuck to their subjects and did not permit their truth-searching minds to wander into the so-called social sciences.

That, I claim, was a great step forward; for it is something rather new in human history to permit untrammelled research in any branch of science. The mind of the agrarian age was definitely set against it. Until very recent times, it was everywhere supposed that knowledge is handed down, not dug up; and that those who want the truth should go to old texts, not to newfangled test tubes, to discover it. And this agrarian-age mind, of course, is still with us, breaking out occasionally in strange, atavistic gestures. In Tennessee, as I mentioned, it drew the line at the teaching of biology; whereas the leading industrial minds drew it only at the teaching of history, morals, economics and sociology—unless that teaching were indoctrinated by them.

But time passed on. Social evolution continued to function in America, even if we did not permit our students to watch its operations; and there were such natural resources here, and so much human initiative released for their exploitation, that America developed wealth and power such as the world had never known. Among other things, we developed machines that were so productive that they could, if operated at capacity, supply every

American not only with necessities and comforts, but with many luxuries of life.

This power, however, was in the hands of those who knew how to get it—not in the hands of those who knew what to do with it. By all the rules, it seemed, they had a right to the power that they now possessed; and, like George the Third of controversial memory, they thought in terms of what seemed to them their divine right and not in terms of the actual human facts. The fact was that these machines were not only able to supply the masses of Americans with an abundance of goods, and provide them all with lasting economic security, but they were so productive that their products could not be disposed of unless the masses were somehow enabled to purchase them, and their economic position made so secure that, instead of saving their money, they *would* buy what they wanted.

In the contest for personal wealth, however, no effective provision had been made to furnish the losers with buying power. Those who got the buying power were supposed to keep it, excepting as they gave it away in charity; and it was now in the hands largely of a little group of prize winners who, no matter how much they might indulge themselves, could not possibly purchase enough of the products of these machines. And if the products of the machines could not be sold, obviously, the machines had to be slowed down.

So there we were. America had become so productive that the masses sunk to poverty. The land of opportunity became a land of bread lines. The nation where everybody had hoped to get ahead of everybody else, presently began to get nowhere very rapidly. All this, not because of anyone's evil intentions but because, with all our science and all our boasted practicality, we didn't know the facts which now most needed to be known.

We hadn't permitted ourselves to learn them. Business men told the schools that they mustn't teach such facts; and the schools turned out graduates who became successful in the fight for power but had little or no understanding of how the power could now be used successfully.

For years, then, America looked to the leaders of industry and business to lead the country out of this wholly unnecessary depression; and for years, those leaders just ran around in circles, trying to solve the problem of how 120,000,000 people could avoid starvation if they happened to have an oversupply of food, or of how they could keep from freezing if they had more coal, cotton and wool than was necessary to keep everyone warm.

It wasn't that they weren't educated. Many were highly educated, but only on one side. They couldn't take the machine anywhere because they had anchored it to a fixed idea. That's what made them travel in circles. The machine was built by science. The fixed idea to which it was anchored was taken bodily from the ancient texts. The machine was ruthlessly social. The idea was sentimentally individualistic—an impractical idealization of rugged individualism. These leaders, then, could not lead America because they could not see America as a society in which it would be necessary to institute social controls, but saw it rather as an arena in which 120,000,000 ruggedly individualistic gladiators were expected to battle for supremacy.

I am not talking socialism. I don't believe in it. I believe in competition and the freeing of individual initiative, and I believe in profits to stimulate enterprise. But it doesn't matter what I believe. What matters is the truth about America, especially about American business, industry and finance. Just as it was once necessary for business progress that the physical sciences be studied and taught with objective realism, it has now become imperative that the social sciences be studied with the same objective realism; and just as the former situation demanded academic freedom for the physical scientists, the present situation demands academic freedom for the social scientists.

This suggests to me the great contribution which the secondary schools can make to better business and industrial conditions; and I am not forgetting, when I say that, that educators cannot be independent of their uneducated employers, and are almost certain to lose their jobs if they antagonize the powers that be.

There is no contradiction in this; for leaders cannot remain leaders very long after they cease to lead; and even financial power ceases to be financial power when those who possess it have no idea what to do. And that, precisely, is the situation in America today. The old leadership has gone. Organized business in America, and organized finance, have revealed their helplessness in the hour of great peril. They not only failed to initiate any program by which business could carry on, but they were unable to follow and to co-operate when such a program was initiated.

Leadership, therefore, must pass to other hands; and just now it is rapidly passing to economic illiterates whose hearts, at any rate, seem to respond to the needs of the masses, however incapable their heads may be. One man gains upwards of twenty million followers by promising $200 a month to everybody as a reward for becoming sixty years of age. It is economically unsound, of course, but under present conditions it is almost futile even to say so, because it is not more economically unsound than the attitude of the United States Chamber of Commerce and most of our trade associations, who persist in approaching our present problems with the logic of an age which has forever passed away.

Another man gained millions of worshipful adherents by promising to divide up our capital. One might as well try to solve the railroad problem by giving everybody a box car. Such suggestions could not get a hearing, we may be sure, if the opposition had a workable plan for transportation. But if the opposition insists that railroads should be run in the interest of those who have grabbed them, and haven't sufficient social understanding even to see where *their* interests lie, we can hardly blame the public for preferring some other economic vagary.

It seems to me, therefore, that there is a peculiar opportunity at present for educators who really dare to educate. Whatever may have been the case ten years ago, America is now old enough to be told the facts of life. Those who would not permit this heretofore have either lost their power or are fast losing their power; and the masses of America, not our erstwhile rulers, are going to decide our issues now.

Will they decide these issues upon prejudice, and upon the

sense of the injuries which they have endured? Or will they decide them according to the facts? That depends largely upon our schools—especially upon our secondary schools; for it is in high school years, as a rule, if not in the high school textbooks, that the mind reaches out to comprehend the more mature relations of life. It is then, especially, when the boys and girls begin to think of their careers; and whether they will be careers of social service or social irresponsibility depends largely upon their educational guidance.

It is in those years, largely, that criminals are produced, even though we merely intend to produce go-getters. It is then when idealism makes its greatest appeal; and whether this idealism is to be fortified by truth, or cruelly shattered later by collision with reality, depends again on educational guidance.

Teachers teaching youth, moreover, do much to teach their parents. In times of rapid change, especially, parents do go to school to their children, if for no other reason than to try to keep up to date. Once let our youth, then, become really acquainted with the actual setup of this machine age, and all America is likely to hear about it. If the schools teach dogma, of course, and the dogma happens to be in conflict with the dogma of the parents, the parents, being voters and taxpayers, may be expected to rebel.

But I see little danger in that. In the first place, you educators do not want to teach dogmas. What you want is freedom to find and teach the facts. If your theories are wrong, you want to know it; and even if you feel confident that they are right, you know that the unquestioning acceptance of any theory does not constitute education. You do not want to tell your students *what* to think. You want to teach them *how* to think—how to separate truth from error—which means in the last analysis, how to find facts and how to use them for the achievement of a more abundant life.

And the average American parent today wants a more abundant life. The average American parent, moreover, is no longer committed against all reason to those ancient theories of rugged individualism. The depression has just about cured the masses of any such fixation. The danger now is, not that the masses will insist upon a repetition of the old preachments, but that they will accept any half-plausible panacea which is held out to them, regardless of how economically unsound or socially disastrous it might prove to be.

When the masses believed devoutly in the divine right of kings, it was dangerous for any educator to challenge the theory. Our early Americans were quite unanimous in their devotion to this dogma; but because they were actually living in a new kind of a world, the time came when they could not believe it any longer. Then educators got the chance to challenge the theory without losing their right to remain educators; and American educators have been freely teaching a very different theory ever since.

It was not necessary in those early days to challenge the claim of the divine right of capital to conduct itself without social responsibility. For capital, in early America, did not have much social responsibility. The masses in those days could make a living, quite independently of what the capitalists did or did not do. For land was abundant and free; and the way of life for the average person in those early days was to settle on the land and produce a living directly from the soil.

But that is not the way of life in this machine age. Even our modern farmers do not and cannot live that way. We are all dependent for our living now upon the continuous functioning of the machinery of production and distribution. To supply our needs, we must buy; and to be able to buy, we must each sell something—our products, our services or our labor power. To live in this age, then, we must all have money. Unless the masses *are* amply equipped with money, the machinery of capitalism can no longer be kept in successful operation, and there is not only desolation and unemployment among the people but no profits for capitalists. The life and security of all America, therefore, now depends upon how money is used.

Instead of recognizing these facts and acting upon them, however, we Americans have tenaciously clung to the theory that those who have accumulated money have an inalienable right to use it as they themselves see fit. They may even do nothing with it; or they may hand it down to their children, as the kings handed down their supposedly divine right to rule, even though the inheritors have no sense of social obligation and no understanding of social needs.

Many of our most sincere publicists and statesmen even maintain that this attitude is the only truly American attitude toward money; and that any deviation from this attitude constitutes a violation of our ancient liberties. Their position, of course, is understandable. Reasoning from tradition, instead of from the facts, they could not change their notion of what constitutes Americanism just because America had happened to become an entirely different kind of civilization.

The possession of money in old agrarian America did not carry with it the control of the means by which the masses got their living; and since the masses could go on living, regardless of what the capitalists did or did not do, the masses *were free*. Riches, nevertheless, were highly desirable, and these free Americans naturally wanted the liberty to become capitalists if they could, and to do with their money as they might see fit. When America had completed the transition, however, from the agrarian age to the machine age, the masses of Americans were no longer free to go on living unless the process by which they now got their living was kept in continuous operation, and farmers could sell their products and workers find jobs.

The old American freedom, then, was gone; and there could be no new American freedom until this new process, upon which Americans now depended for their very lives, could be made dependable. It is the effort to achieve the only kind of freedom which Americans can now have which these traditional thinkers call un-American.

I am not suggesting revolution. I am trying to avoid it. Everyone who observes the facts, however, must recognize that such a situation is intolerable and must lead either to revolution, or to such an education as to the true function of money so that money will certainly be used in ways which will bring to Americans generally opportunity for gainful work and for the enjoyment of the products of their labor.

This is as necessary for business as it is for the wage earners. Success for every legitimate element of our population now depends upon our understanding the social character of this machine age, and instituting such social controls as are necessary to make our marvelous modern processes continuous and dependable. Whether we wished it or not, America has now become, not merely so many united states, but a united people—united in everything excepting an understanding of their unity.

We have become one economic unit, no element of which can be lastingly prosperous unless all legitimate elements are prosperous. Business cannot sell more than its customers can buy, and since the machinery of production has become so productive, business cannot again become genuinely prosperous unless the masses of workers and farmers are buying abundantly. This was not true in the agrarian age, nor was it true in the age of transition when the classical economists studied the haggling in the market and imagined they were studying world economy. It was not true when our great social mechanism was in the making and when, therefore, it was socially imperative that as much as possible of the currently produced wealth should be used for capital purposes, and there were economic if not humanitarian reasons for leaving the masses in poverty. The policies that were good and practical and workable in those days, however, are impractical and impossible now; and many of the principles which then seemed basic are now no more valid than the dreams of Utopians. Not, in fact, so valid; for the Utopians, at least, expected to go *on* to their Utopia, while these traditional thinkers are hoping to go *back* to theirs.

In the old days, when capital was so sorely needed, it was right and proper that schoolchildren should be taught to save. In these days, when we are able to produce so much, and when the necessary saving can best be achieved by social co-operation, the masses should be educated to buy.

Ceaseless labor was then a virtue and could be taught as

such. Now, the sooner we take it easy, and make the kilowatts do the work, the better it will be for all concerned; that is, of course, if youth is properly educated for the leisure which the kilowatts can give.

To concentrate on making a living was always practical, up to a few years ago. In this Age of Plenty, however, such concentration is stupid. It is now time for youth to concentrate on making a life; since, by accepting the facts of the machine age and acting upon them, people can *make a living* with so little effort.

As to what it takes to make a life, you educators are in a far better position to judge than I. If the masses are to be free to live freely, however, instead of having to subordinate all other human aspirations to the task of earning a living, our marvelous new mechanism of production and distribution must be operated according to the actual laws of its being, and not according to anybody's inherited prejudices. To teach those laws, the violation of which brings poverty in the midst of plenty, now becomes the first duty of our schools. Until we operate this mechanism according to those laws, *whatever they are,* there can be no lasting recovery, and consequently there will be all too little opportunity for our younger generations.

We may be sure, then, that youth will want to learn those laws, if the schools provide the opportunity. From this angle, economics can no longer be a dismal science—no more dismal than learning how to drive a motorcar.

We have, I grant, all sorts of theories as to how the machine age can be operated, whereas we have no trouble in agreeing as to how machines are operated. But that is the point. We never disagree disastrously on anything which we study from the fact-finding approach. From that angle, conflicting theories do not worry us; they stimulate us, rather, to find the facts.

We have had conflicting theories of chemistry and physics; but we never got anywhere in either science until we quit fighting to defend our theories and liberated our minds to discover whatever could be discovered. It makes little difference, then, whether our teachers sympathize with this or that political or social movement. What matters is whether they are fact finders and whether they have the capacity to help their students find and face the facts. We have so many theories, indeed, that there is only one platform upon which we can unite, and that is the platform of fact-finding research.

From that angle, we can now teach any truth; and we have now reached a stage of economic evolution when only the facts will do.

The time has come, then, when you teachers can secure the right to teach, if you yourselves courageously assert that right.

The time has come when we must even have the facts about the Constitution of the United States. If it was not handed down from a holy mountain as the only perfect and unchangeable formula of government, I believe that we should let our youngsters find it out. Let them find out that the Constitution itself contains definite provisions for the making, if necessary, of an improved Constitution. If they think that they can produce a better document, by all means let them try; for there is no eternal law which man has been able to discover, which keeps them from trying to do as much for their generation as the Fathers did for theirs.

In our social blindness, to be sure, we business men did our best to keep the masses from developing any social understanding or any sense of a common goal; and we saw to it, as far as we were able, that the schools should not prepare them for any intelligent, co-operative mass action. We even resented it when workers organized for a common end, and we said the very idea was alien and un-American. But all that mis-education must now be undone; for until it is undone, the very machinery of capitalism cannot work. Capitalism needs a new mind, even among its workers. It can no longer use the type of mind it once insisted upon the schools turning out. We thought we needed cringing obedience when what we needed was self-respecting co-operation. We thought we wanted adoration when what we really needed was constructive criticism. Above all, we thought we wanted workers to be individualists who, while loyal to us, would all be ambitious to get ahead of their fellow workers; when what we really needed was a nation-wide body of workers who, while willing to co-operate with us in any sound industrial program, would be ambitious to get ahead *with* their fellow workers.

But why cry over spilt milk? The time came—that's all—when we built up such a productive mechanism that it could not be operated unless it were operated for the common good. We didn't know how to run it that way, so we shut it down; and we, seemingly, with the kind of education which we insisted upon the schools giving us, have not yet developed the social initiative necessary to start it up and keep it going successfully and lastingly. That is now the task for the schools—to find and reveal the facts of actual human relations in this machine age which cannot go ahead with any lasting success until we are prepared to go ahead together. I envy you your great new opportunity.

Unlearning Business *

FELLOW STUDENTS:

I address you as fellow students for a very definite reason; and I hope that you will listen to me only as you would listen to a fellow student.

You may have supposed—those of you who are preparing for a business career—that I would speak to you out of the richness of my business experience and lay down the rules which, in that experience, I have found to be successful.

But if I were to do that, it would be mostly bunk; for I got most of my business experience in a world which no longer exists. If I were to tell you how I got ahead in *that* world, it wouldn't do you any good. If you want to know how to drive a modern car, you don't go to someone who can tell you, out of the richness of his experience, the tried and true principles by which he once succeeded in chauffeuring a horse and buggy.

If you are going to do business, you will have to do it in this new world; and I haven't lived in this new world any longer than you have. It is stranger, in fact, to me than it is to you.

To be sure, you may not know as much about business as I do. But you have the advantage of not knowing so much that isn't so. I have been constantly embarrassed in my later years by having to spend so much time unlearning things which were true enough when I learned them but which aren't true now and, in all probability, can never be true again.

My world, for instance—the world in which I gained my business experience—was a world of rich and poor; and it was taken

---

* Address before the School of Business Administration of The University of Buffalo, Buffalo, New York—December 9, 1936.

for granted by almost everybody that it must always remain a world of rich and poor.

Oh, yes, there was a middle class too: that is, a class of people who were either getting rich or getting poor.

The people of all classes, as I remember them, were generally uncomfortable. The rich were uncomfortably rich. The poor were uncomfortably poor. The middle class were uncomfortably middle class.

It was commonly said, to be sure, that there were no classes in America, because so many people were going back and forth from one class to another; much as we might now say that there are no states because so many people are travelling from one state to another. It wouldn't be exactly true, but there is some truth in both observations.

America, in my day at any rate, was a highly competitive civilization, and everybody knew it. Strange to say, it was also a highly co-operative civilization, but few if any ever stopped to notice it. We assumed—most of us—that life was a race, in which everybody would naturally try to get ahead of everybody else; but we never actually organized our work on any such principle.

We did things in a big way here. When we wanted to do a *big* job, at least, instead of hiring a few men to work a long time, we hired a lot of men to get it done in a hurry. But that meant that the work must be carefully planned so that each worker's task would dovetail as exactly as possible with every other worker's task. By such scientific co-operation, we discovered, Americans could produce wealth faster and more abundantly than could the people of any other country. It was only in the distribution of this wealth, not in its production, that we hung tenaciously to the individualistic, competitive, life-is-a-race theory.

That is, we organized our work in America but we didn't organize the pay. When we thought of employing anybody, we thought first of what he was qualified to do. But when we thought of paying him, we knew of no way of paying him according to the value of the work he was able to do with the help of modern machinery. We paid him, instead, and assumed that we had to pay him, according to the *price* of his labor; and the price of labor was determined, not by how much wealth a man could produce but by how many other people wanted his job.

If many were out of work—thousands, say, racing to get one job—the price of labor was down, and the wages of the successful applicant were very low, no matter how valuable his work might be. If we paid more than this market price for labor, we figured, some competitor who bought his labor at the market price would undersell us and drive us from the market.

This, it was supposed, was an unalterable law of economics. One of our greatest business leaders, in fact, when asked if he thought a dollar a day enough for a workingman, replied that he supposed it was if that was all the man could get.

Not only were wages low in my world, therefore, but the hours of labor were long. I can remember when twelve hours a day was the general rule in factories. And when agitators attempted to organize labor unions, with the idea of demanding a ten-hour day, do you know what we employers said?

I think you can guess. We said that they were threatening American liberty. We said they were conspiring against the American way of life. And we even sent our agents into the most poverty-stricken sections of Europe, and we contracted with steamship companies to bring over shiploads of immigrants, so that our American way of life might be continued.

I do not mean when I engage in these reminiscences, that employers in those days were especially greedy or cruel. I mean simply that they were business men, following the tried and true principles of business. They weren't heartless. They simply did not know that business could be conducted on any other principles.

When they accumulated money, they were often very generous with it. It was an accepted convention in our best circles that the rich should give money to the poor. Not enough to hurt them, to be sure, and not enough to undermine their characters, but enough to keep them alive—and poor.

Rich men, also, built palaces and private yachts, and lived expensively, often, according to Veblen's law of conspicuous display. That is one of the things which made them so uncomfortable; but instead of being criticised for this, they were usually commended. Every palace they built, it was pointed out, made work for the builders; and it was generally believed, in those days, that it was rather nice of anybody to make work for others. It not only brought wages to these workers, it was pointed out, but by leaving fewer people out of work, tended to raise wages generally.

You have no trouble in these days, of course, in detecting the bunk in that; but in our day, we called this economic law. In our home lives, to be sure, we were never brought up to make work for Mother. In our homes, in fact, we were taught to eliminate as much work as possible, either so that we might save time for reading or recreation, or so that we might get time to do other things which needed to be done, but which couldn't be done if we spent unnecessary time in doing our necessary work.

But we didn't think of America as we would think of our home. We thought of America as our oyster. We didn't think of business as the system by which Americans were now getting their work done. Our business, as we understood it, was to get all *we* could get; and it was generally assumed, by rich and poor alike, that if one group or class did get more money, some other group or class was bound to get less; and that the only compensation for this was either that the rich should then give money to the poor or hire the poor in producing luxuries for the rich.

Now, when I say that that world has passed away, I do not want anybody to think that I am condemning it. It was a good world. Moreover, it was a necessary world. It was a world of transition between the agrarian age and the machine age; and if those who directed the transition did not always know what they were doing, it remains true that they did a good and necessary job.

If they had given all their money to charity, or if they had spent all their profits in hiring workers to do unnecessary work, that transition could never have been made; and it is a mighty good thing for society, everything considered, that the tycoons of the past fifty years were either too selfish or too sensible to do any such thing.

At any rate, they wanted even bigger incomes than they had; and to get those bigger incomes, they invested the bulk of their accumulations, neither in charity nor in self-indulgence, but in larger, better and more efficient industrial enterprises.

If it had not been for what was called the selfish, greedy profit motive, America could not have built her transcontinental railroads. The capital for these railroads largely came from Europe; not because Europeans wanted to help America but because they wanted to get rich at America's expense. Those railroads, however, enabled Americans to do so much more than they could have done without them, that America soon produced great surpluses over and above the amount necessary for the subsistence of her people, and these surpluses were used as capital for the launching of other enterprises.

If the masses of Americans had actually received all that they produced, no such accumulations of capital would have been possible; for the masses were poor, and they would have spent the extra money in more food, more clothing and better living conditions. Most people aimed to save a little if they could, of course, but a very large part of the capital necessary for the building up of our machine civilization came from the underpayment of labor—from the fact that the people generally had no opportunity to consume the full product of their toil.

The greatest mistake that we can make, however, is to assume that principles which once were true remain true forever. We may not like the idea, but we owe our present opportunities in America—especially the opportunity for a full, rich life for everyone—to the fact that much of our business has been predatory in the past and has followed the principle of exploitation. On the other hand, although we may equally dislike the idea, business cannot be successful if it follows that principle any longer.

For this is a new world. This is a world unlike anything which has ever gone before. And if, as fellow students, we can discover what has caused the change, then we can learn how to do business in the years ahead of us.

I spoke a moment ago of the way that rich men, by building palaces and buying private yachts, made work for the poor. But they also made work for the poor when they started a shoe factory or a textile mill; and the poor, as a rule, did not care very much which kind of work they got, if only the pay and the conditions of employment were equally good.

There was a vast difference, however, in the two kinds of employment; and if we can only keep that difference in mind, we may be able to discover the nature of our new economic order.

There was nothing new whatever in the rich enjoying luxuries. That had been the rule since the year one. There was something new, however, in the building and operation of great, power driven machines for the manufacture of things in general use. That was a process which had begun only with the beginning of capitalism. Not only that, but it was a process in which there was something new, and in which there had to be newer and better methods, decade after decade and year after year.

If a man wanted to show how rich he was, he could "live like a king." That is, he didn't have to economize. He could have a retinue of servants not doing much work which helped to produce real wealth, but just wearing uniforms and bowing as the great man passed. But that wasn't any way to get rich. It was a way to get poor. It is the way, incidentally, that a nation gets poor—having great retinues of people not doing any wealth-producing work or working at best with a minimum of efficiency. The other way of employing man power—employing it in the most efficient production of things in general demand—was the way in which these rich men had managed to get rich; and it was the way in which America was becoming rich.

And it was a constantly new way. It had to be; for our machines and our systems of management under the pressure of competition, were constantly being improved; and if one uses last year's methods in this year's business, some competitor who uses this year's methods is pretty sure to get the business.

Rich men, then, while they might be as wasteful as sin in their personal expenditures, had to see that their factories were more and more efficient; and this, although neither they nor their employees realized it, inevitably led to one of the greatest changes in the whole history of civilization. It led in the end to mass production; and with the advent of mass production, our traditional theories of money-making all became invalid.

Mass production was the most economical form of production. It was the sort of production which was sure to dominate the market, if only there were a large enough market to make mass production practical. But there could be no mass production of private yachts, as very, very few could afford to buy and operate a private yacht. There could be no mass production of palaces. There could, axiomatically, be no mass production of anything exclusive. There could be mass production only of things which great masses wanted and which great masses could buy.

It seemed to us, when mass production first blazed across our business horizon, that it was an invention which had its origin in the brain of Henry Ford. Ford himself knew better. He saw that mass production was the inevitable development of machine production. He saw that machine industry could be successful and factory owners could make profits only as they adopted more efficient, less wasteful methods. Where Ford differed from the average business man of his day was mainly in this: All had to run their businesses on this principle. If they were running large factories, they had to produce something for which there was a large demand; and they had to adopt better and better methods of production. It remained for Ford, however, to perceive from this that such a system could not continue unless the mass consumer could buy and enjoy more things; and the masses of Americans, he noted, were largely wage earners and farmers, who simply could not buy automobiles unless the price were brought within their capacity to purchase them.

When his business associates told him how much other cars were selling for, and how much, therefore, he might charge for his, he simply wasn't interested. And even when his engineers and factory managers told him the lowest price at which, according to their figures, Ford cars could be sold, he was still not interested. It was their job, he said, to find out what price millions of people could pay, and then find out how cars could be produced and sold profitably within that price.

Ford discovered how this could be done, and that was the death knell of the old capitalism. From that day to this, learning how to do business has largely been a matter of unlearning the things which we had learned before, and which, until industrial evolution had reached this stage, had been essentially true.

When we look back at this development now, we can easily see that no other result was possible. The constant improvement of our machinery had to result in more and more production; and a constant increase in production must one day lead to mass production; but mass production without mass distribution and mass consumption is unworkable. This was the inevitable course of industrial evolution under capitalism and free enterprise; but capitalists as a rule did not study capitalism; and instead of preparing for the inevitable, they customarily opposed it.

Had they studied capitalism as an evolutionary process, they must have seen that they could not continually increase the production of shoes unless more people could buy more shoes; and they could not continually increase the quantity and improve the quality of machine-made clothing unless more people could buy more and better clothes. It was noted, to be sure, that the American masses were becoming better dressed; but this was unintentional as far as business was concerned. At least we did not organize to accelerate the process.

Instead of organizing to make sure that the masses could buy and have more things, in fact, we customarily organized in our chambers of commerce and our trade associations to oppose the movements of labor and of agriculture to achieve more buying power.

On the one hand, we were hiring more and more people to produce more and more things in general demand—more and more things which could not be produced unless the people generally could buy them—and on the other hand, we were using all the powers at our command to prevent the people generally from getting them. Not, however, because we were greedy and cruel but because, in our understanding of the situation, this course was a business necessity.

But don't, I beg you, be too hard on us; for in the early stages of capitalism, as I have tried to point out, this course was necessary. It was only in the later stages that it became stupid. So long as industries were mostly engaged in producing the bare necessities of life, it was neither necessary nor wise in a business sense that labor should get more than a bare living wage. Everybody, of course, had to have food, shelter and clothing—enough to keep him alive and working. Thanks to the introduction of machinery into farms and factories, however, the time came when everybody did not have to be engaged in the production of food, shelter and clothing, and millions of our workers could be spared for other work.

Conceivably, these displaced workers could have then become household servants. But in that case, we would have had no railroads and no further progress in our factory development, and even the relatively rich, in that sort of civilization, could not have a very high standard of living. Capitalism found a far better way of hiring workers who, because of the introduction of more efficient machines, were no longer needed in the production of the bare necessities of life. It was to employ them, first, in the building of still more efficient machinery and, secondly, in the production of things greatly desired by the people generally, but not physical necessities.

As the new machines came into operation, of course, there was a rapid increase in the output of these comforts and luxuries, and that made a higher standard of living a business necessity. But before the new machines could get into operation, there had to be great accumulations of capital; and there couldn't be a sufficient accumulation of capital if the standard of living generally were too high.

It *was* a business necessity, therefore, in the building up of capitalism, that the standard of living generally be low. It was a tried and true principle. What rendered it untrue was the actual operation of these factories producing non-necessities.

These were the factories producing shoes, clothes and household furniture of a higher grade than necessary for working efficiency; also the enterprises producing such unheard-of luxuries as bathtubs, hot and cold running water systems, even telephones and electric lights. Such enterprises could never have become profitable, if America's masses had been held down to a bare subsistence income. But think of what followed.

Thirty years ago, when an agitator wanted to rouse the rabble against plutocracy, it wasn't enough to call a man a plutocrat. To drive his point home, the plutocrat had to be pictured as "riding in his automobile." The automobile today, so far from being the symbol of plutocracy, is now our symbol of mass production: that is, the symbol of production *for the masses.*

And this, I wish to point out, is a normal development of capitalism. It all came about, however, by an equally normal unlearning of the average capitalist's conception of capitalism. It is true that the development of American industry made this higher standard of living possible; but the thing we need to remember is that the higher standard of living—that higher standard against which our capitalists have traditionally fought—made the development of American industry possible. And yet we capitalists, as a rule, not only opposed the labor unions demanding greater buying power through higher wages, and farmers' organizations demanding equality with industry; but we also did our best, as a rule, to keep prices up, thus preventing the buying public from buying enough to keep our industries in profitable operation.

When the railroads and the public utilities demanded higher rates, who as a rule opposed their demands? Strangely, not our business organizations, although if the public paid more than necessary for any service, it would obviously have less than otherwise to spend for other things, and all legitimate business would suffer.

It wasn't business, but an outmoded theory of business, which caused these companies to demand these higher rates. When lower rates were forced upon our utilities, in fact, the lower rates often led to such increased patronage that the utilities were saved from the bankruptcy which they had been virtually wishing upon themselves. And only last year, we know, the people of the United States, through their government, had to compel our eastern railroads to lower their transportation rates and make more money.

How, then, can we business men, with this sad record behind us, advise the younger generation what to do? We succeeded, in many instances, in spite of ourselves. America became prosperous, very largely, in spite of what organized business did which tended to prevent it. When Henry Ford launched the first big experiment in high wages, business generally was alarmed and angry, and said almost the same things against Ford that were recently said against President Roosevelt. They charged him, particularly, with "upsetting the wage level," which to them seemed treason to business; although, had we been analyzing the facts, we must have known that increased production necessitates a larger market and therefore more buying power: and we did see, after it had happened, how the great high-wage automobile industry had contributed to general prosperity.

Our great steel industry, however, fought to the last against the abolition of the twelve-hour day. The greater success which that industry has enjoyed since 1920, it owes, in the first place, not to its own directors, but to the great steel strike of 1919 and its investigation by the Inter-Church World Movement. And yet, if business men had been considering the facts, they must have seen not only that increased production demands increased consumption, and therefore higher wages, but that it necessitates more leisure in which to consume the increase. Our steel industry has largely depended for some years now upon the automobile industry; and the automobile industry has depended for its development largely upon the fact that American workers do not have to work twelve hours a day and therefore do have time to go motoring.

But what does all this mean? It means a whole new world for all of us. It means that business, to be successful, can never again revert to its outgrown theories. It means, in fact, that we must now do consciously the things that we have heretofore done unconsciously, but, because we did not understand the process, have interrupted it and brought on periodical depressions.

It means, at first, that we must concentrate on the job of raising the standard of living throughout America, especially among the lower-income groups. It means that we must organize to eliminate unemployment; and we must find a way of excluding from our ranks anyone whose business practices tend to produce unemployment. Anyone, for instance, who does not pay sufficiently high wages to enable his employees to do their share of buying; and anyone who demands such a long workday as to destroy the leisure now necessary for adequate mass consumption.

We must organize, also, to eliminate unnecessarily high prices for any necessary service, which means the elimination of waste in the whole process of production and distribution. If business in general is to be prosperous, we cannot permit *any* industry to be laggard in this respect; for if coal miners and textile workers cannot buy automobiles and radio sets, the automobile and radio industries will surely languish and all other mass production industries will tend to depression.

But this, when we stop to analyze it, means that it is our business as business men to do the very things which, in the past, we have been organized to oppose. It means that we must establish the right to work—the right of every American to find a job, not merely to look for one. It means that we must establish, also, his right to high wages—the highest wages which the best possible organization of the job will make it possible to pay. A mere living wage, we must all see, would not do now. We must now establish the worker's right to live in comfort and even relative luxury; for living on any lower scale would bring on unemployment. And it means that we must establish his right to leisure and to economic security, not only in old age, but in case of any unemployment caused by necessary adjustments and which, to do our best, we cannot prevent.

I said that business *must* do this, for the only alternative is the end of our present business system. I do not assume to tell you just how business must do it; for in that, as I have said, I am only a learner. But the task is unescapable if our business system is to last. It is inherent in our industrial progress that these things must be achieved; and if American business does not achieve them, the American masses will achieve them through some other agency.

For this is the day of the masses—the day when the exploitation of the masses is no longer tenable. The masses everywhere are keenly sensing this, even though they may not be able to analyze it. They know they have a new power in their hands. They know they can overthrow governments and institutions. In almost every country they are on the march—in some, to be sure, behind leaders who seem to be leading them into war and chaos—but nowhere, in this new world, are the masses meek. Even in America, we have recently had a dramatic illustration of this. Practically all the powers which had been in undisputed control of public opinion virtually ordered the American people to go one way. And the American people went the other way.

What will happen now depends very largely upon how much business can unlearn, and how long it will take to unlearn it. But you, who are preparing for a business career, cannot, of course, afford to take my word for this. I may be wrong in every conclusion I have reached today; but if I am wrong, it is up to you and your teachers, not merely to assume that I may be wrong, but to find out where my error is.

You cannot, in fact, afford to take anyone's word—neither the word of business leaders nor of business teachers. This new world is *your* world; and since it is the only world in which you can do business, it is up to you to find out how it is put together and exactly what its human relations actually are.

The fact that one does not like this or that business theory is entirely irrelevant. Even though organized business and organized business teaching may still be unprepared to accept a new truth, that will not make it any the less true. Wrong principles are wrong principles, no matter how recently they may have become wrong principles; and the more we learn about how to do business upon wrong principles, the more it must unfit us for a successful business career.

On the Eve of the Election *

FRIENDS AND FELLOW CITIZENS OF THE UNITED STATES OF AMERICA:

(With the emphasis, please, on "United.")

At such a moment as this—one of the most momentous turning points in American history—why in the world should you be listening to a Boston shopkeeper, who in his whole life never held any political office, never ran for any political office and never received and never asked for any political favors?

I know, of course, that you did not tune in to hear me. I know, moreover, that if you are an angry partisan on either side, you won't see any sense in anything that I shall say. In spite of the heat and fury of this campaign, however, I am convinced that the great majority of us are not angry partisans on either side. In the main, I think, we *are* friends and fellow citizens.

That's the strangest thing about this whole campaign. The hottest, bitterest, maddest campaign within our memory has come at a time when the United States are more united than they ever were before, and when the people of the whole nation have become more conscious of their common interest.

In former times, Easterners may have wanted one thing and Westerners another; or employers have wanted one thing and employees another. But the New Deal, and the terrible times which gave birth to the New Deal, changed all that.

We now see the business necessity for higher incomes for the masses.

---

* Address delivered at 11:30 P.M., Monday, November 2, 1936, over a nation-wide hookup of both the National Broadcasting and Columbia Broadcasting Systems, as part of the final rally of the campaign to re-elect President Franklin D. Roosevelt. The four speakers in this "Democratic Hour" were the President, Mr. Filene, Senator Wagner, and National Chairman Farley.

If the clothing and textile industries are depressed, or if farmers cannot sell their products profitably, it wouldn't help the situation any to increase *my* income, for the simple reason that my income is already large enough to enable me to buy all the clothes and all the farm products which I happen to want. But if we increase the incomes of the lower-income groups, enabling *them* to buy all the clothes they want, or all the farm raised food which their children need, it would boom the clothing business, the textile industry, American agriculture, and all work-giving production as they have never boomed before.

And we voters are practically unanimous in wanting such things to happen. If the Republican party were to come out definitely against higher incomes for the masses, not one Republican voter out of ten would vote the Republican ticket.

Until March, 1933, however, neither party had ever worked out any plan for achieving business recovery by increasing the buying power of the people generally. Neither party, in fact, had any idea that any such plan could be evolved.

That is the great meaning of these great new times. Heretofore we assumed, whether we were Republicans or Democrats, that if we increased the income of one group, it was necessarily at the expense of some other group.

But that isn't true any longer. I'll say that these are new times.

I'll say more. I'll say something which may shock a lot of Democratic partisans. It's this. If the American people and American business fully understood the meaning of these times, it might be perfectly safe to make Alfred H. Landon president.

But new times always demand a New Deal. Furthermore, when we come to new times, we come to them with thinking shaped by the old times. In the beginning, then, new times are times of widespread confusion; and to launch a program applicable to the new times requires not merely vision and understanding, but leadership of the first magnitude—leadership which cannot be swayed from its definite purpose by the buffeting cross-currents of special interests and of Old Deal thinking.

None of us thinks the New Deal perfect. Nor has it been completed. But what we want to know is this:

1. Is it in accordance with these new times? That is, has it aimed definitely to increase the buying power of the American people generally?

2. Has it worked? Has it helped to bring us from depression to prosperity?

3. Do we want the various innovations which have gone to make up President Roosevelt's New Deal?

Do we, for instance, want unemployment insurance? Undoubtedly we do, although it was a political innovation which could never have been enacted in Congress excepting for the strong leadership of President Roosevelt.

Unemployment insurance was not a program in itself. It was a vital part of the New Deal which had become necessary—as necessary to business as it was to the unemployed. For unemployment insurance means *assurance of employment*. The thing that makes unemployment spread like a plague is that the unemployed can't buy. By enabling them to buy, however, even though unemployed, they will keep up such a demand for goods as to maintain employment. What the workers will get from unemployment insurance, then, is not merely the amount which they put into it, nor the amount which the employers are compelled by law to add to this. What they will get will be more regular employment—more wages—many times more money than the whole sum contributed.

Next, do we want old-age insurance? Undoubtedly we do, and for the same reasons. It isn't merely a humanitarian issue. It is part of the New Deal in these new times. Old-age insurance has now become necessary to business, to labor and to successful farming. If the old can't buy enough to live well, we business men can't sell enough to do well, which means that masses of those who are young, strong and able to work cannot be employed.

For the same reasons, the vast majority of the American voters also want other things which the New Deal gave us, namely, government co-operation with farmers, protection of bank deposits up to five thousand dollars, and adequate relief for all the victims of our traditional Old Deal way of doing business when, because we had become able to produce so much, that traditional way had brought us to the worst depression in our history.

Upsetting tradition, however, is a pretty serious thing; and it must be admitted that powerful interests, wedded to tradition, do not want the American people to have all these things; and it is interesting to note that these interests are unanimously backing Governor Landon for the presidency, although Governor Landon himself seems to favor most of these New Deal measures and, I believe, is quite sincere in his position.

Can anyone guess why this is? These interests met, we must remember, only a year or so ago, in a convention of the National Manufacturers' Association, and drew up a platform denouncing all of these things which the New Deal has brought to us—even denouncing social security and calling for a return to rugged individualism—which means: each man for himself and the Devil take the masses who are not employers and therefore do not and cannot control employment. And yet today, although they have not changed their minds, these Old Dealers are unanimously backing Landon.

There's a reason. To favor a New Deal is one thing. To put it over in a time of national confusion is another. Roosevelt put it over.

Landon promises that he will do the same things, and do them much better; but he also promises that there will be no *must legislation.*

In other words, he promises bounties for farmers, but promises that he won't insist upon them. He favors social security, including unemployment insurance and old-age insurance, but he won't use his powers as President to push such measures through.

That lets him out. That suits the special interests exactly. If their candidate stood on their platform, he couldn't get many votes anyway. So they don't care what Landon favors, if he will only keep this one sacred promise, and not insist as President Roosevelt has insisted, that the New Deal must go through—that we must as a nation go forward until the masses of the American people are secure in their right to work, in their right to buy, and their right, in this age of abundance, to buy abundantly.

Can we not see, then, why this campaign has not been a campaign of discussion of New Deal principles or of New Deal measures, but a campaign of bitterness and hatred on the part of traditional, Old Deal business minds—and on the part of interests, it would be well to remember, who own and control many of our larger newspapers?

Why has the President been denounced as a dictator although, on the very face of it, if there were a dictatorship, no administration measures could be annulled by the Supreme Court and no such political opposition would be permitted?

Why has the opposition shrieked about the Constitution versus the New Deal? They know that we reverence the Constitution—Republicans and Democrats alike; but we reverence it because it *was* a New Deal at a crisis in our national life when new times had made a New Deal necessary.

Why all this hysteria about departing from the American way of life, when the American way of life is, and always has been, a way of rapid change?

And why all this cry about the costs of the New Deal when, by increasing our national net debt by six and a half billion dollars, we have already increased our national income by twenty billions in a single year?

There's just one reason. Traditional thinking—not real business thinking.

We business men wanted recovery, and we got it. But we lost something, which I have always thought we should lose. *We lost control of America.* We are doing much better in a business way than we did four years ago; but if the New Deal is completed, and all Americans are guaranteed the right to work and to buy abundantly, we business men cannot be their bosses any longer. To succeed under the New Deal, we must become their servants. We must live up to the old command: "Let him that would be great among you be the servant of all."

Now, we need not get angry because some business leaders are not yet ready to accept any such great change as this. All we need to do, when we vote tomorrow, is to say whether *we* are ready for it. Do *we* want business to become our servant? Or do we want it to become our master once more?

That is why, on the eve of perhaps the most momentous election in our history, I haven't said a word about party politics. Nine out of ten of us, at least, want what the New Deal, under President Roosevelt's great leadership, has brought us; and if we haven't lost our heads as the special interests have hoped by now we would, nine out of ten of us will vote for President Roosevelt's re-election—not as Republicans and Democrats, but as friends and fellow citizens of one United Nation.

Capitalism and the Consumer Co-operatives *

MR. CHAIRMAN AND GENTLEMEN:

Some of my friends have apparently been puzzled by what seems to them my sudden interest in consumer co-operation, after a lifetime devoted, as they remind me, to private business.

I see no cause for mystification. In the first place, I have always dealt in consumer goods and therefore had to have consumer co-operation. In the second place, in company with the great majority of American business men, I have always done everything I could to keep my business from becoming private.

In Webster's Collegiate Dictionary, the first definition of "private" is "of or concerning an individual person, company or interest": then, "sequestered," "secret," "secluded," "solitary," and "not publicly known." None of us, I am sure, wants his business described by any such words as those.

We business men believe in publicity. We believe that what we are doing is in the public interest, which is only another way of saying that the public *has* an interest in our business. And unanimously, we business men, no matter what we have to sell, are interested in securing the co-operation of our buying public.

So far from being opposed to consumer co-operation, then, every modern American business man is strongly in favor of it. He not only wants his customers to co-operate with him, but he wants to co-operate with his customers. He knows he can't even continue in business if he doesn't.

He may not, of course, want to co-operate one hundred per cent. He may want to compromise. He may imagine that he

* Address at conference of the International Association of Sales Executives, Hotel Biltmore, New York, N. Y.—April 3, 1936.

can make more profits, for the time being at any rate, if he doesn't do everything possible for his customers, but just gives them, let us say, fairly good service instead.

But that attitude, as we all know, is dangerous. For some competitor may be so anxious to sell to our customers that he won't stop at mere fair service. He'll go the limit. He'll make his prices as low as he can, and he'll sit up nights thinking out some better ways to serve. Not that he is unselfish. He may be very selfish. But he wants a market, and it is inherent in our competitive business system that the methods of service which give the best values do capture the market.

This is all so elementary that one almost feels like apologizing for dwelling upon it. There is a reason, nevertheless, why one must dwell on it; for our competitive business system is now under challenge. Even in America, many of our business leaders have become so alarmed that they are going into politics in a big way, to defend the rights of business against the encroachments of government ownership and the menace of communism.

Now, I don't object to business going into politics; and I am quite as much opposed as are my fellow business men to the theories of government ownership, of socialism and communism. But let us be realistic about it. If we want to defend capitalism against socialism or against the encroachments of unfair competition by government in business, let us be clear as to what it is we are trying to defend. Are we trying to perpetuate the system which has made it possible for us to thrive? Or may we not be seeking only to perpetuate our position in that system—our individual business, our established ways of doing business—even appealing to government, perhaps, to defend our present holdings against the normal hazards of capitalism itself? *We can't do both of these things.*

If we try, for instance, to fix prices so that inefficient industries may continue to make profits, we are choking the very life out of capitalism. We may take such a course as capitalists, in the interest of our special capitalist investments; but it is a course under which capitalism cannot survive.

Capitalism can survive only as, under free and fair competition, we are constantly impelled to discover and apply better and better methods of production and distribution.

Naturally, in the progress of business, we must defend our individual rights; but once let business men get it into their heads that it is their right to make profits by withholding service, or by the continuation of methods under which the best possible service cannot be given, and they become the worst enemies of our present capitalistic system.

There is one and only one way by which a competitive business can achieve lasting success; and that is by giving better and better values to its buying public. And there is one and only one way by which our competitive business system can survive the encroachments of government ownership, or successfully defend itself against the menace of revolutionary movements. That is by giving better and better values to the buying public generally.

The real argument against government ownership is not that the government has no right to engage in business; for the government of these United States belongs to the people of these United States; and if the people can use it for the purpose of providing better service in any line than we business men are giving them, the people will do it, whether we business men say they have the right to do it or not.

All governments, we must know, engage in business to some extent, and none of us denies their right to do so. But to what extent? If we study the facts instead of arguing theoretical rights, we may find our problem greatly illuminated.

If we study the facts, we must discover that the principle involved in the actual practice of government ownership has nothing to do with whether the business concerned is public or private. Bread is at least as necessary to the public as, say, postage stamps; but the government is in the postal business and has not invested very heavily as yet in bakeries. Telegrams and telephones, surely, are as public as letters and postal cards; but the government is in one business and has kept out of the other, not according to any fine distinctions between the two services, but because the telephone and telegraph companies are giving good service, whereas nobody was giving adequate postal service when the government undertook the job.

There is a real objection to government ownership and operation of business, but the fact that it infringes upon the rights of investors, if it does do so, is not to the point. When the government contemplated carrying parcels as well as letters, spokesmen for the express companies pleaded for the rights of widows and orphans, dependent as they said for their very living upon express company dividends. But it didn't do any good, and there's a reason. They thought they were spokesmen for the *business way* of doing things, but they were not. For our business system can live only as it eliminates its dead investments, just as any other organism must eliminate its dead cells. To plead for the right to draw dividends, then, simply because money has been invested, is not pleading for our business system but against it.

Livery stables by the thousands went out of business when the motor car arrived, which was obviously tough on widows and orphans who owned livery stables. Something doubtless should have been done for them; but nothing could be done for them on a *livery stable basis* without violating the basic principles of capitalism, as well as the basic principles of common sense.

The real argument against government in business is not that it is too radical, but that it is too conservative. Because a government can make up any deficit by taxation, it conserves too many practices which ought to be eliminated. You and I can't do that. If you and I manage our businesses badly, our businesses are eliminated. Therefore, we must improve our methods. Therefore, we must give better service.

Thousands of independent merchants were forced out of business when the chain store arrived, and the plight of the little man became a problem. This problem, fortunately, is being solved, but not in the way that the spokesman for the little man usually suggested.

His idea was that the chain stores ought to be taxed out of existence, to save the investments of the little fellows. Something, to be sure, has been done along that line; but everything that has been done has not only been a direct blow at the buying public, through subsidizing inefficiency, but a direct blow at our capitalist business system and a direct blow at the little man himself.

Wise little men, however, instead of crying out for the protection of their outmoded stores, have been dealing with the facts of this ever changing capitalist order, with the result that they are in many cases outsmarting and outselling the centrally owned chains; and they have done this in the only way it could be done, by giving better service to the buying public than their big competitors were giving.

No one little man, acting independently, could do this; but by organizing voluntary leagues of little stores, and arranging that all the stores be served by one central organization, the little man has not only again gone into business, but has gone into Big Business quite as definitely and quite as successfully as any big capitalist can.

Now where do the consumer co-operatives fit into this picture? Do they, as some seem to assume, constitute a new menace to business? Or are they merely a menace to continued inefficiency in business? The answer is all important. For business is being menaced by so many things just now that one more menace might easily be the straw that breaks the camel's back. On the other hand, if these consumer co-operatives result in giving more service to masses of consumers than they could otherwise get, they may prove to be the very salvation of our business system, a bulwark of defense against socialism, communism and dead, dull, bureaucratic operation of industry, whether by the government or by shortsighted capitalist cartels.

It is quite natural, of course, that individual retailers, noting the rise of these co-operatives, should see in them a threat to business—another hand reaching out to grab their customers and their profits.

But I wonder if anybody remembers the depression. *That* was trouble—real trouble—for all of us; and yet it wasn't because the hands of competitors were grabbing our profits. It was because there weren't any profits for either them or us to grab.

We couldn't make profits in those days—not because others were making them but because others weren't. If only some great, new, profit making industry had come along, we would all have welcomed it. The more successful it was, the more people it would have employed, and that would have meant better business opportunities for all of us.

Our trouble was that we could sell so little to a people who were so largely broke. We couldn't be successful unless the masses of Americans were successful; and they couldn't be successful unless they were regularly employed. On the other hand, we couldn't employ them unless we could sell our products; and the foreign market had been so shot to pieces that our only possible market was the market of these masses at home. So no great new industry arose; and under the circumstances, none could arise.

It wasn't that our masses didn't want to buy our products. Their wants were greater than ever, and they would gladly have bought everything that we could possibly have produced, if our industries had been running at full capacity and employing every available man and woman in the country. The only reason they didn't buy on such a scale was that they couldn't. They were either out of money or had so little that they were saving it to tide them over the depression.

And because the masses couldn't buy, industries shut down, unemployment increased and incomes generally dwindled. Because the masses couldn't buy, businesses couldn't meet their obligations and the banks became involved. Because the masses couldn't buy, moreover, there were few further opportunities for capital investment, so our money largely remained idle; and finally, because the masses couldn't buy in adequate volume, securities held by the banks so shrank in value that the banks became unsafe, and millions of Americans not only lost their jobs but their savings too.

Yes, our business system was menaced. We were close to social revolution in the spring of 1933. We may have differences of opinion as to what the New Deal Administration did to carry us through that crisis, but there can be little difference of opinion as to what the trouble was. The trouble was solely our inability to sell in accordance with our enormously increased capacity to produce; and this inability to sell was not due to any saturation of the market, but to the inability of the American masses to buy the things which we all wanted to sell and which they were eager and anxious to have.

That some of us were not selling consumer goods makes no difference. No one wants capital goods for themselves alone. The only reason there *are* any capital goods is that people want consumer goods. The only reason that people work at all is that they want goods and services. Capitalism rests upon buying and selling, and goes up or down in accordance with our ability to buy and sell. In its early stages, it was not necessary that the masses of consumers buy very much; for our machines were crude and relatively unproductive, and the need of the hour was for more capital with which to launch bigger and better machines. In its later development, however, the machine became so productive that a smaller and smaller part of its total product was needed for capital purposes, and a greater and greater total consumption became the basic need if the capitalist system were to endure.

Of course this meant that the system would have to change. Being a living growth and not a mere institutional formula, if it didn't change it would surely die. If we are interested in its preservation, then, we must become interested in whatever course will now tend to increase mass buying, mass employment, and mass enjoyment of consumer goods. Capitalism has no greater enemies than those capitalists who, in their concern for some supposedly divine right to make profits by withholding service, do not plan in such times as these for increased mass buying.

As everybody knows, I have constantly urged the nation-wide organization of business to raise wages—to raise them as a business investment—so that our money could return to use instead of remaining in stagnant pools. But business hasn't got around to that yet. If we can reduce the costs of production and distribution, however, so that the mass consumer can purchase a greater volume of our industrial products, we shall be working toward the same end. But such a course *is* consumer co-operation; and if consumers take it on their own initiative, they co-operate with business for maximum business prosperity, by bringing about more production, more employment and thereby a still greater market and more opportunities for capital investment.

Of course, if one goes among the thousands of workers and farmers who are now studying and experimenting with consumer co-operation, he may hear a lot of harsh words about capitalism and the capitalists, and he may hear talk of substituting a co-operative system in its place.

But capitalism, as it progresses, must become more and more co-operative. It isn't that we become angelic. We merely become confronted by the fact that we can't make a go of business in days like these unless we do serve the consumer more and more effectively.

Consumer co-operatives, on the other hand, if they are to succeed, are under the same compulsion as any other business to do better and better. If they don't they will lose their membership, quite as definitely as any standstill store will lose its customers. They can't make up their deficits by taxing the public any more than any so-called private business can. They must engage the best possible management. They must employ the most extensive fact-finding research; for they can no more afford to operate according to the notions of their well-meaning but inexperienced idealists than business can afford to continue operating according to the old, inherited business traditions.

This all points, to be sure, to great changes in our capitalist order. But they are the changes which result from growth—from keeping abreast of the times—not the decay which inevitably must set in when we attempt to conserve our no-longer-adequate formulas.

If we refuse to go forward—if we do not permit capitalism to go on to this new and greater development—we may call ourselves conservatives, but we shall conserve nothing of any use to us. For we cannot stop science and invention. We must employ the most efficient methods of production; and if in doing this we do not arrange things so that we can sell according to our capacity to produce, all that we can really conserve is poverty, unemployment and business depression.

Many imagine, to be sure, that we can go on to further periods of prosperity and yet, because of our progress in labor saving technique, continue to have widespread unemployment. The idea is not only cruel but futile; for no social order can be maintained unless it provides an opportunity for its masses to earn a living; and capitalist production has already reached such a stage of efficiency that the masses must consume abundantly if our industries are to operate at anything approaching capacity.

Instead of worrying over the rise of these consumer co-operatives, then, business men who keep abreast of business change will welcome them as reinforcements in the struggle against depression, and as insurance for the continuance of our capitalistic business system. A few years ago, many bankers opposed the Credit Unions, which are uniformly successful financial co-operatives, lest the movement might take some share of the credit business out of their hands. All intelligent bankers know better now. They are now co-operating, and for good reason, with the Credit Unions; for they know that masses initiated and trained in the sound administration of money and credit will not be led into such movements as the Townsend Plan or schemes to share our wealth by parceling out our capital. Similarly, let the masses come to understand and to practice sound principles of distribution, and they can be depended upon to oppose the wastes and losses to all legitimate business which result from inefficiency and graft. And in the meantime, we may be sure, they will not take any business from any private distributors who can give the public better service than they. On the contrary, by enabling the public to buy more than it has been buying, they will increase production, increase employment and increase the opportunities for business in every line. Business men, I believe, when they fully understand the facts of our business evolution and fully understand the real menace to capitalism, will give these consumer co-operatives their heartiest co-operation.

Our President and Our Newspapers *

American newspapers are the best newspapers in all the world, but there is one interesting piece of news which they are not telling.

In the spring of 1933, when business was prostrate and our banks were closed, these newspapers as a rule were loud in their praises of President Roosevelt. But now, when the papers themselves are heralding the story of returning prosperity, most of them are denouncing the President and declaring that the business revival which is occurring under his Administration *cannot* occur under his Administration.

One might suppose that this is because another presidential election will soon be due and that the editors of these papers are generally Republicans. But that doesn't explain it, as every newspaper man understands.

We cannot tell, when we read an editorial, what the writer of that editorial really thinks. Let the owner of the newspaper give the word, and a Republican editor must as a rule write Democratic editorials, or a Democratic editor must write Republican editorials; that is, if they are interested, as many are these days, in holding down their jobs.

We cannot always tell, when we read a newspaper, what the *owner* thinks. As a rule, however, we *can* tell *what the owner wants us to think*. And for very definite reasons, the owners and financial backers of most of our larger newspapers do not want the masses of America to understand what the Roosevelt Administration has been really doing.

Whether the Roosevelt Administration is right or wrong, we must admit that this is a serious situation. In America, at least

* Address over a national hookup of the Columbia Broadcasting System—December 21, 1935.

theoretically, the people rule. What kind of government we have depends upon their votes; and how people vote depends upon how well they understand the issues at stake. Daily, they read their newspapers because they want to keep informed; and they read them, not only for the news, but for interpretations of the news —for some understanding of the meaning of events.

And yet, in a great national crisis, in which our national Administration, working for a better distribution of wealth, has somehow come into conflict with the great financial and Big Business interests, it turns out that our newspapers—the very source of the average voter's information and education—are usually owned and controlled by these same special interests.

But it isn't a conspiracy. The story is much more interesting than that. Getting angry, moreover, won't help us in the least. Admittedly, there is great confusion, but confusion cannot be dispelled by blindly fighting it. All that we really need to do is to understand the situation. Then we may discover that it isn't altogether bad.

Our typical, modern newspaper *is* a Big Business. Big Business did not buy up our papers so that it might have a mouthpiece. Our papers became big, rather, in the same way and at the same time that other businesses became big; and they became big *because* other businesses were becoming big.

People sometimes sigh for the so-called good old days of journalism when a newspaper was a personal mouthpiece for its individual owner; but our modern Big Business newspapers print more news and more accurate news than those old personal organs could ever print; and this has been due very largely to the growth of advertising.

When our factories became bigger, they had to have bigger markets; and they sought these bigger markets, largely, through newspaper advertising. To answer the need, however, newspapers had to have a large circulation; and they got this larger circulation, as a rule, in two ways—by printing more and more accurate news and by regaling their readers with entertainment, sensation and thrills. Little by little, however, it was discovered that yellow journalism, while it might achieve a big circulation, did not get the *kind* of circulation most valuable to advertisers; and ever since then, our American newspapers have tended to print more, and more accurate, news.

Many people are saying just now, of course, that what we need is a press which will be at least fair toward the Roosevelt Administration—a press that will dare to represent the masses of Americans. But they don't say how we are going to get a big newspaper, which will not at the same time be a big business; and so long as our Big Business leaders are angry at this Administration, it seems to me that we must expect the average Big Business newspaper to be just about as angry as it is.

If the average paper were distorting the news, the situation would be far more serious than it is. But that isn't the trouble. As far as the news columns are concerned, there is at least more impartiality than there is in any other country with which I am acquainted, and more than there ever was at any previous period. It is only in the editorials and special articles that the newspapers show signs of losing their heads.

If you read in the news columns that business is reviving, and you read in the editorial columns that it is being strangled by the Roosevelt Administration, which statement will you be likely to believe?

Our business leaders are obviously angry because the Roosevelt Administration has spent so many billions for the relief of the unemployed that it has not been able to balance the budget.

Well, this is a free country; and newspaper owners are human and have as much right to be angry as anyone else. The newspapers, in their news columns, have told us where the money went; and we all know that the President was as anxious as the newspapers that the budget should be balanced. It was only a question of *when* it should be balanced.

If he had balanced the budget when these angry newspaper owners wanted him to balance it, millions of Americans must have starved to death. He had to let the budget wait or let the starving millions wait. If anyone is angry because he did not let the millions starve, I suppose we must let him be angry. But we can do our own thinking about it.

So I am not attacking the newspapers. I am glad I live in a country in which the press can attack the Administration, and even attack it angrily and unfairly. If we were to stop unfair criticism, we would soon be stopping all criticism, and American liberty would be destroyed.

Nor am I worrying about President Roosevelt. Washington was attacked so bitterly and unfairly that he declared he would rather be in the grave than in the Presidency; and Franklin Roosevelt has not been assailed more bitterly than was Abraham Lincoln. Our nation, however, remembers Washington and Lincoln and has utterly forgotten who their critics were.

All that we need to do is to understand the nature of these attacks. The real interests of business have not been hurt, as the news columns bear daily witness. But the *feelings* of our business leaders *have* been hurt; and when our feelings have been hurt, we are not in any mood to weigh the facts.

In all history, up to a very few years ago, the rich could be rich only if the masses remained poor; for there wasn't and couldn't be enough to go around, and we knew of no way by which enough could be produced.

The privileged classes, then, made a religion of their privileges. Some were benevolent and some were cruel, but they made much of their divine right to rule and were almost uniformly angered when that divine right was challenged by democracy. Under capitalism, capitalists gained the privileges, and they looked upon those privileges as *their* divine right. For many years, indeed, if the masses had had a high standard of living, it would have been impossible to accumulate sufficient capital to develop our modern, almost magically productive machines; and every administration, even in democratic America, was compelled to think first of the needs of capital.

When our machines became so productive, however, that their output could not be sold unless the masses were able to buy it, that old attitude of capitalism no longer worked. Coolidge prosperity turned into Hoover depression, not because we changed our ways, but because we didn't change our ways when a change had become absolutely necessary.

There had to be a New Deal, if we were ever to be prosperous again. Some way had to be found to get sufficient buying power into the hands of the masses, so that they could buy the now enormous output of our machines. Unless that were done, business must continue in the dumps, our machines could not be operated at anything like their capacity and millions must therefore remain unemployed. Hoover naturally couldn't see this. He can't see it yet, and is still insisting that the way to prosperity is the way which he tried, and which sank us further and further into depression until, although we had more money than ever, our banks were forced to close and, although we had more of everything than ever, America was on the verge of starvation.

Neither, perhaps, did Roosevelt see what the trouble was; but Roosevelt promised to find out, and he did. Every act of the Roosevelt Administration, then, has been an effort at least to get adequate buying power into the hands of the masses of Americans so that, by their buying, they might keep business good and keep themselves employed.

The N.R.A. was such an effort; and if business had acted on its real interests, instead of on its feelings, it would have co-operated in the N.R.A. to make wages high enough to enable the masses of wage earners to buy in such abundance that every employable person could be employed.

Not our real business interests, then, but our traditional business minds felt hurt and robbed of their supposedly divine right. Now they are making open war, not only against everything which the Administration has done but against everything which it has been trying to do.

Against unemployment insurance. Against old-age insurance. Against any concerted plan to raise wages, and now even against the spending of billions for relief of the unemployed; when, if the billions were not being spent, millions of Americans would be starving and business would be getting worse instead of improving as it now is.

The Administration, we must know, did not want to spend all that money, and such appropriations would have been unnecessary if American business—which happens to own and control so many of our American newspapers—had been willing to co-operate in the New Deal.

The feelings of business are all against Roosevelt; but the facts of business are all on the Administration's side. The facts, fortunately, can still be found in the news columns—the feelings in the editorials and special articles. Whatever we think of the fight, we must admit that it is uniquely interesting. And we needn't worry overmuch; for, in any protracted war between feelings and facts, there is always an excellent chance that the facts will win.

Youth and Our Economic Superstitions *

MR. CHAIRMAN AND MEMBERS OF THE NATIONAL STUDENT FEDERATION:

Before I speak about "Youth and Our Economic Superstitions," I wish to say a word about two other superstitions.

First: a prevailing superstition concerning youth.

Second: a widespread superstition concerning superstition.

We frequently hear youth referred to as the "Younger Generation." That isn't so; and to assume that it is so confuses our thinking, especially on the problems of education.

The so-called younger generation, to be sure, is composed of our younger individuals. But a "generation" is a social, not an individual, term. As an individual, I grant, I have had more years than you, and more individual experience behind me. Socially, however, your generation is more mature than mine. You have more social experience in your background.

You young people will solve your social problems, I am sure, much more successfully than we of our generation solved ours. But that isn't anything to gloat about. You ought to do a better job than we did. We are handing you all of our mistakes. Former generations, to be sure, handed us *their* mistakes, in much the same way; but you have their mistakes and ours too as data to begin with, whereas we had nothing but theirs.

And let me say it is a rich legacy which we are leaving you; for I doubt that any generation in human history ever bequeathed to the next generation a richer lot of mistakes than we are handing down to you.

Furthermore, you have the advantage of knowing that they

---

* Address before Tenth Annual Congress of the National Student Federation of America, Parker House, Boston, Massachusetts—December 29, 1934.

are mistakes. You know, for instance, that war is a mistake. We didn't know that. We had to prove it by making the biggest war that had ever been made. Yours is the first generation in history which has started its job with the definite knowledge that in war the victor loses quite as much as the vanquished. In this and in many other lines of social experience, you are obviously more mature than we.

Now as to that superstition concerning superstition.

Many of us who pride ourselves on being realistic imagine that superstitions have come down to us from ages in which there was no realism. That is a superstition.

It is a superstition, in the first place, to suppose that any of us are or can be thoroughly realistic, and it is a superstition to suppose that ancient beliefs which now seem superstitious were necessarily superstitious at the time they were formulated.

The superstitions of today are not the superstitions of yesterday. More often, they are the formulas of yesterday, which applied very well to the conditions of yesterday but which must be edited and recast if they are to become applicable to the conditions of today.

Most of our prevailing superstitions contain some element of truth, and were doubtless useful at the time that they were formulated. It is still bad luck to walk under a ladder—if there is someone on the ladder wielding a paintbrush and splashing the paint. It was frequently fatal in the Boer War for British soldiers to light three cigarettes with one match; for by the time the third cigarette was lighted, the Boer sharpshooters often got their range.

Then there is the superstition of American individualism. There was some foundation for that too, although, if we wish to be very literal about it, human beings could never be human beings if they were unreservedly individualistic. To be human, they had to participate in human life, and human life has always been very largely social.

To be really human, for one thing, they had to have a language; and by no possibility could each individual have his own individual language, for the simple reason that if other people did not share one's language, it wouldn't be language. It wouldn't be a means of communication.

Similarly, we have always had to have codes of conduct—not a special code for each individual, which would be no code at all and which, therefore, would make human life impossible.

Nevertheless, the early settlers in America had to depend so largely for their living on what seemed to be their own unaided efforts, that they became relatively individualistic; and there was no bunk or superstition about their individualism. Nor was there anything destructive about it. It made them self-reliant. It helped to build character.

If I find myself on a new continent, and the only way that I can get my dinner is to go out in the woods and shoot something, I'm going to do it. And if I do do it, I may not only achieve something to eat but achieve a sort of spiritual experience as well. It is likely to give me a thrill of self-reliance. I may exult in my own prowess. I may feel my independence of other people; and I may go on to my other problems with more confidence and more power than I would have had without this experience of discovering my ability to take care of myself. Strictly speaking, it might not be self-reliance at all. For I didn't make the gun, and without the gun I might be helpless. I relied, therefore, not only upon the gun and the gunmakers, but upon the original inventors of firearms, the discoverers of gunpowder, and the generations which preceded them, who, although they had no guns, still developed projectiles and the art of hunting. My theory of self-reliance, then, might be demonstrably inaccurate; but my experience of what I *called* self-reliance might still be a valid and valuable experience.

But suppose there *are* no woods in which I *can* hunt game. Suppose I need a dinner as much as ever, but all I have is my theory and my gun. And suppose I try to apply the law of forest individualism to the streets of Boston. I might make a living that way for a while. Some gunmen do. But they do not develop any worth-while experience; and the more they try to apply this old formula of individualism to these new conditions, they not only become menaces to society but utterly detestable as individuals.

Or suppose, instead of a gun, I own a great public utility, or an industrial or mercantile corporation. That's when this superstition of individualism gets to doing the most damage. For such things are obviously social in character, and my individual ownership of them cannot erase that fact.

I am not preaching. I am simply calling attention to obvious facts. If one is operating any social mechanism, he must operate it in the light of his social responsibility or he will become a social menace. Incidentally, if he does not so operate it, but operates it instead for the exploitation of the human community, his success, like the success of the gunman, is likely to be very short-lived.

It is the law of this machine age that a social mechanism must be operated to serve the community; and if we are so blinded by the superstitions of individualism that we cannot understand that law, we not only injure the community but, in the long run, destroy our chances for individual success. To make a rapid transit system permanently profitable, we must provide the whole public with the best possible transportation at the lowest possible cost. The same principle applies to every industry and every business. By high rates and high prices, we may squeeze the public for a time; but the inevitable result is to drive patronage away and wreck the very properties which we meant to guard. The American railroads today are impressive monuments to the superstition that railroads exist primarily for the benefit of those who own or those who direct them.

Your generation, I am sure, will not wish to destroy any real human values. What is good, what is applicable in individualism you will wish to preserve; but to preserve the real values of individualism, it seems to me, you will have to uproot these superstitions of individualism.

Whether individualism is the most accurate term to use or not, we human beings are not all alike and we do not want to be. We object to regimentation; and we would object rightly, I believe, even to prosperity, if it tended to mold us all according to the same pattern. Unless we deal with realities, however, as far as it is possible for us to deal with reality, instead of swallowing some formula of an age that is past, we may find ourselves regimented by our very efforts to escape from regimentation.

I know some superstitious souls who think that social planning is unlucky and that, if they engage in it, they'll surely come down with regimentation or some similar disease. As a matter of fact, of course, if there were no social planning, we would all be regimented. If we did not develop some degree of co-operation, we would all be forced into the same mold.

Even the most primitive agriculture and the most primitive industry required some degree of planned co-operation between man and man. Without industry and agriculture, however, we would all have to become hunters; and we'd have to hunt with our teeth and claws, which would require so much of our time and energy that none of us could possibly spare any time or energy for anything else. That might be individualism, but it would be beastly individualism; and we would all be regimented on the level of the beasts.

It wouldn't be rugged individualism. It might not be rugged enough even to perpetuate the race, to say nothing of giving it any human satisfactions. It was by social planning that man was able to become dominant over animals which were individually far more powerful than he and far better fitted to survive. And it is only by more and more social planning that man can conquer those forces which drive nations to war when they do not want to fight, and keep individuals in a desperate struggle for existence although they have a machine in their hands abundantly able to provide economic security for all.

Youth is often told, I know, that its aspirations are impractical, and that wisdom consists of concentrating as soon as possible on the stern business of making a living. Well, there was some sense in that—once. But that was in the days before the machine age when, if one did not give the bulk of his time and energy to making a living, he ceased to live and incidentally ceased to aspire. If we examine the facts of the machine age, however, instead of taking this ancient talk too seriously, we shall see that the machine age makes it possible for the masses everywhere to get an abundant living, without devoting the bulk of their time and energy to the task. For the first time in human history, then, the so-called younger generation may now actually achieve the liberty to live in full harmony with human aspiration.

Youth surely wants liberty. But what is youth going to do about it? Does it want this new and greater liberty, or will it be content to follow the superstitions of liberty and to wear liberty's old clothes?

This is the machine age. Do you want liberty to live in the machine age and to achieve the satisfactions which the machine age makes possible? Or, do you want the liberty to live as if it were not the machine age? You can't achieve that sort of liberty, but you can lose all liberty by trying to achieve it.

The American pioneers were rather realistic on this subject of liberty. But their realism may become our superstition. They took advantage of *their* opportunities. If we want real liberty, we will have to take advantage of *our* opportunities. They had a raw continent in which it was possible for almost every family to take up land and, by hard and steady and lifelong labor, produce its living directly from the soil. We have a machine age of almost magical efficiency. We know how to run these machines. We do run them occasionally, in fact; and when they are running, the results are marvelous.

Why don't we keep them running? Superstition—that's all; and chief among these superstitions is the superstition of liberty. We haven't been looking for the real liberty which this machine might confer upon us, but for the formula of liberty which the self-contained farm once conferred upon those early settlers. Because these modern industries are not self-contained farms, however, they cannot be operated as if they were. *Because* we have tried to run them as if they were, they wouldn't run, excepting by occasional jerks and starts; and when they didn't run, capital, labor and the consuming public all lost their liberty.

It isn't my purpose here to suggest how this machine can be made to run so that every American may be able to enjoy a more and more abundant life. I simply say that it can't be run by superstition. If you want real liberty in this machine age, you've got to operate the machine according to the facts of this machine age; which means that it is necessary not only to discover the facts, but to train the mind to respond to facts instead of to the fears which are nurtured by superstition.

Just now, for instance, many good people who think that unemployment insurance would be a fine thing, if we could only afford it, are staggered by what they believe to be its tremendous cost.

Is there any sense in that attitude? None whatever. Nothing but superstition. If they would think in terms of the facts, they would discover that the whole cost of insurance is the cost of administering it. Insurance is a system of spreading losses, not of granting bonuses.

Imagine running a life insurance company on the theory held by such timid souls. Imagine warning the agents not to insure so many applicants because the company can't see where all the money is to come from to pay all the policies which will certainly mature.

The money will come from the insured, of course. That doesn't mean in life insurance, however, that the money paid for deaths comes from the dead; and it doesn't mean in unemployment insurance that money paid for unemployment comes from the unemployed.

The fact is that unemployment, because it doesn't produce what the unemployed might be producing, is a loss. If we do not prevent unemployment, we must suffer the loss; and we must not only suffer the loss in nonproduction but somebody must care for the unemployed. Expecting the unemployed to shift for themselves is not only unthinkably cruel but economically fantastic; for the unemployed, even if they did not riot and destroy our social order, would continue to be nonproducers; which means that they would not and could not buy the products of industry. Business therefore could not sell and industry could not continue to make these products, and more workers therefore would become unemployed. Unemployment, however, unlike death, is preventable; and unemployment insurance, therefore, is not merely a scheme for spreading the losses involved, but of so bringing the loss to the attention of all concerned that all concerned will organize to prevent unemployment. Directly, it would prevent much unemployment by enabling the unemployed to continue buying and permitting the employed to spend the money which they would otherwise save to tide them over periods of unemployment. Beyond that, however, it must accomplish much more by inducing employers, in their own selfish interest, to organize more and more employment.

Now let's repeat the question: Where is all the money to come from with which to change our present unbearably expensive way of dealing with unemployment?

Our notions of money are simply loaded down with superstitions. Where does money come from anyway? The prevailing notion seems to be that it comes from pockets and that its rightful function is to remain in those pockets. If we examine the facts, however, we shall make a startling discovery. It is that money is a medium of exchange.

The purpose of money is to facilitate exchange. When money is not used for that purpose, it ceases, temporarily at least, to be money. Money in our pockets, then, is money temporarily out of commission. Real money is the money which is going into our pockets and coming out.

We have to have more money in the machine age than in any previous age, solely because we have to have more exchange. The ancient farmer on the self-contained farm could live sometimes without hardly seeing a dollar from month to month. The farmer in this machine age, however, has to get money if he is to live well, and may get to thinking therefore that money is wealth. If he were to think again, however, he would realize that he couldn't live well merely by taking in money. In order to live well, it is equally necessary to pay it out.

It is when business men, bankers and manufacturers get to thinking of money as wealth that the machinery of exchange breaks down and all society, including those business men, bankers and manufacturers, comes to grief. It is then that we have unemployment; and money, not being used to facilitate exchange, largely ceases to function.

In 1929, many people wondered who got the money which they lost. Because there was as much currency in November as there was in September, many imagined that there was as much money as ever. But there wasn't. Money being a medium of exchange, the volume of actual money at any given time is determined by the volume of exchange which is occurring at that time; and just how real even that money is depends upon the reality of the exchange which is being effected. For money is a symbol of wealth; and if the money is to be truly genuine, the exchange must be an actual exchange of needed goods and services.

Which brings us to a widespread superstition, not about money, but about wealth itself. Frequently we get to thinking about wealth as things—especially things that people want. But that is a little to one side of the facts. Wealth consists of things which people want *and which are available to them.* There may be many things on the moon which we could use if we could get at them; but until we can discover a way of getting at them, we cannot reckon them as wealth.

The superstitious supposed that there was as much wealth, at least, in America, after the Wall Street crash as there was before, even if there wasn't as much money. There were, in fact, as many things; but because the people who wanted those things could not get them, those things had really ceased to be wealth and even those who still possessed the things were poor, not rich.

Our farmers had millions of bushels of wheat, and wheat is surely something which people want. Millions of families in India and China, in fact, were starving at the time. But this wheat was not available to those who wanted it, and it ceased, therefore, to be wealth to those who owned it. One could almost reckon a Kansas farmer's wealth at that time by the amount of wheat he didn't own.

But when the New Deal proposed to correct this situation by the simple means of increasing the buying power of the masses, all the superstitions concerning money and wealth bristled in revolt. People thought that money was something to accumulate, not to pay out; although if it were not paid out, it most assuredly could not come in. In their superstition, many even forgot that exchange is necessarily a two-way process, both within the nation and internationally. Business men prayed for a heaven in which they could sell more than their customers could buy; and the National Manufacturers' Association prayed for some miracle which would enable them to carry on mass production without their enabling the masses to consume its products.

America is groping its way out of some of these superstitions today; but they still remain in the back of our business thinking, forever inhibiting the actions which it is imperative for us to take. It is the job of youth, today, to approach this problem free from all such inhibitions.

I do not know, and do not much care, whether you are radical, liberal or conservative. But I know that you are younger than we, with all the fire of youth, and yet that *you are a later and therefore socially more mature generation.* In that lies our promise of a better world. That fact, it seems to me, is the very foundation of our faith in human progress. Because of that, we were able to find our way out of the dark ages, with their ignorance and their cruelty. It was not that the people of any generation did or could become wholly enlightened, but that the succeeding generation carried on.

I know also that you are not overburdened with reverence. You couldn't see the wreckage which our generation has made and still retain the superstitious hero worship with which *we* began. That's all to the good. You will know, at least, that successful men are not necessarily supermen, and you will not look up to them as patterns for *your* lives.

You will understand that nobody, not even your professors, can be wise enough to tell you *what* to think; and that what we need for human progress is to learn *how* to think—how to free ourselves more and more from the spell of worn-out formulas and how to find the truth and follow it.

But this, instead of decreasing your faith in humanity, will only strengthen it. For you will know that *all* the great achievements were accomplished not by perfect supermen but by faulty human beings, with the co-operation of other faulty human beings.

You will want to be successful, no doubt. But, freed as you are from so many social superstitions, you will understand that success does not come from power *over* our fellow men but from power *with* our fellow men. You will not, then, be forever trying to get something for nothing, either as a ticket holder in the sweepstakes or a stockholder in some corporation which is overcharging the public. As you study the facts of the machine age, I am convinced, you will see that it cannot rest on gambling and speculation but that it must be founded on the principle of human service.

I say this in spite of the outburst of petty gambling in America today. I do not think we can rightly blame our youth for that, when we of our generation have done our worst to make you believe that the mere possession of property, although not earned and not used for human service, is entitled to receive rewards.

A social order with that conception of property created a great structure of debt which all but strangled our economic life. It issued credits for war and everything discreditable, and tried to establish the principle that these debts, although they were seriously interfering with our progress, were still immortal.

They weren't. The debts died on our hands, and more of them are dying day by day. In our superstition, however, we have so far refused to bury them and write them forever off humanity's books. We seem to be leaving that rotten job to you.

I believe, however, that you will not flinch. You will not tolerate a social order with so many economic corpses lying around. You will bury the dead and turn to the building of a better world in which there will be no profits except the earned profits that come from real service and no privilege except the privilege of participation in the upward march of human life. I am not thinking of any Utopia or any Perfect State. Nor am I thinking of ultimate reality. I am thinking of the upward struggle through and beyond our superstitions and an ever nearer and nearer approach to Truth.

What's Next in Advertising? *

MR. CHAIRMAN, MEMBERS AND GUESTS:

The late Nineteen Twenties were not the golden age of advertising. That was the age of brass. The golden age is just ahead of us.

Advertising will improve from now on, both in quality and in quantity; and as it improves in quality it will improve in quantity. How rapid this progress will be, however, will depend largely upon how rapidly we can forget what we knew in 1928 and 1929.

For our basic problem today is distribution. I am sure that no one who has been observing business developments of late will challenge that statement. In this machine age, where our capacity to produce is necessarily increasing from year to year, our problem is the problem of effecting a larger and larger distribution of goods and services.

That is why we must have more and more advertising. But it is also why the advertising technique of 1928 and 1929 is now of relatively little use to us; for an important part of the advertising of those days was not designed to increase the *total* volume of distribution.

An important part of that advertising, for instance, was the advertising, not of goods and services, but of alluring offerings in stocks and bonds. Stocks and bonds, to be sure, have to be advertised, and I do not mean to criticise their being advertised. The fact remains, however, that the large-scale advertising of stocks and bonds, in 1928 and 1929, resulted in the American masses investing billions of dollars in stocks and bonds *at a time when it was vitally necessary to our prosperity that they should have been purchasing goods and services instead.*

---

* Address at Annual Convention of the First District of The Advertising Federation of America, Hotel Garde, New Haven, Connecticut—November 9, 1934.

Had the masses bought goods instead of securities at that particular time, our industries could have continued to run and the masses could have kept their jobs. Since they bought securities instead of goods, however, the production and distribution of goods was necessarily reduced; which caused such unemployment and such a further reduction of the market for goods as to impair the value of even the best of those securities.

I am not, of course, blaming advertising men for this. Advertising, then as always, was the voice of business, but business was dumb. I am simply noting the facts. That bull market was created largely by advertising—much of it very skillful advertising—but the total result was not to help business but to wreck it.

One of the dominant notes in advertising, in those days, was what was known in the profession as the Snob Appeal. It was based on the theory that the public wouldn't mind being gypped, if it were gypped stylishly; and that the price of things, therefore, was not a matter to be given much consideration.

In every city, there were many stores, large and small, trying to sell exclusiveness instead of goods; and many restaurants were so interested in providing swank that they often neglected to provide good food.

Now it can't be denied that some people made money for a time out of such rackets. The fact remained, however, that business could not sell more than the public could buy; and if the public paid more than it was necessary to pay for anything, it was left with less money than it might have had with which to purchase other things. In so far, then, as this Snob Appeal tended to increase prices, or to turn the attention of business from the necessity of lowering prices, it tended to decrease the total volume of business, to increase unemployment and to hasten the depression.

Incidentally, it may be well to remember, it was those business organizations which did emphasize low prices which made the most notable success even in those mad years. It was Ford and Chevrolet, Woolworth, Grant and the other nation-wide chains, who made the greatest profits and stood up best when the depression came; and it was those organizations which went in strongest for the Snob Appeal which most frequently failed during the lush years or were first to fall when the financial cyclone struck.

The purpose of advertising is to sell goods and services. Let us not get away from that basic truth, or we'll never be able to discover what was wrong with advertising then, or what course advertising must now take.

Advertising became necessary wherever it was necessary to find a market; and large-scale advertising became necessary when it became necessary to find a great market—necessary often to *develop* a great market, even if that necessitated a re-education of the public and a considerable change in its buying habits.

It was mass production which caused advertising to become the tremendous business which it eventually became. Mass production had to have a mass market; and if it could get this market by advertising, the advertising more than paid for itself. It paid not only the producer and seller, but the buyer; for with a mass market, providing an adequate outlet for economical mass production, goods could be and were sold at lower prices than would otherwise be possible.

There was one factor in this situation, however, which some producers and some advertisers overlooked. Advertising or no advertising, it was impossible to sell more than the buying public could buy; and the buying public obtained its buying power from employment—employment either as wage earners, farmers, professional people, or managers, organizers or promoters of some business service. Many, to be sure, obtained their buying power from interest, rents and dividends. Unless there was general employment, however, and unless real values were continuously being produced and distributed, these incomes from interest, rents and dividends tended rapidly to disappear.

In that situation, it became necessary not only to increase the market for our machine products, but to increase the capacity of the masses to buy. Unless this was done, in fact, the market could not be increased, and business could not go on. In fact, it was *not* done and business did *not* go on. It went back. That isn't theory: it's history.

I am not asking advertising men to adopt any new principles. I am not even asking them to *favor* the New Deal, which is designed to provide the masses with the buying power which they must have if advertising is to get results. All that I suggest is that we apply some well-known principles to some very new conditions, and that we recognize those evolutionary forces which made this new deal necessary.

Intelligent advertising men have long recognized that even large-scale advertising of dishonest goods cannot build up a business; and they have insisted that the product which they are asked to advertise shall have some value. We must now also recognize that large-scale advertising of goods offered at dishonest prices cannot build up business. Intelligent advertising men will insist, therefore, that the goods they are asked to advertise shall have *adequate* value: that is, that their prices shall be honest.

When I speak of honest and dishonest prices, I do not mean that profits must be limited to such and such per cent. An organization may place an unfair tax upon the consumer and make no profits at all, or it may cut its prices in half and make more profits than ever. We can never tell, therefore, whether prices are fair or unfair merely by the profits which show up. They are honest prices if they do not take more than it is necessary to take from the consumer's dollar. They are dishonest prices if they do.

For *all business and all employment* now depend upon the Mass Consumer's Dollar. If the consumer pays ten dollars for something which can be produced and profitably sold for five, he will lack exactly five dollars of providing all the employment which he *might* provide; and unless people are generally employed, the market for every business is in danger. This wasn't always so. It is so only in a world of mass production—in a world in which we have improved our methods to a point where we must sell to the masses or the whole machinery of production must shut down. This is so largely because advertising has made it so; and what to do about it is something which advertisers have simply got to learn.

A few years ago, we were talking about the "New Competition." We figured that each industry was competing against every other industry for its share of the consumer's dollar, on the theory that, if the masses spent their money for automobiles, they couldn't buy clothes. We know now that that theory was slightly cockeyed; for if the masses didn't buy automobiles, millions would be thrown out of work and have no money with which to buy clothes. Every legitimate industry helps every other legitimate industry. The more the masses buy, in this kind of a world, the more they *can* buy. It is our wasteful methods of production and distribution—methods which necessarily make prices higher than they need to be—which so cripple the consumer's dollar that even the more efficient industries cannot secure an adequate market for their products.

That is why nation-wide planning had to come, and why it must go on, regardless of how it may upset many of our traditional notions. That is why we will have to have unemployment insurance, old-age insurance and health insurance for the masses, and why we must go much farther in providing the masses with buying power than our much-criticized Administration has even thought of going yet. It is not the radical element which will demand this. It is we business men who will demand it—when we once wake up to the full meaning of the situation which now exists. Soon we shall begin to look upon low wages as indecent; and upon prices which are higher than they need to be as treason to our social order. Then we shall not tolerate waste, either in public or in private business, any more than we would think of tolerating incendiarism; and we will look upon unemployment as a social disease to be stamped out at any cost. All this, remember, not because of any sudden conversion to higher moral principles, but because we can't help seeing what we shall see—that to be successful in this mass production world, we must supply the needs of the masses, and supply them more and more abundantly.

With such a business development inevitably ahead of us, can anyone believe that advertising has seen its best days? Advertising has just begun. For advertising is the voice of business, business is just passing out of its infancy, and all the advertising we have yet learned has been more or less in the nature of baby talk. To create and to develop this new market, which need be limited only to our capacity to produce—and to educate the masses to the possibilities of such a market—that is the big job for the advertising profession.

I am not preaching. I am not trying to lay down new rules of ethics, nor am I worried about our present ethical standards and ideals. I would prefer to put the whole problem on a practical business basis and ask what kind of advertising will this new turn in the business situation demand?

Will it require more truth in our advertising or more clever dissembling? Or will it simply require more ballyhoo which, if not literally fraudulent, still hints of satisfactions which the actual goods cannot supply?

It seems to me that these questions must answer themselves. But let us look at some samples of present day advertising and see if they seem to meet the practical requirements. Here is an advertisement presumably designed to induce more and more people to smoke a certain brand of cigarette. There is nothing literally fraudulent in the ad. It doesn't state outright that this cigarette is a tonic, or that it builds up a run-down body, and gives the smoker a new lease on life. It simply says, in effect, that this and that well-known athlete was all in as he crossed the tape, or as the gong sounded or as he completed some record-breaking performance. But then he smoked one of these cigarettes and—look at him now!

My impression is that that kind of advertising has about six more months to run. Nothing at all moral in my reactions—I'm simply looking at it from a business point of view. For all the public can get out of a cigarette is a smoke; and the suggestion that it can get a bracer or a cough cure, or even a welcome into Newport or Palm Beach society, by smoking some particular brand of cigarettes, must in the end become a boomerang. This cigarette, for all I know, may be the best cigarette on the market; but if so, intelligent advertising will do its best to tell the public why.

There is a store in Boston which gets out some simply terrible advertisements—if the purpose of advertising is to build up business. Just look at this:

SALE BEGINNING FRIDAY
MEN'S SCOTTIE CHEVIOT
SHIRTS—$1.40

Our Regular Price Up To Now And Again
Monday—$1.75

FILENE'S

You see, I'm not playing any favorites. Most of us business men get absent-minded now and then and, instead of advertising, we just go through the motions of advertising. We have learned by experience that advertising pays, and we seem to assume that anything which *looks* like advertising will pay.

Such an announcement as this, however *is positively not an advertisement of Filene's store.* It is a warning to the shirt-buying public, rather, not to visit us before Friday or after Monday with the expectation of getting any such value as this. And it is a warning, also, not to buy other things even on Friday and Saturday, but to wait until we offer those other things at prices at which we cannot continue to offer them.

I believe in bargains, and I believe in advertising bargains. I believe even in selling goods below cost, if we have been foolish enough to stock our shelves with goods which the public will not buy from us at a price which gives us any profit. In our Automatic Bargain Basement—which is by far the most profitable part of our store—we even give to charity all goods which, for any reason, are not sold within a month of the day when they are first offered for sale.

In our advertising, however, this frequently slips our mind. Because somebody offers something at a special price for three days only, we think we must do the same. It's up to us, we think, to lose as much money as he does in bribing people to visit our establishment, even though this act of bribery automatically and inevitably puts those people on their guard and conceals from them the real service which we are regularly trying to give.

Such advertising isn't fraudulent. The bargains which they offer, in the case of reputable department stores, are *real* bargains; and the only person who is really cheated by the advertisement is the advertiser. Nevertheless, the ads are not truthful, because they offer a false reason for trading at the store. If stores are not profitable, they cannot serve the public. The buying public knows this; and it knows that it can get its money's worth only if the system under which the store operates is a profitable merchandising system.

It pays to take the public into our confidence through large-scale advertising. It pays to let them know not only of our good guesses but of our mistakes—of the things which we bought which we cannot sell for the price we paid for them, and which, therefore, we are offering, for business reasons, at less than cost. But it doesn't pay, and it can't pay, to give the public the suspicion that it is being lured into some special sale, not because the sale is profitable to us but because we hope that, once in the store, they will buy other things as well.

Intelligent, courageous, truthful advertising pays. And if advertising has had some setbacks of late, it may be well to examine our ads for the purpose of finding out just how intelligent, just how courageous, and just how truthful, they are.

And that means examining them, not from the standpoint of 1880 or of 1920, but of 1934.

It took real courage for the Wright Brothers to make that flight at Kittyhawk; but there isn't much courage involved in the flying which I do today. It took courage of the first magnitude for Galileo to assert that the earth moves around the sun, but any timid soul can be emphatic on that point now.

Truth, likewise, doesn't stand still. A statement is true or false, not by any absolute standards, but to the degree that it corrects, or fails to correct, the misconceptions of the past. This goes for advertising, quite as much as it does for astronomy or biology; and the kind of advertising which was relatively courageous and truthful ten years ago may be both timid and fraudulent today.

It required real business courage, for instance, not many years ago, to appropriate a million dollars to advertise a single commodity, selling perhaps for ten cents. But after it was demonstrated, again and again, that this sort of advertising returned huge dividends, such appropriations did not require courage. What they required, seemingly, was simply more and more attention to the science and the art of ballyhoo.

I do not mean to ridicule ballyhoo. It was an inevitable development. It was a period which expanding business had to pass through. All that we need to do about ballyhoo is to understand it. When we do understand it, we shall discover that the very thing which made ballyhoo successful is now making it unsuccessful; and the technique of advertising, from now on, will largely be a matter of finding out how to get away from ballyhoo.

One man with a horn may attract considerable attention; and if he has goods to sell, he may use the horn to advertise the fact. When a sufficient number of competitors provide themselves with horns, however, his horn will not be quite so effective; and it is only natural, then, that he shall think of getting a bigger horn. It is when everybody gets a horn, and everybody concentrates on the problem of getting bigger and bigger horns, that we have the age of ballyhoo and the necessity, from the standpoint of advertising, of getting out of it.

It will require courage to try something else. It will require fact-finding and *courage to follow the facts*. It will not, however, mean any decline in advertising. The discovery of the automobile, although it did result in the closing of a number of livery stables, did not bring about a decline in transportation.

There is a limit, after all, to the business which can be drummed up by mere noise; and that limit is reached when there is so much noise that no particular noise can be heard above it. There is no limit, however, to human wants, nor to the science of supplying human wants, nor to the news which people want to hear as to how these wants may be supplied.

It is to be remembered that every article of common use by the masses, or that would be in common use if the price were brought within the buying power of the masses, is going to be produced by mass production, which of course will necessitate mass sales. To secure these mass sales, however, and to secure them quickly enough to serve the needs of mass production, the only device which can be employed is mass advertising.

This advertising, however, must be news; and the news, to serve this business purpose, must be as accurate and as truthful as it is possible to make it.

Time was when all that the buying public expected of a trader was that he should announce his arrival with whatever noise he chose to make. He lied about his goods, but the public expected him to do so, and buyers expected to match their wits with his. The only reason they quit trading with crooks and tricksters was that they discovered some trader who was not quite so crooked, and whose word could in some measure be relied upon. The whole progress of business, from that day to this, has been progress in the direction of serving the public, instead of exploiting it, and keeping faith with the public instead of lying to it.

There is no other line which can mean progress. There is no other way to build up business. There is no other course which advertising, to be successful, can take.

One of these days, then, and I think it will be in the near future, some great business will undertake to tell the buying public all that the public really wants to know. It will not only tell the good qualities of things offered for sale but it will tell the truth, and avoid making any sale which should not be made, if the interests of the consumer are the first consideration.

If we *could* hide the truth from the consumer, perhaps, there might be business excuses for continuing the old pretense. But we can't. The consumer is already getting wise, by his experiences and by information brought to him by his own organizations. The public is learning the truth about our goods. It is learning the truth about soap and toothpaste and razor blades. These are all good things, and much can be said for them. Nothing, in fact, can be said against them which could prove more harmful in the end than some of the things which their advertisements have recently been saying. I am not married, I admit, because she said "No"; but I am morally certain that she would still have said "No," regardless of the kind of razor blade I used. And I swear to you, as an employer, that I never have discharged a salesman because he did not use a certain kind of soap.

All this is nothing against advertising. It is simply a reference to the kind of advertising which can lead nowhere and which, in the end, must alienate the public instead of winning its confidence. Whatever may have been successful in the past, we are entering a very different social order now. If business is to be profitable in this new order, the public must be served helpfully; and all businesses and all business operations which do not so serve the consuming public must be eliminated. Advertising, then, which is the voice of business, must become primarily the Voice of the Consumer, which is a tremendously greater and more important role than it has ever played before.

The New Relations Between Business and Government *

A few years ago, American business men were thrilled by a phrase.

As is so often the case when people are thrilled by phrases, the phrase didn't mean anything. It was:

"Less Government in Business and More Business in Government."

Now, that phrase sounds all right, but the words do not make sense.

If you had asked the business men who were worshipfully repeating this slogan just what they meant by "business" and by "government," they would quite generally have agreed, I think, that business is *trading for profit* and that government is the *orderly arrangement of human affairs.*

But what then becomes of the precious slogan?

LESS ORDERLY ARRANGEMENT OF HUMAN AFFAIRS IN BUSINESS AND MORE TRADING FOR PROFIT IN GOVERNMENT.

Thrilling, is it not?

But we took it seriously. That is what was the matter with us. We not only sold goods but elected presidents on that issue.

This, I wish it understood, is not a partisan criticism. Both of our political parties were suffering from the same kind of nervous disorder, under which the phrase I have quoted seemed for the time being to be sense instead of nonsense.

Many a man has looked back to the doings of the night before with considerable mystification. Why did he wear his coat inside out? Why did he climb that lamp post and throw his shoes at the

* Address before The American Academy of Political and Social Science, Bellevue-Stratford Hotel, Philadelphia, Pennsylvania—January 5, 1934.

traffic cop? And the only intellectually satisfying answer is that *it seemed like a good idea at the time.*

But what has really happened in the case of this poor penitent? There are new relations now, apparently, between him and government as represented by the man in uniform. For a moment last night, he was seemingly superior to the government. The policeman was simply a nice bright target at whom one, if he felt that way, would just naturally want to throw his shoes. But things seem altogether different in the morning; and the gentleman in question, if his head is not yet quite clear, may remark that times have changed.

On further reflection, however, I think we must agree that, although times have undoubtedly changed somewhat during the night, the significant change has been, not in the times, but in the man. He is under government regulation now, whereas, for a few moments during the night, he did not seem to be. But he is not in a new world, not even in a new era, in the sense that many people use the term. For there never was a world or an era, excepting in this poor fellow's imagination, where it was either logical or right for him to exert his sturdy individual initiative in the way he did.

It is necessary to draw this fine distinction between objective and subjective changes, if we are to discover the really new relations between business and government. This *is* a new world in which we are now living, but it is not a world which came suddenly into existence last March. This *is* a new era, but the era dates from the development of trade and of mass production processes, not from the passage of the Recovery Act. The N.R.A. and the other parts of the President's program have not repealed a single fundamental law of the social order of 1929 or of 1919. They have simply *recognized* the fundamental laws of that order —laws which for the time being were cheerfully disregarded.

The recognition of our responsibilities in a machine age has come upon us suddenly, after three or four years of headache; but the responsibilities existed long before they were recognized. They existed in previous administrations quite as definitely as they exist today; and had we then looked realistically at the world in which we were living, we would have taken much the same attitude, and much the same course, which we are taking now.

But we did not look at our machine world realistically. We looked at it, on the one hand, according to the patterns of thought which had been developed in agrarian and patriarchal civilization, and on the other hand according to our own inflamed imaginations.

When democracy decreed that the people should rule, instead of the sovereign, it was easier for many of the people to become imbued with a sense of the *majesty* of their new position than with a sense of its responsibility. The people were now sovereigns, they reflected, and being sovereigns sounded attractive to such democrats. They could not, however, actually become kings; but they could get drunk and tell themselves how big they were; so millions of them did just that, and democracy was almost lost in the shuffle.

Similarly, when modern machinery made it not only possible but imperative from the true business standpoint that the masses should live lives of comfort and of leisure, traditional thinking and inflamed imagination kept us from grasping the real nature of the problem. The masses were almost unanimously willing to get rich, and they had no end of energy to devote to the process; but each tried to get rich in the new order according to the formula by which people had become rich in the old order. Many, indeed, *became* rich, and a hundred millionaires grew where one had grown before; but millions of the masses were trampled in the process and lost their buying power, the machinery of production choked with its own product, unemployment spread like a pestilence and the world starved in the midst of plenty.

New conditions were forever creating new human relations. But we had no labels, no tags, with which to distinguish these new relations from the relations which had formerly existed; so we put our old tags on them and let it go at that. This is a very easy thing to do. It saves time. It saves thought. It keeps us for a while in a fine romantic frenzy and renders us immune from sobriety. But the formula cannot abolish the facts which it ignores. If the facts could only be abolished, if evolution could be fooled, or if natural law would only take cognizance of our state of mind and govern itself accordingly, then we would never have to wake up and no New Deal would be necessary.

The law of life in early America was that families should support themselves on the land; and our codes and statutes were derived mainly from that law of life. That wouldn't have been the law if there hadn't been any land; and when, in the course of human events, life became organized so that not many American families could possibly support themselves on the land, it ceased to be the law, and any pretence that it was still the law was fantastic. We Americans, however, hugged the fantasy. Actually, we organized our affairs away from the self-contained, little-community principle into a system of great collective enterprises. When we thought of law, however, and when we thought of government, we simply slapped the little-community tags on the big-community processes and called it a day.

We still insist, for instance, that it is up to every man to support his family. Nothing can take the place, we say, of individual initiative. Now, that's true, but it doesn't happen to have anything to do with the case. Individual initiative (and I'm for it) cannot accomplish anything by itself. It has to have something to act on. With all due respect to the American pioneers, they couldn't have raised a single turnip with their individual initiative alone. They had to have land in order to raise turnips and they had plenty of land.

The modern American, in order to support his family, usually needs a job; and modern American jobs, as a rule, are not jobs which can be created on the initiative of the modern American worker. Somebody, to be sure, has to initiate these jobs. But they are now initiated mostly in business and financial offices, and sometimes in laboratories devoted to business or scientific research. Each individual, on his own initiative, may still start an independent business in which there will be little independence and less business or may still go out and sell lead pencils on the street corner, or offer to do chores around somebody else's house. But not many could support their families by such activities. They could not solve the problem of living, as the early American could solve it when he settled on the land.

The trouble now, it must be kept in mind, is not that the land has all been taken up. What has happened is that we have changed from an agricultural to a business civilization, in which everybody, including the farmers, is dependent upon the institution of trade. There is as much individual initiative as ever in America (more, in fact, for there are more Americans than ever); but for individual initiative to be economically effective now, it has to be applied within the mechanism of modern production and distribution.

Most of our talk, then, about our once having lived in an era of individual initiative and now approaching an era in which we must dispense with it, is simply beside the point. We are not even changing from a planless to a planned economic order; for there could be no economic order without constant planning. The patriarch had to plan. The Indian tribes had to plan. The early American pioneer had to plan, and the business man has always had to plan.

What is happening now is simply an effort to make our plans fit in with the actual facts of present day conditions, instead of slapping ancient labels on the new conditions and then planning according to the labels. One process exerts as much individual initiative as the other; but planning with relation to the realities is *one* thing, and planning with relation to our superstitions or our states of mind is another. It required planning to climb that lamp post, but the plan was not socially feasible.

In the days when industry was developing in America, under the auspices of an agrarian tradition, government went on as usual trying to effect an orderly arrangement of human affairs. The development of industry, however, brought on a whole new batch of human affairs with which the institution which we called our government did not try to deal. There was, therefore, increasing disorder. Strikes, for instance. If anyone had said that it was the province of government to eliminate strikes, he would scarcely have had a hearing. It was not considered the business of government to study strikes and to find out what they were.

So the government contented itself with trying to police strikes, and the disorders grew. The government was supposed to be impartial, but there was a joker in that. One might think at first that, the government being democratic and there being so many workers and so few employers, any partiality which the government did show would be shown toward labor. But hardly. The real situation was that the government, if not actually bribed and corrupted, was trying to be impartial as between the property rights of employers, which the government thoroughly understood, and the right of the workers to get a decent living in the only world in which they could possibly live; and that was a right which our agrarian minds did not understand.

So far as the government was aware, there *was* no industrial order. It was something entirely new; and the government got its ideas not from studying new conditions but from studying ancient precedents. From the standpoint of government, then, industrial relations were nothing to worry about. There were, as always, just a lot of people. Some of them were doing well and some were not, but they would all have to obey the laws which grew out of human experience when human relations were what they were, regardless of what they might have become in the meantime.

The political government's attempt to keep its hands off from these new human relations did not result in universal satisfaction. There had to be government in business, for one thing, whether the visible government furnished it or not. So an invisible government furnished it—an invisible government composed of employers and financiers. The invisible government presently controlled the visible government. It furnished the campaign funds. It exerted financial pressure on legislatures and courts; and it not only misgoverned the country at large but it misgoverned the very enterprises which it was designed to protect and brought them very often to ruin.

Even the business giants, our great captains of industry, did not, it now appears, know what the actual new relations which had been set up by business were. Although production increased so rapidly that new markets were absolutely imperative, they kept wages as low as possible and thereby kept buying power at a minimum.

They, too, were obsessed by the agrarian tradition; and instead of perceiving the general interdependence which the new order had brought about, they looked upon finance and industry as private fields for them to farm. Nevertheless, somebody had to make the laws governing this new world; and until somebody did do it, that invisible government, bad as it was, could not be overthrown.

There is nothing new in government decreeing the hours which workingmen shall work. The invisible government did *that.* It decreed that men should work twelve hours, so that there would always be a sufficiently great surplus of unemployed to keep the market price of labor down. What is new is that our government is again becoming visible; and it is *our* government again, in fact as well as in theory. It is *our* government because it is at last visibly dealing with the world in which we really live.

To keep government out of the production and distribution of life's necessities is, of course, impossible; but were it possible, it would be equivalent to keeping government out of human life. Under the old conditions, when our visible government was forever trying to follow its famous "Hands Off" policy, it was always finding its *hands full.* Because it refused to deal with the cause of strikes, it was kept busy with their effects. Because it did not deal with the problem of unemployment, it had to deal with the plight of the unemployed. Because it had nothing to say about the distribution of wealth, it was constantly confronted with crises caused by inadequate distribution, which some stick-in-the-mud traditionalists still refer to as "overproduction."

There is much loose talk at present concerning the passing of our liberties, and the thousand and one ways in which our government is now supposed to be interfering with our lives. One would think, to read some of the comments, that every American was once free to go his own individual way, but that we have now come upon a time when we cannot budge an inch in any direction without bumping up against some governmental regulation. The fact is that we are now on the march toward freedom; and there is more liberty in the United States today than there has been in many decades.

In early America, people could not go in any way they happened to feel like going. They might have felt like flying, but they couldn't fly. As in every other human society, past and present, they had to accept the restraints of existing conditions; and the greatest freedom which any government could bestow was the freedom to live according to some code which took full cognizance of actual conditions.

So early Americans, if they were not slaves, were free to go the agrarian way, under such laws as might be necessary in an agrarian age. Because people understood the agrarian age, however, most of them naturally obeyed its laws, and did not consider such necessary obedience as any curtailment of their freedom. When we came into the machine age, however, we did not understand its laws. We did not know that we would now be compelled to find an entirely new way of life. Incidentally, we lost our old freedom, but we did not realize it at the time, for agrarian freedom was still on the statute books and absent only from actual life. We could still till the soil, the only difference between us and the early settlers being that, although we were employing vastly more productive methods, we couldn't make a living out of agriculture and they could.

Because we did not know the laws of the machine age, we could not establish any code of human procedure which would not inevitably bring us to disaster. Desperately, frantically, we passed millions of laws, and our government became big and bulky and expensive. Not until today, however, have we adopted the expedient of relating our visible government to our new and necessary way of life.

I have set forth this general statement of the new relations of business and government, rather than attempting to deal with a multiplicity of details, because unless one sees the whole picture, each detail is pretty sure to mystify him. He may then think of each code, and of each new restriction of business practice, as one more curtailment of our liberties; whereas, if the codes are based upon actual fact-finding, and the restrictions are not imposed by an outside power but are inherent in the nature of the new conditions, they will prove to be the Way to Liberty.

Since the machine age is an age of invention, and of constantly increasing ability to produce, the first principle of its government must be to provide for adequate consumption. Granted that it is dangerous to tinker with the currency, we know that the traditional dollar will not avail us now, and we must devise a medium of exchange which will certainly facilitate such an exchange of goods and services that poverty will be abolished and the masses everywhere be assured of an ever increasing standard of living commensurate with our ever increasing ability to produce.

The dollar heretofore has been fundamentally an agrarian dollar. It was a dollar to be spent only if its owner could not get along without the thing he spent it for, and to be saved mostly for purposes of investment. It was a dollar to be loaned, upon certain property as security, and to draw interest whether the borrower used it successfully or not, or whether, as in war, he used it solely for purposes of destruction. And it was a dollar to be handed down, with all its accrued interest, and its interest upon interest, generation after generation, to serve as a perpetual drain upon our productive activities, until in the course of time the world became so burdened with debt that it could not carry on its normal functions.

One of the necessities of legislation, then, is an amortization clause in every long-term debt, limiting the life of such a debt to the life of its usefulness. Another is the absorption, by inheritance taxes, of those fortunes which place power over millions of lives in the hands of irresponsible, inefficient, untrained persons whose sole claim to this vital power is based not upon anything which they contribute to society, but solely on what they have received from society.

I cannot see, as hard as I have tried to follow the arguments of those who favor it, that we need any legislation looking toward the elimination of profits. If production and distribution are once organized for the greatest possible human service, the wages of such organizers, I believe, will be higher than ever. Profits, it seems to me, are the legitimate wages of capital which is being used for human service. It is the accumulation of profits into useless and even dangerous reservoirs of disservice against which our new civilization must guard.

It is one of the possible eventualities, of course, that the profit system will be destroyed. But if it is destroyed in America, I am sure, it will not be destroyed by Communists or technocrats. It will be destroyed by those very business men who believe most profoundly in the profit system and are shouting the loudest about individual initiative. If these men cannot see that the President's Recovery Program is their program—*their* way out of chaos—but insist instead upon some program in which business shall not be organized and co-ordinated to serve, the Administration may be caught in the logic of events and be forced farther and farther to the left, even to a program which will leave private business out of its calculations. At present, however, I see no danger of this. Practically all America seems to be behind the President in his great effort to discover the underlying laws governing production and distribution and thus to effect an orderly arrangement of the processes.

Many seem mystified at present because our Administration in this crisis has sought counsel from professors instead of lawyers. It was inevitable. When we want to discover precedents—the established practice—we must consult lawyers. When we must learn about things which are not yet known, we must go to men of science.

It should be remembered, in every study of the new conditions, and the new relations, therefore, between business and government, that something vastly more significant is aimed at than a mere redistribution of wealth. No redistribution of present wealth, however inequitably it may now be distributed, can solve our problems. What we want is security and continuity in the operation of our economic mechanism, and the assurance that more productive methods will always bring greater benefits and greater leisure to the masses. To the masses this naturally seems attractive. To the business man it is imperative; for if the masses do not buy, and are not provided with both the power to buy and leisure to consume, business can never again be profitable.

There is no mystery about this whole procedure. We are simply effecting an orderly arrangement of the world in which we live, instead of trying longer to live in that world under the laws governing a world which has passed away. We are rather belated in getting at it and our tardiness has already cost us one world war, and one depression which was in many respects more devastating than war.

This is a world of mass production, and it must become a world of mass consumption. This means that everybody must do his part—as a consumer. That and that only will keep production running smoothly.

As to where the necessary funds are to come from, there is no very serious problem. For money is not wealth but *a medium of exchange of goods and services*. Let us once agree as to the goods and services it would be mutually profitable for us to exchange, and it will not be difficult to find a medium.

We must use money and credit, and we must devote our business and financial thought to the one aim of promoting mass consumption. It won't cost anything. What costs us more than we can pay is nonconsumption. Where there is no consumption, there can be no business, no production, no income to pay for anything. Only where there is maximum consumption, can there be maximum income and maximum ability to pay for everything, including the cost of government.

Business and government, then, must co-operate in eliminating unemployment and in arranging for an adequate income to those too young and those too old to work, lest by their failure to consume, they clog the wheels of industry. They must also plan together to eliminate waste, so that human labor may produce the greatest human results. Merely employing everybody will not do; for if labor is employed ineffectively, its wages and its plane of living must be low.

In the past, when business did not perceive the business necessity of increasing mass buying power in accordance with every increase in industrial productivity, labor was rightly suspicious of efforts toward efficiency. Many employers who believed in high wages, indeed, have been afraid to pay them, lest their competitors would not do the same. Only by governmental co-operation, then, and by official enforcement of the plain law of prosperity, could prosperity be created.

We have been living for several generations now within a business civilization; but we have had no understanding of what business is for, and business has remained uncivilized. We thought we were governed by the Almighty Dollar, but that dollar became so drunk and disorderly that it could not solve our human problems. No wonder. It was a Financier's Dollar, and business is not for finance. Sometimes it was a Producer's Dollar, and business is not for production. But now we are beginning to understand. We are learning that business is for the consumer—the mass consumer. Only with that understanding, and only as we exalt and reverence the Consumer's Dollar, can we effect an orderly arrangement of human affairs.

We may have thought in the past of business and government, as if they were two separate and mutually jealous entities, each telling the other: "Thus far and no farther shalt thou go." But that picture must vanish now. Business is trading for profit. Government is the orderly arrangement of human affairs. Unless this trade is a real trade, however, unless it is an actual exchange of human services, and unless the transaction is profitable to all concerned, it is not good business. On the other hand, unless the government does bring order into the processes upon which the life and welfare of all of us depend, it cannot long remain the government. It is in that light that the new relations of business and government must be perceived.

Business and the Wage Problem *

MR. CHAIRMAN AND GENTLEMEN:

I wanted to make this talk short and sweet, but I'm afraid it's going to be sour. I haven't been able to discuss the wage problem yet without saying something which sounds to some employers like a sour note.

"It's all baloney," a listener told me recently. "It's all right to *talk* about high wages. Everybody knows that high wages can buy more than low wages, *but where do I get off?* Business is rotten. I'm not making a cent. If I added two cents an hour to the payroll, I couldn't pay my rent—and then I have to sit and listen to you telling about the business advantage of paying higher wages."

Well, I am not heartless. Such criticisms hurt. If you want to know just how that fellow made me feel, perhaps you can think back to the time when you participated in one of those "Buy Now" campaigns, and you were accosted by somebody with a seven dollar bank balance who asked you if he ought to buy a coffin on the installment plan and use his seven dollars for the first payment.

You were right, of course, in urging the public to buy now; and if the public had spent its money at the time, it would probably have improved business so that everybody would have had more money to spend, including this poor chap with seven dollars standing between him and starvation. But it didn't work out that way. Those who had a little money hung on to it; and all of us campaigners, deep down in our hearts, knew that under their circumstances we would do the same.

---

* Address before the Commonwealth Club, Fairmont Hotel, San Francisco, California—February 6, 1935.

And I know, in this present discussion, that if I can't raise wages, I can't. I have the deepest sympathy for such critics as the one I quoted; and if I can't show definitely how wages can be raised, I ought to be told to shut up.

This man was in the overcoat business. Although the thermometer was below zero, it was the overcoat business which was so rotten.

Why was the overcoat business so rotten in such cold weather? Was it because everybody had a suitable overcoat? *No!* That's why I'm here. That's why I am harping on the same old subject. The fact is that millions of American citizens at that very moment were *cold*. They'd have given anything they had, almost, for a good overcoat.

The trouble was that nobody would trade a good overcoat for anything these American citizens had.

But what did they have? What did they have that might have been traded for good overcoats? Did they have anything which other people could use advantageously if the trade could only be facilitated?

Yes, they did.

They didn't have any money. They didn't have any jewels. They didn't have any more of the necessities of life than they needed to keep themselves alive. But they had something—something of great value—something that millions of Americans would have been glad to make use of. The overwhelming majority of them, at least, had knowledge and power and skill. Most of them knew things that none of us know. Most of them could do things that none of us can do.

I, for instance, have to have coal, but I would be up against it if I had to get the coal myself. Even if I knew how, I couldn't wield a pick and shovel. But many of these fellows could mine coal, if anybody would let them. Their trouble was that they couldn't get a job.

Why couldn't they get a job? Was it because Americans had all filled up their cellars and nobody needed more coal? *No!* Millions of Americans at this same time were cold, even when they went indoors. *They* wanted coal and would give almost anything they had to get it. But all they had was their knowledge and power and skill. Some of them, for instance, knew how to make overcoats; but the people who knew how to make overcoats went without coal and the people who knew how to mine coal went without overcoats, and the overcoat and the coal businesses were rotten.

What was the basic trouble? Why couldn't we facilitate exchange among these groups who were so abundantly able to supply one another's wants? It was because they were *short of money.*

What is money? *Money is a medium of exchange.* Its purpose is to facilitate exchange. Obviously, however, there either wasn't enough money in the United States at this particular time or else it wasn't being used for that purpose.

May I digress just a moment, so that no one will think I'm arguing for inflation. Most of us, I think, felt that we were rather short of money, and some of us possibly felt that the government should issue more; but while I do not intend to enter into a discussion of the currency here, I must ask two simple questions.

When does our country have a lot of money and when is it short? Do we get a lot of money by issuing a lot, or is there some other factor which governs the actual volume of our currency?

The answer is that there is a lot of money when there is a great volume of exchange. In good times, we use relatively little currency. We write checks for the bulk of our transactions. We issue our own money—money which serves the purposes of exchange. On the other hand, when the volume of exchange is low, governments frequently indulge in currency inflation only to discover that the currency issued does not do what money is supposed to do. I do not mean this as an argument against currency reform. I simply wish to point out what we all must know, that our basic problem is the problem of exchange—not the problem of discovering a perfect medium.

What we want to know here is why exchange was blocked—exchange between the miners and the overcoat makers and the hundreds of other groups, the blocking of which made our businesses so generally bad. Why were these millions short of money? Was it because they had had some money and spent it?

That seems logical, doesn't it? That is, if we forget what money is. It's like saying, however, that a man doesn't know anything because he has used all the knowledge which he had. If these folks hadn't spent their money, it wouldn't have been money. Money is a medium of exchange, and anything which is supposed to be money but isn't being used to facilitate exchange ceases for the time being at least to be money. If these workers, then, had saved their money when they had it, instead of buying overcoats and coal and things, those businesses would simply have gone bad before they did.

It is possible, of course, for a man to lose his knowledge, but not by using it. He can lose his knowledge, and become utterly unaware of everything—by a simple sock in the jaw. Workers likewise can lose their money by a sock in the pay envelope.

We cannot lose money by using it for all that it is worth. We can lose it only by not using it or by using it for something less than our money's worth. Money, being a medium of exchange, must keep going and coming. If it stops coming, it stops going; and if it stops going, it necessarily stops coming. To facilitate exchange to the limit, of course, we must have reserves. We must have banks, insurance, appropriations for emergencies that have not yet arisen; but even our savings must be managed in ways which facilitate exchange or they will die on our hands.

Let's get back, then, to my friend, the overcoat man, and see if there is something in all this which may apply to his predicament. Out of the goodness of his heart, he wants to raise wages. Out of the badness of his business, he wants to reduce them. His greatest costs, he says, are wages and material. If he could only cut wages ten or twenty per cent, he feels, he could make a profit; and because he could make a profit, he could keep his business going; and because he could keep his business going, he could continue to employ his workers; whereas if he continues to pay what he is paying now, or if he were to raise wages, he is certain that he will have to lay them off. Isn't half a loaf better than no loaf at all?

"Well," I asked him, "Why don't you save on your material? Why don't you make coats that go, say, seventy-five per cent of the way around the customer's body?"

He saw immediately that he couldn't do that. He couldn't do it, regardless of how much less it would cost him, because he couldn't sell the coats. But that's his only trouble now. If he could only sell enough coats, he assured me, he could raise wages.

"If you could sell enough coats," I asked, "would you raise wages *enough?"*

"What do you mean *enough?"* he asked.

"Well, when are wages high enough?"

"Enough for what?"

I was glad he asked me that. Let's figure it out. When are wages high enough to suit the purposes of business? When are they high enough to purchase enough overcoats to make the overcoat business good? And to purchase enough of the other necessities and comforts of life to make all our other businesses good?

I confess that I don't know. What I know, however, and what we all know, is that wages are not high enough for that today. Yet, the wage earners and farmers constitute the masses of our customers and the only possible market large enough to solve our business problem. I'm not now discussing the farm problem, but the same general principles hold. Unless we can get buying power into the hands of these masses, there is no chance on earth for business recovery, and the only buying power which the wage earners can get is the buying power which they find in their pay envelope.

The government, of course, by taxation, may keep these masses alive. I'm not saying a word against these billion dollar relief plans—either in direct relief or in the carrying out of good and useful but tremendously expensive projects. But all this by itself cannot revive business to the point where it will generally be good. Nor can the mere printing of more money revive business. The government might print carloads of money and give a million dollars to every citizen, but the money wouldn't be any good because it could not affect the exchange of goods and services.

The only thing that can revive trade is employment on the scale which American business could and would employ, if the American masses had sufficient real money with which to buy our goods. And the only way that the wage-earning masses can get sufficient money to buy these goods, to create this employment and to bring prosperity all around, is through higher wages.

Let my friend reduce wages in his overcoat factory, and let his workers even consent to the reduction in the hope of holding their jobs, and what will inevitably happen? In the first place, every competitor will find it necessary to reduce wages too; and every employee in the whole industry will necessarily be buying less than he is buying today.

Less of what? Less of everything that all our businesses have been selling them—little as that happens to be even now.

That will be a sock in the jaw to all of us. The loss of this trade alone may be enough to put a number of business men in the red. They'll have to retrench. They'll think about cutting wages. And among the other casualties, we may all be sure, there will be thousands and thousands of American citizens who will give up buying the overcoats they intended to buy; and by that time, my friend will feel that he is obliged to give us another sock by cutting wages once more.

I don't like to be sour, and I hate to put it as unfeelingly as that. And if he has to do it, I know, he has to do it, even if it does bring down ruin upon everybody, including himself. That's the way, in fact, that we all did business for years and years and years. When business for any reason got to going down, we all got busy pushing it down by cutting buying power—by cutting wages. Each did it, of course, to save himself. Nobody could blame us for that; only, unfortunately, nobody in the end was benefited.

But here's a cheerful note. We don't have to do business in that way any longer. Something has happened, recently, which too many of us have overlooked—something which, if we make up our minds to use it, can pull us out of this vicious circle and into a spiral which goes up and up and up.

I mean our N.R.A. codes. . . . Yes—that is what I said—

the N.R.A. codes. In these codes today is our great opportunity. By using these codes as they may be used, we business men may solve this problem of wages in a way that will bring business, in the near future, to new heights of prosperity.

Today, of course, the codes are only in their infancy, and many of them seem to be rather messy infants. What is wrong in the codes, however, is what we business men have put there. The big news is that, for the first time in history, American business men can now act together, particularly upon this problem of wages; and we can enforce the decisions which we make. All we now need is a better understanding of wages as the buying power of the only market which can be big enough to pull us out of this depression, and keep us out.

Long before we had our business codes, Henry Ford and many others proved that paying higher wages could be made profitable. In the depression of 1921, we in Filene's kept wages up in accordance with a practice we had established years before. To do it, however, we were forced to go over the whole business as we had never gone over it before, in a determined effort to effect savings and to introduce more efficient methods. We thought we had been efficient, but what we found surprised us. *Because it had become necessary* for us to improve our methods, we found ways to do so; and we made more sales and more profits during those two depression years than we had ever made before.

In this last depression, on the other hand, Filene's yielded to the general pressure to reduce wages. In my judgment, it was a grave business mistake, but I was outvoted. I cannot prove, of course, that we would have done better if my policy of maintaining the wage scale had been followed; nevertheless, the principle has been well established that the necessity for paying high wages keeps management on its toes, whereas the effort to save expenses by reducing wages tends to turn our attention in the wrong direction.

With business under business codes, however, we need have no misgivings. If every competitor is forced to pay the same higher code-wages that we must pay, we are left in relatively as good a position as before. But all will be competing in a larger market—

a market made larger not merely by our own contribution but by the raising of wages throughout the whole industry in which we are engaged. We may sell little more, to be sure, to our own employees; but they will be buying much more from business generally; and because more goods are sold, there will be more employment, more wages and a larger market for *our* goods.

We not only get back the money we pay out, then, but we get back more. For money appropriated to higher wages creates more buying power, which creates more employment, which creates more wealth—more things which can be exchanged for profit. That's where we business men come in. If we do not use our money to facilitate exchange, however, things are not sold, things therefore are not made, there is therefore less employment and less buying power for our customers—and that's where we business men pass out.

But that is only one phase of our new business opportunity under the codes—when, of course, we take these codes seriously and begin to use them in the way they can be used. If a single business can sometimes effect economies more than enough to pay for wage increases which it has made—if it is forced, in fact, to discover better methods because of this wage increase—think of what a whole nation-wide industry acting as a unit might do. Then think of what all industry, organized under a nation-wide, interindustrial code, might do.

Great as are the present wastes within the businesses which we business men individually control, our greatest wastes, after all, are in the *structure of business itself* over which, heretofore, there has been no control. The codes, fortunately, do not mean government control. They mean business control of this structure of business—if business only gets ready to exercise such control. Business could never do this heretofore, because it had no authority to stop practices which were ruinous to business; and it was always a case of government control or no control whatever.

But what a difference now, if we only understand our opportunity. To be sure, when we first started to make these codes which, under the New Deal, could now be made binding, we were so bewildered in many cases that we even tried to fix prices, and decreased mass buying power at a time when the one thing needed was a great and organized increase.

Every time we raise prices, we thereby reduce wages; and even if we raise wages at the same time, we are not likely to repair the damage. For most of us have more customers than we have employees; and when we reduce wages, we merely cut the wages of our employees whereas, when we raise prices, we cut the wages of all our customers. The only safe rule to follow, then, is for business to lower prices while it is raising wages. Prices are best lowered, however, by competition. Our need, therefore, is to leave prices in fair competition while taking wages out of competition.

How high we can make wages, I do not know. The higher we can profitably make them, however, the more prosperous will business be; and with the economies which business can and will even be forced to make, not merely in our separate factories and stores, but in the whole hitherto disorganized process of production and distribution, we know that we can bring wages to hitherto unknown heights, develop a mass market which has scarcely yet been touched and create such prosperity as business has never known before.

That we do not do this is clearly the fault of business and of our business organizations. Business is in a bad way now only because, instead of organizing according to the actual facts of the present situation, we have carried over into this age of plenty those principles and traditions which could apply only to an age of scarcity. To sell what modern industry can produce, it must be sold to the masses. Our one great, basic, business problem, then, is how the masses can get sufficient buying power to keep business good; which means—because our machines are necessarily more and more productive—not merely increased wages but constantly increasing wages.

In our chambers of commerce and other business organizations, however, we have not yet got around to organizing for this definite objective. We still think of wage increases as a concession—as some sort of additional expense to us. Wages, therefore, remain too low for our purposes. We can't keep our machines running; and unemployment—which is the absence of buying power—blocks every move we do attempt to make. And because we do not organize to end this unemployment in the only way it can be ended, we still find ourselves burdened with supertaxes for the relief of the unemployed.

This depression, then, is strictly up to us. We can get out of it at any moment we are ready to get out. To get out of it, however, *and to stay out,* we must organize, in our chambers of commerce and our trade associations, to solve this wage problem, not according to any ancient tradition of wages, but according to the facts of this new machine age.

The A. B. C. of the New Deal *

Mr. Chairman and Gentlemen:

We cannot comprehend any legislative program merely by studying the program. To grasp the meaning of any political policy it is necessary to understand the conditions which the policy is designed to meet.

The New Deal marks a turning point in American history, but these Administration measures did not cause the turning.

When night comes, we may go to bed; and, when morning comes, we may get up. Going to bed and getting up are two very different policies, and it would be futile to argue as to which is the better policy. Whether either one is right depends upon what time it is, and what the times demand. We will surely become confused, however, regardless of what time it is, if we once imagine that our going to bed and getting up is what causes day and night.

The so-called New Deal is not a new way of solving an old problem, but an effort to solve a wholly new problem—an effort to cope with a new historic situation.

If there has been no great basic change in human history, then we need not worry much about the New Deal, one way or another. No political government, autocratic or democratic, is of itself likely to inaugurate any great change in the habits and characteristics of the social order which it assumes to govern. If there *has* been a basic social change, however—if our customary way of life has become no longer possible—it is the task of government to discover formulas by which the nation may go on.

And that was the situation which confronted President Roosevelt in March 1933.

* Address before the Providence Chamber of Commerce and Brown University, at Brown University, Providence, Rhode Island—May 23, 1934.

In saying that, I want it understood that I am not blaming the depression upon President Hoover.

I am a Democrat, but it is nauseating to me to hear habit-bound politicians of my party trying to convince themselves and their constituents that the depression was the direct result of the Republican party's policies and would have been averted if we had only known enough to elect good Democrats.

It makes me feel something as I used to feel when I heard Republicans talking about prosperity as *Republican* prosperity!

The depression came because American civilization could not go any further in the direction in which it had been going.

We had got to the end of the road—and the road I speak of was not only approved by both Republicans and Democrats, but it was, in the main, the right road and, I believe, the only road which America, up to a certain period, could have taken.

There came a time, however, when we could not go any farther in that direction.

We seemed to have everything which was necessary for progress. We had more power in our hands than we had ever had before. We had ample resources. We had an abundance, in fact, of almost everything which Americans seemed to need; and we had machinery and scientific managers, and no end of willing, skilful workers capable of producing a still greater abundance. Our storehouses were fairly bursting with food. We had clothing enough to supply every man, woman and child in the country, or so it seemed. At any rate, our experts said there was a surplus. They said that there was an overproduction of everything.

And American civilization was utterly unprepared to meet any such crisis as that.

On the face of it, the crisis may have seemed absurd to all of us. The *logical* time for a people to go hungry is when food is scarce—not when there is more in sight than was ever seen before. And the logical time to deprive ourselves of things in general is when *things are scarce*—not when they are more plentiful than ever.

Nor was it, as some might suppose, that these things were owned by the greedy rich who didn't want the poor to get them.

These things were owned in the main by people who were poor and wished they could think of some way to get rid of them.

Wheat, for instance, and beef, pork, cotton, potatoes, fruit—they were owned largely by farmers who couldn't meet their mortgage payments. Millions of suits of clothes were owned by manufacturers and dealers who were going bankrupt because they kept on owning them, when they wanted somebody else to buy them, and own them, instead. Thousands and thousands of stores all over the country were piled high with goods owned by people who frantically longed to quit owning them at the earliest possible moment.

Nor is it true that they wouldn't sell these things unless they could make a profit. Naturally, they preferred to make a profit, but thousands of manufacturers and merchants were willing to carry on if they could only break even.

Our mechanism of production was better than ever, but our mechanism of exchange had broken down. Because we couldn't exchange these things, we couldn't go on producing them—we certainly couldn't continue to hire millions of workers to go on producing them. So we laid off millions of workers, only to discover that exchange was clogged up worse than ever. Only when the workers were spending their wages regularly for goods had we had prosperity. After they lost their jobs, they had to quit buying; and the more we laid off, the more we had to lay off. Everything we did, in fact, instead of getting us out of our trouble, only seemed to get us further in.

It was natural, under the circumstances, that a lot of people began to blame the big, bad bankers. But while the big, bad bankers have enough to answer for, we can never understand that depression if we think that they brought it on.

The good bankers, in fact, did much more harm than the bad. They didn't mean to. There is no sense in blaming them. They merely did what all Americans expected them to do and what all Americans, as a rule, wanted them to do. That is, they collected the savings of the people and arranged to have them invested in the sort of investments which, by long experience, had proven to be safe and sound.

This was the course which had enabled America to make such progress; and if we hadn't come to the end of the road, it would have enabled us to make still further progress.

There was a limit—that was all—to where such a course could take us. When we reached that limit, we simply had to change our way of doing business or stop doing business. We didn't change our way, and we stopped.

Many, I know, criticise the New Deal, although they admit that it seems to be beating the depression, because it is so different from the deal which brought us *to* the depression.

They don't, of course, put it just that way. They say it is different from the course under which America became the most prosperous civilization in world history.

But they neglect to note the nature of that depression. It was not a depression which was brought about by doing things poorly. It was brought about, in the main, because we did things so well. It was because we were so efficient, both in the factories and on the farms. It was because we were organized to produce so much more than we were organized to consume.

If, at any time in our previous history, we had been organized to consume as much as we produced, we would never have had the depression.

But neither would we ever have had prosperity on the scale we have had. Nor would we ever have developed an economic mechanism which could by any possibility produce enough for everybody. The point is that *when* our economic mechanism *could* produce enough for everybody, our whole economic situation underwent a revolutionary change.

The secret of that mechanism was modern power, plus modern machinery, plus modern scientific management; and these were all developed by the use of capital along the lines approved by our good bankers.

Pardon me if I indulge for a moment in some very elementary economics—principles so basic that some of our financiers have long ago forgotten them. We cannot understand what really happened to America, however, and we cannot grasp the necessity for such a completely new deal, unless we do remember them.

In the first place, money is not wealth; it is merely a medium of exchange of wealth; and the mere putting of money into any enterprise could not by itself develop the enterprise. What is really invested is wealth—the things which people buy with their money—especially food, clothing, shelter and physical supplies.

We were once, for instance, an agrarian nation, almost entirely agricultural, and if we consumed all we raised from year to year, we must have remained an agrarian people. But we didn't. We learned to save food and other things beyond what we consumed on the farm; and it was these products of our farms—not mere money—which enabled us to build our first factories.

What we actually did, of course, was to sell these farm products and get money for them, and then, probably, we put the money in a bank. But when the banker loaned the money to somebody who wanted to build a factory, it was used very largely to buy the food which thrifty farm families had saved and to feed workingmen who were engaged in producing not things to consume but things with which to increase production.

The factory builder may not have thought of this. All he thought of was that he needed labor and material and supplies. But his labor had to eat, so he had to give wages to his workers so that they could buy food and other necessities. And the people who produced the materials and supplies had to eat, even if they did not raise any food directly; and what they ate was paid for out of the money which they received for the materials and supplies.

If we keep this in mind, we may be able to see what was really happening as America was evolving from an agrarian to a machine civilization. We were always *saving* an important part of the things which we produced. But what we were really saving was not money, and the very act of saving was not what it seemed to be at all. We were not saving things for a rainy day, nor things to be consumed in our old age, as squirrels might store up nuts for winter.

Little or no food *could* be saved for very many years. Even clothing so saved would soon get out of style. Nevertheless, wealth was being saved by being converted, as it were, not from things into money, but from things which people needed for their own personal consumption to things which nobody cared to consume but which would make it possible to produce consumer goods more rapidly.

No farmer, for instance, could eat a mowing machine; but if he ate all he raised on the farm, he might never be able to buy a mowing machine or anything else which would make it possible for him to raise much more than he had been raising. By going without some of the food he produced, however, and selling what he went without, he might be able to buy machines which would enable him to produce much more food.

That, in effect, is what the American farmer did; and as he improved his methods of production, he became prosperous. Then he went on improving his methods of production and did not become so prosperous. By the time he had improved his methods so that he was producing more food than he could sell, he became very poor indeed.

And all America, particularly during the past fifty years, was going through much the same process. We were organized to increase production. That was the only practical way by which anything much could be really saved; and although in later years it seemed that we became extravagant, we actually became more and more saving; and, instead of consuming all that we produced, we set aside a larger and larger part of it for the building up of more and more efficient methods of producing wealth.

But that process could not go on forever. The fact that financiers were not acquainted with any other process could not save us. Inevitably there would come a time when our machines would become so productive that, unless we arranged for a larger and larger consumption of these machine products, they could not be operated profitably, and further investments in more and more machinery could not possibly result in saving.

That time came—that's all. It came with a bang in 1929; but those who think the crash was due entirely to that optimistic bull market are likely to miss the point. It would have come inevitably if there had been no bull market, for there wasn't any other known way to invest our savings than through perfecting and expanding our machinery of production.

Theoretically, of course, our financiers might have seen the necessity at about this time for doubling or tripling the wages of American labor and thus increasing the market for American goods. But our financiers had not studied *finance:* they had studied only that kind of financing which had been required during the period which had just ended.

They urged everybody to save more resolutely than ever. That, they said, was how they got their start, and it was—by everybody's saving and investing the savings in more ways of increasing production.

And that was the way—although they did not realize it—by which these same financiers would now get their finish.

I am speaking, remember, not of the bad bankers, but of the good ones. A few villains could never have messed things up like that. It was the good bankers, who, by referring to the policies which had once been so successful, urged our employers to cut wages and to lay off workers at a time when only universal employment at higher and higher wages could have saved the day.

Not that they wanted to do it. They said it had to be done. And it did have to be done, and it will always have to be done, in any civilization which is struggling to change from an agrarian to a machine civilization. It does not have to be done, and it is disastrous to do it, in a civilization which can produce an abundance for everybody.

Soviet Russia had to do it. Russia had practically no machinery and no credit. Their system of production was mainly a peasant system by which, even if everybody were employed and the masses were to consume all that they produced, the standard of living would still be very low. If they were ever to have a higher standard, however, it had to go still lower. For they needed machines, and the only way they could get the machines was through going without a large part of the little which they were producing, and using it largely to feed and clothe and care for the labor which would be needed in the production of power and machinery and equipment.

I said I did not wish to attack President Hoover. I think it was rather fortunate for America, when this crisis arrived, that we had the sort of Administration which we had. For President Hoover, by holding firmly to the old formulas, demonstrated conclusively that the old formulas were now utterly hopeless.

Banks, for instance, were failing rapidly, early in the Hoover Administration; and if this had been due to some ordinary mishap, instead of to the great revolutionary change which had come over us, the Hoover policy would have been the correct policy. What was really causing the banks to fail, however, was that we had emerged from the era of scarcity, in which it was necessary to give first attention to the capitalization of more and more schemes for production, to the era of abundance in which it was necessary to arrange for consumption by the masses of the enormous volume of things which it was now possible to produce. If this were not done, business could never again be profitable; and savings advanced to enterprises which could not be profitable would necessarily be lost. Of course the banks failed; for banks engaged in this losing game would necessarily tend to fail.

Without blaming Mr. Hoover, then—because it was not merely the Hoover policy but the traditional American policy—we may remember how the Hoover government came to the aid of the banks. It loaned them more money with which to continue this failing process so that, when they eventually did fail, they failed in a bigger way than they could possibly have failed without this government backing.

The farmers, too, were generally losing money because they were producing so much more than they could sell; and the government loaned them money with which to raise still bigger crops which they could not sell. And the farmers also succeeded in failing in a bigger way.

Well, we all remember the final crash. It did not come until months after Mr. Roosevelt's election; and my impression is that Democrats were quite as unprepared for it as were the Republicans. It cannot be claimed that even President Roosevelt knew what to do; and he took the first opportunity to confess to the American people that he did not.

What he did know, however, and what all America by this time seemed to grasp, was that the old, traditional policies could not longer be relied upon. Some new way had to be tried. And although this idea did not dawn upon America until the black moment when every bank in the nation had closed its doors, it more than offset the gloom caused by the bank holiday and America experienced its first real surge of hope in years.

A new way had to be found. The New Deal came because a New Deal *had* to come; and only as we understand that, can we grasp its A. B. C.

The job might have been bungled. America might have been thrown into chaos and revolution; but out of it all, eventually, we would have to organize an entirely New Deal.

How well the job would be done—and how much suffering and chaos might be avoided in its doing—depended mainly on just one thing. It depended upon how good a leader this incoming president would prove to be.

Neither Washington nor Lincoln ever faced a more serious crisis in the history of our nation. Surely it was no time for partisanship. It was no time even for quibbling over details. If Roosevelt could measure up to the demands of leadership, it was now up to every American who had any sense of the seriousness of the situation to see what we could do to back him up.

Well—fortunately—our leader did not know what to do. If he had known what to do, he could not have been our leader; he would have been the leader merely of those who agreed with him.

But he decided to find out what to do; and when he did that, all Americans, excepting those who do not believe in acting according to the facts, could acknowledge his leadership.

He could make mistakes—yes. So can all fact-finders. But when we follow the policy of fact-finding, we can correct our mistakes as we discover that they are mistakes, and we can, therefore, profit from our mistakes. When we merely follow tradition, however, and do things in a certain way, because that is the way things have always been done, we perpetuate our mistakes. And when we fail, we continue to fail, because that is the way that people have usually failed.

It became apparent at once that President Roosevelt was not content to find out what presidents customarily do, not content to go to practical politicians for counsel. Our practical politicians, like our financiers, undoubtedly knew a lot, but most of what they knew had recently ceased to be so, and the President had to have the facts of a situation in which nobody had yet had any experience. So the President took counsel of fact-finders—men of research.

We called them his Brain Trust, and the politicians were sure that such a name would bring both the professors and the President into ridicule. America, however, did not seem to mind. America seemed to welcome the idea of having brains in politics, and the laugh eventually seems to have turned the other way.

I do not think this audience wishes me to go into details of all the Roosevelt policies. There is no time for such an analysis, and it would only obscure the issue if it were undertaken; for many of these policies have had little or nothing to do with any eventual New Deal.

Many of them, necessarily, have had to do, not with the reorganization of our economic mechanism so that it can function in an era of abundance, but with emergency relief and with first aid to those injured in our financial and industrial crash.

In the early days of the depression, we tried to care for the unemployed by passing the hat; and when increasing needs were confronted by diminishing incomes, we tried to make the employed care for the unemployed by sharing their work and dividing their pay. Eventually, we had to resort to taxation. Fifteen million citizens and their families simply cannot be allowed to starve; and if they were allowed to starve in any country—including America—they would tear down the social order first.

This emergency relief program has, of course, been expensive, but it has been unavoidable; and it has been less expensive in the long run than any mere passing of the hat could be. Something at least will be salvaged from it. For millions, instead of being recipients of private charity, have been honorably employed in public works. The necessarily hasty organization of such enterprises has no doubt worked for inefficiency in many ways. On general principles, however, I am sure that America has been solidly behind these programs; for they are demanded not only by every humane impulse but by ordinary economic sense.

There is also the President's financial policy, which can only be mentioned here. Many may honestly disagree with certain details of that policy, and it would serve no purpose for me to declare that these critics are wrong. We can all agree, however, upon three points:

First, it is a good policy if it works.

Secondly, since the President is committed to a fact-finding program, he will not continue a policy which does not work.

Thirdly, whatever errors, if any, there may be in this policy, the alternative from which it saved the country was a policy of paper money inflation; and saving America from that kind of inflation, must be eventually recognized as an incalculable service to our social order.

In a recent study trip through the country, I myself was surprised to find so little opposition to the President's gold policy, on the part of both business men and bankers. Many admitted that they did not understand it, but they were confident that it was carefully and cautiously worked out; and they were usually agreed that our going off the gold standard was inevitable because of the disruption of our foreign trade by the depreciated European currencies.

But it is not in these policies that we can find the A. B. C. of the New Deal. It is rather in the N. R. A. and the Agricultural Administration.

Private business, we are constantly reminded, has been saddled with all sorts of restrictions. Employers are no longer free to say what wages they shall pay their workers, or how many hours they shall be compelled to work. And while all this, say the critics, may be defended as an emergency measure, it is obvious that business is again reviving and the Administration should now remove the restrictions and let us resume our customary way.

Now there is some truth in these contentions, but permit me to state them in another way.

Private business has *always* been saddled with restrictions. Employers were *never* free to say what wages they should pay their workers, or how many hours they should be compelled to work. There is no such thing as abstract liberty, either in business or in life. The only liberty which is possible for any of us is liberty to deal with the facts; and we could not continue along the old road because the old road didn't go any further.

Let me ask if any employer in this audience ever paid his employees all that he would like to pay. None of us ever did. Business wouldn't permit it. If we did anything like that, our competitors would put us out of business in no time. Some of our competitors, we know, were pretty mean. They always hired their labor for as little as possible and worked their employees as long as possible—*and they set the pace for us.*

It amuses me nowadays to hear people talk about business being regimented, and about its being under a dictatorship.

It was in the old days that business had a real dictator—and it was the meanest chiseler in every line who did the dictating.

He was the one who regimented us and had us all doing the goose step. When he cut wages, we all cut. We might not have liked it, and we might have hated him, but we jumped to attention and clicked our heels whenever he gave a signal.

We must surely remember the great effort made by President Hoover, at the very beginning of the depression, to maintain wages and buying power. He called hundreds of employers into conference—modern, progressive employers, with vision and understanding and deep wells of human sympathy—and had them all agree to act in concert to maintain the wage level. They all, or pretty nearly all of them, went back and ordered wage reductions.

Why did they do that? It wasn't because they wanted to. It wasn't because they weren't sincere when they promised that they wouldn't.

It was because somebody did it. It was because the *chiseler* did it; and when the chiseler did anything, the public spirited had to follow suit.

The New Deal is not restricting business. It is liberating business from the domination of the chiseler by removing wages from competition.

Business, to be sure, is still under restrictions; and whatever happens it will continue to be under restrictions, just as any people who have dethroned a tyrant must continue to have some sort of government. The question for business men is not whether business shall or shall not have a government, but what kind of government shall it have?

Shall it be a government of nation-wide codes, to achieve the objectives which it is now necessary to achieve? Or shall it be a mere continuation of habits and traditions, wholly unrelated to our new needs and whose only justification is that *they are habits and traditions* to which the mind of business has become accustomed?

I think I can give the answer. In spite of the senseless clamor which is arising here and there, I believe that American business men are in the main alive. I believe they have not forgotten the depression, and that the real lessons of the depression are becoming more and more apparent. I believe they are coming to understand that business cannot sell more than its customers can buy, and that the most urgent need of business is the maintenance and the constant expansion of mass buying power. I think they realize that this cannot be achieved unless wages are raised, unemployment eliminated and the masses endowed with more leisure to consume; and I think they realize that these goals cannot be achieved unless business is liberated from the rule of the chiseler. It seems to me, therefore, that American business men, instead of merely submitting to the codes of business, will soon be fighting aggressively for the extension and perfection of those codes, and calling upon labor to organize on a national scale to the end that progressive business and progressive labor shall co-operate on every front to achieve their common aim.

This, of course, would require a considerable reorganization of labor, which was originally organized to fight employers because, under the conditions which then existed, no other course was possible. Under the New Deal, however, another course is possible, and progressive labor leaders consider it most desirable. It cannot be taken, however, until business does organize to pay the highest wages that can be paid, and to build up mass buying power in accordance with our ever increasing ability to produce and the business necessity for more and more sales, and it cannot be taken until labor definitely and always acts on the fact that business can pay higher wages only out of profits.

Of course, I don't know when all this will happen. I cannot say for sure that it will happen. It is conceivable, at least, that traditional thinking still has such a hold upon us that business will attempt to resume the old way once more.

I can say positively, however, that business will not *get anywhere* through any such scrapping of the New Deal. We may go back to the old road, but we cannot take it any further than it goes; and we came to its end long before President Roosevelt was elected.

We can, however, go back to the class struggle. We can blast every human hope which the New Deal has aroused. We can notify labor that everything is off, that we shall employ whom we will, when we will and how long we will, at whatever wages any chiseling competitor thinks he has to pay. If we can do this and get away with it, we can reduce mass buying power. But we can't sell goods in any consequential volume. We can't keep the wheels of industry going. We can't keep the masses employed.

And that means that we can't get away with it.

Fifteen million Americans were out of work in March 1933, and countless others were working on part time for wages upon which their loved ones could scarcely keep alive. Yet there was no revolution. There was no uprising. The masses patiently endured and hoped and would not listen to revolutionary agitators. *Why?*

It was because the American masses still had faith in America and in the American business system. Now is the time, if we wish to do it, to destroy all that faith. All that is necessary, to bring to America all the social disasters which European countries have been experiencing, is to abandon the course upon which we have so successfully started and turn our backs upon nation-wide economic planning.

I am not intimating that we must concur in every Presidential policy. I am not asking that we refrain from criticism. I think it is quite possible, in fact, that all the various special agencies, including the N. R. A. itself, will give way to better plans.

But the A. B. C. of the New Deal will remain—and it is the A. B. C., not the other letters of the alphabet, which is arousing all the present opposition. To give up the business and industrial codes is to give up progress and to turn our backs upon the facts of industrial evolution.

Thanks to the New Deal, American business is recovering; and since recovery was its object, it is now claimed that the New Deal should be abandoned.

Well, there is a certain logic in that. If we save a man from drowning by pulling him out of the water, we just naturally throw him back in at the first sign of recovery. That is, if we reason as these critics do.

But there is another way of looking at it. We will not desert the job of bringing him back to life because, in his first semiconscious mutterings, he tells us rather angrily to keep our hands off.

Most assuredly, recovery is the objective of the President's program; but business recovery will not be complete until business is able to take care of itself; and it just happened to be a fact of business evolution that business can no longer take care of itself unless it organizes consciously to seek its profits in the greatest possible service to the mass consumer.

When American business does organize for that, it will no longer complain of government interference. There will be no interference and no necessity for it. There will be simply cooperation of labor and capital and scientific management—cooperation also between industry and agriculture—in the interest of all concerned. That is the A. B. C. of the New Deal. It is a deal which leaves nobody out because, in the nature of the revolutionary changes which were brought about by the evolution of the machine, we all became dependent upon one another, and could no longer deal prosperity to some without dealing it to all.

Leadership in These New Times *

FRIENDS AND FELLOW STUDENTS:

I trust we are friends, and surely we are fellow students.

Once upon a time, we used to read in the obituary columns that so-and-so "completed his education" at such-and-such a college. But the phrase, I am glad to say, has about gone out of use.

We now know that if a man's education is finished, the man is finished. Even the justices of our Supreme Court are learning things today.

There is a never ending controversy, to be sure, as to what constitutes an education. Until recent years, our institutions of higher learning were engaged for the most part in providing what they called a broad general education, as opposed to mere technical instruction, while business men argued for what they called more practical courses in our colleges.

As if that which is broad and general could not be practical and that which is practical could not be broad and general.

But it was an interesting controversy. I never could understand it all; but I gathered from one side that an education, to be broad and general, must specialize on Latin and Greek, and from the other, that an education, to be practical, must teach the students only those things which wealthy business men wanted them to know.

Like most controversies of the sort, neither side seemed to have any idea of what the other side was talking about. Few of our business men, for instance, knew Latin or Greek, and they could not argue convincingly as to their educational value. Few, also, knew much about chemistry or electrodynamics. But there was

* Address before Graduate Students of the Massachusetts Institute of Technology, Cambridge, Massachusetts—April 14, 1937.

this difference. They could use any number of competent chemists and electrical experts, if they knew where they could find them, but they hardly knew where they could place those so-called broadly educated graduates, even if they could recite Aristotle backwards.

To make a long story short, the educators won the argument, but the business men won the day. For while the business men might be lacking in education, the educators were likely to be lacking in money, and it takes money to operate a university. So the business men endowed our colleges, and built new ones. It may not have been written in the bond that these colleges should teach what the business men wanted them to teach. Nevertheless, Latin and Greek were soon selling short, while one institution after another set up schools of engineering, chemistry, physics and other branches of applied science.

We business men surely started something when we did that. It hasn't stopped yet, and it isn't going to stop. We simply didn't know what we were doing. If we had known, we can well ask whether we would have done it.

For what we let loose was the principle of fact-finding, in place of the hitherto dominant principle of precedent and obedience to authority.

The argument between classical education and so-called practical education may never have been put upon that basis. But consider what happened.

A century ago, our colleges were largely devoted to turning out preachers and teachers, excepting as their graduates might take up law and medicine. These, in the mind of the day, were the *learned* professions.

One had to learn things, to be sure, to become an engineer or a business executive; but that seemed to be a relatively low order of learning, and not entitled to as high a degree as the classical students earned.

To become a spiritual leader, in those days, one did not have to inquire much as to the special needs of the times. What he had to do was to master the ancient texts, so as to transmit them with due authority to his spiritual flock.

There has been a revolution, even in religion, since then. Many favor this revolution and many deplore it, but that is not the point. The point is, it happened; and it happened because all America, including our theological students, participated in this drift from the unquestioning acceptance of authority to scientific, fact-finding research.

Teachers of that day, also, relied upon authority, and were in turn accepted as authorities. And in the same category, of course, were the lawyers. I am not trying to belittle them. But lawyers were not required to find out what was just or unjust, or to study the changes in human relations which now make acts right or wrong. They also were required only to study the texts and precedents and to abide by them.

Physicians, to be sure, had to engage in research, and they changed their practices according to the facts which they discovered. But from time immemorial, the doctors had constituted a sort of priesthood, so much so that even chiefs and kings were compelled to defer to the supernatural authority of the Medicine Man. A good many doctors, in fact, haven't entirely recovered from this tradition yet.

But an engineer was just a practical fellow. He had no sacred formulas—only mathematical formulas, which could be proved or disproved with a paper and pencil. His only authority was the facts.

That being the case, he had to make good in a way which was not uniformly required of the so-called learned professions.

If a preacher failed to save our souls, nobody blamed the preacher. If a doctor failed to save our lives, we did not hold him responsible, and the evidence was buried anyway. Even if students flunked their courses, that was said to be the fault of the students, not of the teacher. But if a bridge fell down, everybody held it against the engineer. It was his business to operate strictly according to the known and knowable facts.

Now, I am not trying to belittle the arguments in favor of a general rather than a technical education. I am simply trying to trace what happened, so that we may find out, if we can, what is likely to happen next. And what happened was a growing practice in America of approaching problems from the standpoint of fact-finding research; and few if any of us business men had any idea of how far that practice would spread.

For we believed profoundly in authority. We believed, for instance, in our property rights—even in our divine right to use what was authoritatively ours in any way that we saw fit. If we were rich while the masses were poor, we felt no responsibility. We openly declared, many of us, that God had ordained it that way. If a professor of economics, in fact, in one of our endowed colleges, set out to study human relations in the same fact-finding way in which we wanted chemistry and engineering studied, we said he was exceeding his authority. In our technical problems, we wanted solutions based on facts. In our social setup, we did not. The beneficiaries of privilege and traditional inherited rights seldom do.

But we cannot release great new forces in our world and hope to retain the status quo. Machinery, for one thing. When we once arranged to manufacture clothing with power machinery, and compelled American families to abandon their looms and spinning wheels, the institution of the family could never be exactly what it had been before. And when power machinery, producing and distributing to the whole nation, eventually destroyed the independence of the family and caused the people of the whole nation to become interdependent, neither the nation nor the family could be what they had been.

Understand, I am not arguing the right or wrong of this. I am simply noting what has happened. You are living in extremely difficult times. You are beginning your careers at a moment in history when the old authorities have broken down—when the old moral standards and the old political and economic standards cannot be maintained, and when your basic problem is one of discovering, if you can, what sort of a civilization you are going to function in.

Naturally, you are ambitious. But if ambition means to you what it meant to the young men of my generation, you will be merely inviting disaster.

In those days, for instance, we hoped with reason to get ahead of the average person. If we could get enough money together, we had reason to believe that we could keep it, and neither the possession nor control of any honestly won fortune would be questioned. For the authority by which we held our property was still strong. We denied even the right of the government to tax us according to our incomes, and the Supreme Court at that time decided in our favor that the government had no such right.

If you view this from the standpoint of any fixed and unalterable conclusion as to what society ought to be, you may go through life with a headache. But if you view it from the standpoint of social evolution—if you find out the cause and the direction of social change, and employ fact-finding to discover what to do about it, all discouragement and all pessimism may disappear.

Recently, for instance, a shocking thing has happened—a thing simply paralyzing to the minds of business men who have been quick to say what America should be like but have given very little study to the problem of what it is becoming.

I refer to those sit-down strikes. All of a sudden, to hear the employers tell it, their employees have gone mad. They have shown no more regard for the law, apparently, than a crazy man. They have actually invaded their employers' property; not, to be sure, to steal or to wreck, but to remind their employers that they will produce no more wealth until they can come to some agreement as to what sort of division of that wealth is just.

Few if any employers would object, to be sure, to the employers sitting down, and remaining seated until their employees were willing to enter into some responsible contract with *them.* But that's different. The point is that these sitters do not own the places they are sitting on. Those places are simply the places they must go to if they intend to work—that is, if they intend to go on living and keeping their families alive.

There was a time in America when, if an employee was not satisfied with his job, he could go back where he came from; and where he came from, usually, was a piece of land upon which he could at least make a living.

The modern employee has no such choice. If he doesn't work on the job to which an employer assigns him, there *is* no place for him to go, except to some charity or relief headquarters. And so long as that is the fact, we must see how futile it will be to appeal to the authorities.

The authorities, to be sure, may oust the trespassers; but it will solve no problems until we first provide some other space for them to occupy, and it must be some place where they can make a living.

Once again let me emphasize that I am not pleading the righteousness of their demands, or even their right to trespass upon other people's property. I am simply calling attention to the facts. These things are happening. There is a reason why they are happening. It is not hysteria. It is not the presence of agitators. And to assume any such cause for happenings which can be understood only through scientific fact-finding will lead at most to cures that will not cure.

We may depend upon it that in any society in which getting a living has become a collective enterprise, the people will sooner or later act collectively. Collective bargaining is only the first step. Collective and co-operative action, based upon fact-finding research, will follow. In the meantime, a mere appeal to constituted authority—especially if the authority be constituted upon the experience of an economic order which has ceased to exist—will not cure a single evil or solve any of the problems involved.

Please do not assume that I am advocating the defiance of authority, or contending that reverence for authority is not necessary in human life. We never could have had any social order, if people had not looked up to other people as their divinely ordained patriarchs and priests and kings, and if it had not been considered a sin, punishable in this world and the next, to question their decrees. It happens, however, that human society *has grown beyond that.*

Even today, children must learn obedience before they are old enough to learn why or when to obey; but a modern father would only make a fool of himself if he were to attempt to usurp the authority of an ancient patriarch when, in the very nature of the world he now lives in, he cannot direct the lives of his wife and children in such a way as to provide for their maintenance and the perpetuation of the race.

And we have come upon times when private property cannot maintain the rights to which it was once very properly entitled. If we are to have order at all, it must be order based upon the facts of these new times. What is more, the masses of people all over the world have become aware of this.

I do not mean that they have found any solution, or even that they are approaching the problem in a scientific, fact-finding way. But we business men, when we developed a generation of fact-finders, with the idea that they would find ways by which we could make more profits, let loose forces which have so changed the world that the masses could not, if they would, retain their old-time sense of subordination.

This was brought about by the group to which you belong.

You technicians originally appeared in a world of small communities, in which each little community seemed remote from every other community; and by your research, for one thing, you made it possible for them to communicate with one another in seemingly magical ways. You discovered the telegraph, the telephone and the ocean cable. You made the modern newspaper possible. You even made it possible for the human voice to carry around the world on waves whose very existence was unknown, even to the highly educated, a single century ago.

Then you performed equal miracles of travel and transportation. You made it possible for people and their products to go anywhere and to get there quickly. You conquered land and sea and air, and now you are exploring the stratosphere.

More important than anything else, you abolished the need for scarcity on earth. You so multiplied our capacity to produce as to make it no longer necessary for masses to be poor; and you made it quite ridiculous, therefore, for people generally to devote all their time and energy hereafter to the problem which, all down the ages, had taxed their every resource—the problem of obtaining food, clothing and shelter.

Unwittingly, perhaps, you have brought mankind to the threshold of a higher life. And the masses of people, although they may not comprehend it, feel it. They at least see no further reason why they should be mere serfs and vassals, producing the wealth which has made a life of leisure and culture possible only to the very few. And so they have been rising everywhere and demanding things which they never dared to demand before.

In many parts of Europe, the hitherto privileged classes bitterly fought these demands; and there is no doubt that they could have brought the masses to subjection excepting for one thing, and that was the force of abundant production which you had let loose.

In the very nature of this machine order, the masses had to share abundantly in its benefits, else the machines could not run, and there would not, therefore, be profits for their owners. This was so because the machines had become so productive that only the masses, by consuming abundantly, could provide an adequate market for their products. But the beneficiaries of privilege were not fact-finders, as far as the maintenance of those privileges was concerned. In that, they were traditionalists—blind believers in authority, especially the authority of their own private property. And so, all through Europe, there was strife and revolution and chaos. Then there were men on horseback—dictators—determined to quell the disorders even if they did not know the principles of order in this machine age. So there have been renewed appeals to authority—appeals to obey orders because they are orders, with no thought of whether or not they are actually in line with the facts of social evolution.

Technology, based on fact-finding, brought mankind together. Through its development of mass production, it made possible an abundant material life for all, and pointed to the time, therefore, when nation need no longer struggle against nation, nor race against race, nor class against class.

Before this era of universal peace could dawn, of course, there would have to be an understanding by the people everywhere of the great events which were bringing them together as opposed to the age old traditions which were keeping them apart. But technology, in its development of the wire and wireless, of modern printing and publishing and many other devices, provided the means by which the peoples might become acquainted with the facts of their new order and their common interests understood.

These dictators, however, have prostituted all this mechanism of enlightenment to the maintenance of their authoritarian appeal. They do not—they dare not—let their subjects learn the news, else they could not hope to mobilize them once more under the banners of their ancient, warring, tribal gods.

They have also taken over the schools and colleges and universities, to the end that youth may not learn anything which the constituted authority does not want youth to know, and have even decreed that science must take on a tribal character and promise not to discover any truths which might tend to upset their authoritarian propaganda.

But it is all futile, and you who are trained in fact-finding must see that such dictatorships cannot last. Already these dictatorships are falling—falling of their own weight. They can exist only by force, whereas human society can endure only by truth.

No nation which exhausts its man power in building armament can endure; for no nation can endure unless its people endure, and people can't eat armament. It is no accident, then, that the really strong nations today are great democracies, in which, although the people may be hampered by tradition, they have access to the news—that is, to the new facts which have rendered so many of the ancient traditions invalid.

Under the old traditions, there could be privileged classes, and the domination of the masses by the fortunate few. The tradition was valid, however, only up to a certain point—up to the point where fact-finding technique resulted in the development of the mechanism of plenty.

Under the old traditions, war could be a profitable pursuit; for one nation could overrun another, enslave its population and carry off its goods.

Fact-finding, to be sure, has not yet abolished war, but it did make a fool of it. For the fact-finders developed machines so productive that the nations in which those machines were used were soon surfeited with goods, and it became their chief problem to find out how to sell those goods.

They might, to be sure, have sold larger and larger quantities to their own people, if they had only studied the facts of this new epoch and acted in accordance with what they found. But that was against tradition. It was against the tradition of the age of scarcity, under which the masses had always had to remain poor. Nevertheless, because of the new facts, they didn't want the goods of other nations pouring across their boundaries as tributes; nor did they want the workers of other nations to become *their* slaves, producing things for *them* to consume.

If that happened, they reasoned, their own masses would become unemployed; and if they were unemployed, they couldn't earn a living, and if the masses couldn't earn a living they would surely overthrow their government.

Had the problem been submitted to fact-finding, it would have presented few difficulties. All that would have been necessary then would have been to arrange a profitable equitable exchange of goods among the nations, to the great advantage of each. But that, too, was against tradition. In the age of scarcity, it was generally taught and believed that the way to prosperity was to get the best of others, which was the way of war.

No nation, to be sure, wanted war. But because they acted according to tradition, instead of according to the facts, they all went to war.

And because the traditions were no longer valid, all sides lost. There were conquerors, but there were and could be no real or lasting gains.

And the same evolutionary forces which had rendered it impossible to make war successfully now made it impossible to make peace successfully, unless the old traditions were abandoned in favor of fact-finding research. But tradition was old. Fact-finding was new. So the nations tried to make peace according to the traditional pattern, and there was no peace.

Eventually, there was world depression, in many ways more disastrous than the war.

Now we are experiencing recovery in spots; and the voice of tradition is heard on every hand, urging us to make sure that it be a traditional recovery—not a recovery based upon the facts of these new times.

Under the facts, the masses must now be served. Under the facts, they must become not merely abundant producers but abundant consumers of wealth. Under the facts, poverty must be abolished. Under the facts, this whole mechanism of plenty must be dedicated to the utmost possible service and the utmost possible liberation of the whole people, else it cannot be kept in operation and we must all go down once more into the depths of depression, unemployment and poverty in the midst of plenty, with its consequent chaos, revolution and war.

But I did not come here to deliver a lecture on any abstract theme. I am a busy man. I have about all that I can do to attend to my own business; and so, I know, have you, and I would not take my time or yours to discuss any subject which is not of vital concern to each of us.

You may not be preparing for political careers. You are architects and chemists and engineers, expecting presumably to offer your professional services to business men; and although we business men have need of your fact-finding technique, it is useless to deny that many of us are still traditional thinkers as far as these basic problems of all business and of all society are concerned.

In what spirit, then, will you come into our employment? Will you say it is none of your business what your employer thinks, or whether he prefers to follow tradition rather than to think at all?

Well, let me remind you that it is your business; for under the facts of the world change which technology has brought about, we capitalists and employers cannot remain capitalists and employers unless the mechanism and the scientific technique which you technicians have discovered are dedicated to the service of the whole people, instead of to the special service of hitherto specially privileged groups.

The time has come—and technology has brought it about—

when, to be practical, we cannot continue to think within the limits of any special technique. The old educational problem, which could not be solved by argument, is being solved by events. For only fact-finding in the broad matters of human relationship can now preserve society, and save it from the chaos into which so-called conservatism would recklessly consign it.

Almost inevitably, then, you who have been trained in fact-finding will become the business and political leaders of the day that is dawning now. You must not and will not permit our out-of-date convictions to dominate your minds. You will not permit any mistaken notion of loyalty to induce you to follow us if, in your fact-finding, you note that we are blindfolded, and that the way we are going leads to the yawning precipice of economic and social ruin. In the very nature of the world we have entered, *we* must turn to you, not merely for technical advice and assistance, but to find the way of true social progress in this new age.

The American Way of Recovery *

The so-called unemployment problem is not a particularly difficult problem. What makes it seem difficult is the name we give it. It is not merely a problem of unemployment. It is the problem of *unemployment in this machine age.*

At the beginning of the depression, many efforts were made to "employ" the unemployed, particularly in work about our houses and grounds, but none of these efforts had any appreciable effect upon the conditions which we were trying to improve. If the unemployed were given work, we supposed, that would solve the problem. *How* they were employed, or what kind of work they were engaged to do, seemed not to matter very much. Some even supposed that the problem might be solved by the development in America of a sufficiently large "servant class."

Many still find it difficult to distinguish between the relations of master and servant and those of employer and employee in this machine age; and they can hardly discover the difference by consulting the dictionary. To discover the real difference, we must find the difference between the machine age and the ages which preceded it.

In the ancient civilizations, the typical master engaged servants to perform services, either for the master himself or for persons belonging to the household, estate or little community over which the master presided. In these days the typical employer hires workers to perform services for his customers, who may be numbered in millions and scattered over the whole world.

In the old days, to be sure, a few so-called servants were employed by men engaged in trade to produce the things which their

* Address before The Pittsburgh Community Forum, Carnegie Institute, Pittsburgh, Pennsylvania—November 21, 1934.

employers intended to sell. And in modern America, wealthy persons still hire servants to do certain things exclusively for their employers.

There is a vast difference, however, in the two kinds of employment—the kind which was typical of those pre-machine civilizations and the kind which is typical of this. To lump the two together, as we so often do in thinking of the unemployment problem, leads to no end of confusion.

Our very efforts to classify labor according to the classifications which were appropriate to the ancient type of employment, add to this confusion. We speak of labor as "skilled" or "unskilled," as a basis for determining the wages we intend to pay. Actually, there is no way of telling whether a locomotive engineer is more or less skilled than a lady's maid; and if he does get higher wages, it is on some other basis entirely. Similarly, we speak of "physical" and "mental" labor, as if some kinds of labor did not require that the body performing it have a brain, while other kinds do not necessitate the existence of a body.

To classify labor in any useful way, we must classify it according to the wealth which it produces; and personal skill is but one of the elements—perhaps a minor element—entering into this. The truly highest grade of labor in this machine age is the labor which most efficiently serves the greatest number of human beings. Then there is labor which, no matter how personally skilled it may be, is not equipped, organized and managed in such a way as to give such efficient service to so many people. There is also labor which, through no fault of its own, is utterly wasted and does not add a cent's worth to the total of wealth out of which all labor must be paid; and there is labor which is destructive and actually detracts from that total. Since all wages must come out of production, our problem is not one merely of finding employment for everybody, but of *how* everybody shall be employed.

If a man employs a valet, or even a personal secretary, he thinks almost wholly in terms of the employee's individual skill; and since large employers do employ such persons, they are likely to rate employment generally (or try to rate it) in terms of such individual aptitude. These men have often resented what they term the "levelling" attitude of the labor unions, which demand such a high minimum wage, they allege, that it becomes impossible to reward the specially fit with the rewards to which they are specially entitled.

As a matter of fact, the labor unions have come closer to an understanding of the actual economic realities. They have not sought, to be sure, to make their minimum demands the maximum of payment; but they have sensed, more or less accurately, that real economic worth in modern industry depends far more upon the process in which one is engaged than in the individual art of the persons engaged in it. An average worker engaged in an up-to-date modern industry, under the best of management, can produce a lot of wealth; while an exceptionally talented person employed in wasteful processes can not.

Only as people are employed in modern, well-managed machine industry can high wages be paid. Only if the masses are employed as efficiently as they can be employed can the highest possible wages be paid.

Relatively few personal servants can produce much wealth. A young gentleman of leisure may derive some egotistic satisfaction from having a valet who understands his job. But the valet's service is strictly personal, and is likely to consist at best of saving time for a person whose time is not valuable. There are, of course, exceptions. Anyone who could save ten minutes a day for President Roosevelt would be doing a great service to the whole United States, perhaps to the whole world and to future generations; and there would be no economic loss involved in paying such a servant very high wages. The average lady's maid, however, and the average "gentleman's gentleman" cannot produce much wealth, and any wages which they receive are likely to be much more than by strict economic standards they are really worth, no matter how efficient, loyal and hard working they may be.

The cost of everything, including the cost of personal servants, must come out of wealth which is produced, and very little wealth in this machine age is produced by personal servants. Everybody knows this. Everybody understands that, whatever benefits may be derived from this kind of service, hiring such servants is not profitable. To secure profits, one has to employ a very different kind of employee—the kind who serves the buying public. And if one pays wages to the first type of employee, he pays them not out of the wealth which *they* produce, but out of the wealth which is produced by the other kind of employment.

While all this is perfectly obvious, however, it is not usually taken into account in our approach to the so-called unemployment problem. The problem is not unemployment; *it is unemployment in this machine age.* It is not a problem of putting everybody to work; it is a problem, rather, of putting everybody to work in such a way that he can earn and get a good living. The *best* solution of the problem, obviously, would be such an organization of work as will enable *everybody* to earn the *best possible* living.

We may almost measure the prosperity of any country by the way in which ladies of leisure discuss their servant problem. In poverty-stricken India and China, from the standpoint of such employers, the situation is ideal. In Europe, there is also a large, well-disciplined servant class; but, because Europe is industrialized, good servants cost much more money than in the Orient. In America, in prosperous times, such ladies find conditions terrible. This, of course, is because industrialization has gone still further here. In America, in prosperous times, more workers are engaged in operations aimed to give service to the general public; and these operations have made it possible to pay such high wages that the person who demands individual and exclusive service finds it very expensive.

When our economic mechanism broke down, we were all very sorry, and we were all eager as could be to get it repaired at once. It was years and years, however, before we took any real steps toward recovery, for the simple reason that we did not grasp this secret of American prosperity. In so far as the American system was superior to the economic mechanism of any other country, it was superior in this one way—because it was geared to give service to great masses of people instead of to a few, and because

American labor was directed toward serving the American public rather than toward the exclusive service of individuals.

American workers had been doing many of the same things which Asiatic servants had been doing for their masters; but because they were not doing them in the same way and not doing them exclusively for their employers, we even failed to understand that they were the same things and we did not therefore arrange to have the services continued. The fact is, however, that they were not only doing *all the things* which servants had customarily done, but they were doing them so much more efficiently than personal servants ever could do them that they were also able to perform a multitude of services which personal servants never could perform.

In both civilizations, for instance, considerable time was spent by working people on the job of preparing the daily bath for others. In one civilization, however, one or two servants ran out with pails and brought in water; then somebody built a fire and the water was heated to the proper temperature, and the tub was brought to the room selected by the bather and—well, the result was that a few people in such civilizations did manage to get a daily bath.

In America the job was done differently. Here we organized waterworks and modern plumbing and heating systems; and while everything perhaps wasn't ideal from the standpoint of those who delight in having menials about them, Americans generally preferred the American way and we were rapidly approaching the day when every American could have his luxurious daily bath. Most of us became so used to it, in fact, that we no longer thought of it as a luxury, but numbered the bath and the bathroom among the ordinary necessities of life.

The same principle held in almost every other item of service. The essential difference between America and ancient civilizations was that they organized service so that masters could be served, whereas we were rapidly organizing it so that everybody could be served.

When our mechanism broke down, however, because we did not exactly understand its purpose and therefore tried to run it in ways in which it could not run, we thought the trouble was unemployment instead of *unemployment in this machine age.* So we tried to correct it by finding work, and even by making work, instead of finding out what the masses wanted and organizing the masses in such a way that they could supply those wants most efficiently.

And now, people who have failed to comprehend what the American way of working was, declare that we are departing from the American way of doing things in these days of the New Deal. It was really in 1930 and 1931 that we departed from the American way and experimented once more with the ways of the old master-and-servant civilizations. It was then that we began taking workers off from high-power machines geared to serve the whole public, and hiring them to do odd jobs for individuals—cleaning up our back yards, fixing that leak in the roof, putting in an extra flower bed or anything else by which we figured that we might keep someone busy.

Now, this was all legitimate work; but this was not the typically American way of getting such things done. It was the master-and-servant way; and, because we were abandoning the typically American, big-machine methods of providing service, few of us could afford to have much of this sort of work done anyway. If we had kept the big American processes going, we might have found them profitable enough so that a large number of us could indulge in the extravagance of employing individuals to serve us in this exclusive, individual way. But it *was* an extravagance; and if a large part of our work were customarily done by such methods, it would be impossible to pay anything resembling the American standard of wages.

There *was* a typically American way in which a large number of people might have been profitably employed doing these same little household jobs—particularly all kinds of house repairing. But that would have been through the organization in every city of a comprehensive house repairing service, employing modern machine methods under scientific management, in the doing of anything which any householder might ask to have done. By a scientific organization of such work, it would be possible not only to do the jobs better than they could be done by the personal-employee method, but to do them so economically that the cost would be low and the employees could not only receive but earn a high wage. Low charges for the service done, in fact, would have been essential to the success of such a business; for only if charges were low, could enough people use the service to make the use of economical methods possible.

America had developed many such services. Some were well organized and profitable. Others were not. The American tendency, however, was definitely in the direction of organizing service for masses of customers who would have to go without service in any other kind of civilization.

Millions who could not afford to employ servants to prepare their food could and did employ large industries to do so. Those who could not afford to have servants building fires could and did use gas and electricity. In the last two decades, especially, a large restaurant industry had been developed; and while the service in these restaurants may not always have equalled the service which a millionaire could have at home, it was better service than the average patron ever could have had before; and the average employee, even if he were underpaid, still enjoyed a far higher standard of living than could the average person in those countries where work was customarily done without resorting to machine technique.

The American tendency was clearly in the direction of the organization of the masses for the service of the masses. Only in this way could wages be high and the general plane of living rise. Instead of improving the mechanism, however, by finding out what the masses wanted and organizing their efforts to supply those wants efficiently, we tried almost everything else.

We even tried going back to the land and some two millions did go back. But they couldn't make a living on it. They simply carried their poverty from the city to the country—that was all. For the members of a family or of a little group to "support themselves," it was necessary for all to do a lot of work, and the results even then fell short of self-support. The only way by which the masses of any country could ever achieve an easy, comfortable and luxurious way of living was the way on which America had embarked without understanding what it was, and without even noticing that it was the American way.

Under the New Deal, we are simply picking up the American way once more. Now, however, we are beginning to understand what the American way is—that it is not the pre-industrial way under which a master class was served by a working class, but a way by which the masses might employ modern power, modern machinery and modern scientific methods for the greatest possible advantage to everybody.

In this new kind of civilization, it now appears, the employer was not and could not be a master, and his employees were not and could not be *his* servants. If the employer were to succeed as an employer, he had to organize employment, not to the end that his employees would do for him the things which servants traditionally did, but so that better and better service might be rendered to a larger and ever larger public. Neither employer nor employee, however, could at first see this, and each tried to explain the new setup in terms of the old, familiar, master-and-servant setup.

It was not the New Era, but this misconception of the New Era, which so suddenly failed to work in 1929. The new methods were all right—which was amply proved by the existence of such abundance that everybody's needs might easily have been supplied. It was the old notion—the pre-industrial, un-American, master-and-servant notion—which inhibited us from distributing this abundance and amply satisfying our human needs.

Under the old master-and-servant system, if more was to be produced, workers had to work longer hours and they had to be speeded up. Under the new, machine system, the machine, not the workers, had to be speeded up. That is, all lost motion, all wasteful processes and *all unnecessary labor* had to be eliminated; and to the degree that these things were eliminated the machines became so productive that their products could not be sold unless the masses were endowed with more and more leisure to use these products and more and more buying power.

Under the old system, it was necessary from the standpoint of the master class, to keep the servants "in their place." That meant keeping them from consuming the product of their toil—keeping them at work for their masters instead of at work for themselves. Under the new system, however, this attitude toward employment and toward employees did not and could not work. It now became necessary, from the employer's standpoint (although the employer was a long time realizing it), that the workers should not keep their ancient, lowly "place." Especially as trade expanded and as everybody became more or less dependent upon machine production, machine production became dependent upon everybody's buying and upon the masses' having more and more buying power coupled with more and more leisure in which to consume the things which they might buy.

Under the old system, there was a certain logic therefore in making war on labor. Under the new system, the only logical war was a war on poverty and a war on waste. Unless poverty were eliminated, the masses could not buy the enormous and ever increasing volume of products which the machines were now turning out; and unless waste were eliminated, poverty could not be conquered.

Under the old system, moreover, the only way in which the average person could hope to improve his economic status was through saving—through nonbuying—through depriving himself of the things he wanted and needed. Under the new system, it is now appearing, such saving on the part of the masses becomes an economic menace; for the machines could not be kept in operation, employers could not hope for continued profits and employees would surely lose their jobs unless the masses continued to buy more and more and more.

These were the facts of this new American way of doing things. But they were new facts—facts which could not come to light until the machine age had actually arrived—and there were ten thousand years of master-and-servant tradition which was all at variance with these facts. When measured by master-and-servant logic, indeed, these facts themselves became absurd.

How, we asked, can we lift ourselves by our bootstraps? How can we spend our way to prosperity? How can we economize by extravagance?

We could not, of course, do any such thing, in the sense in which the questions were asked.

But, although we cannot lift ourselves by our bootstraps, we can lift ourselves through co-ordination of the powers we possess. We do, in fact, so lift ourselves every time we get out of bed.

We cannot spend our way to prosperity any more than we ever could; but it is true, and it always has been true, that wealth is created only by human effort, that wealth consists, not of money, but of things which human beings need; and that, if human beings do not consume what it is necessary for them to consume, they will presently become unable to put forth any effort toward the production of more wealth. What it is wise to consume, however—what scale of consumption constitutes real thrift and what constitutes extravagance—depends not merely upon what is idealistically and abstractly good, but upon the times. We can all agree, for instance, that children need an education, and that it is wise, therefore, to send them to school. It would be unwise, however, to send them to school at a time when they are urgently needed at home to help put out a fire which is threatening to destroy the homestead.

What it is wise to do depends upon what one has an opportunity to do. In the agrarian age, it was wise to live frugally, and to deny oneself any number of things which might intrinsically be good; for it was only by such rigorous self-denial that any economic security could be achieved. But such frugality does not result in economic security today. It results in unemployment. It shuts off the source of wealth in this machine age. But economic security is as necessary as ever, and saving is as necessary as ever. But we can't get security in the old way; and trying to save in the old way does not result in saving.

It has become necessary now, therefore, since wealth is now produced and distributed by nation-wide collective effort, to learn to save by nation-wide collective effort, and to achieve economic security by nation-wide collective effort.

If the masses now do not consume largely, we cannot keep the machinery of the machine age running; and in spite of our having learned how to produce enough for all, we cannot continue to produce enough to suit anybody. Four years of that sort of thing is enough; and rising to the logic of the new conditions, our America has now determined to establish such economic security for the masses that the masses may buy on a scale which would once have been not only extravagant but impossible. But such seemingly prodigal buying, however, is not now prodigal. It is now thrift, in the best sense of the word, because it is the only course which can now be taken which will keep all our people at work and which will not shut off the even and continuous flow of wealth.

That is the meaning of unemployment insurance, old-age insurance and the other forms of social insurance which, to many, seem so un-American. They are American because America cannot go on without them. They are as American as the automobile, as American as the Declaration of Independence, as American as the spirit of the hardy pioneer to whose initiative and daring we are all indebted.

Yes, I said "initiative." I mean individual initiative. If you prefer, I shall say "rugged individualism." I believe in it as devoutly as any critic of our nation's present effort to adjust itself to the facts of this machine age.

I know it may seem to many that initiative is passing from the individual to government; or that the American people, by relying upon their government, are in grave danger of losing their individual initiative. But this is reasoning from fears instead of facts.

For what, actually, is government? It is the orderly arrangement of human affairs. It is the opposite of anarchy. Whether the government is autocratic or democratic, it is still an effort to preserve some kind of order and establish a code under which all the people may proceed. If there is anarchy—which is the absence of any code—people cannot live co-operatively and therefore cannot exercise individual initiative.

There was government in the wildest sections of the Wild

West. There were codes. There had to be. The codes were not necessarily written; and there may have been no duly accredited enforcement officers. Each person, then, became his own enforcement officer; nevertheless, when he pulled his gun, he had to use it within certain generally accepted restrictions or else the other frontiersmen would unite to liquidate him. As the frontier became settled, these codes became more definite, more particular, and more attention was paid to the rules and by-laws governing their enforcement. But this, instead of meaning deterioration, meant development, progress; for now, unless these codes were more definite, individual initiative could not function successfully.

It is true, I think, that individual initiative has had hard going in recent years, but certainly not because of the New Deal and the effort to introduce order into our economic life through the setting up of nation-wide codes. Individual initiative was restricted, rather, by the absence of any sufficiently definite code although industry had long since passed out of its pioneer stage and could not continue unless there were a definite industrial government, and some orderly arrangement of our economic affairs.

Even business men who could see our economic problem now seemed powerless to do anything about it. Even President Hoover, who saw the necessity for concerted action to maintain the wage level and the public's buying power, was unable to initiate any program by which this could be achieved. Even Henry Ford, foremost discoverer of the principle that high wages are necessary to machine production and foremost apostle of individual initiative, could not act as he wanted to act and as he knew was the logical and right way to act. Instead of cutting wages in 1930, to be sure, Ford spectacularly raised them. He raised them to seven dollars a day. Because there was no code of business conduct, however, or none at least that was adequate to the new condition, this splendid effort failed and even Ford was compelled to retract and cut.

To-day, however, Ford *can* raise wages and does. He can exercise his splendid, American, individual initiative in business because there is a code of business which, however imperfect it

"E. A."
On Shipboard

may be as yet, is already introducing some order into our economic affairs.

I am not criticizing Mr. Ford because he has not studied the science of government, and makes remarks occasionally which would seem to indicate that our government can be kept separate from our way of life. For Ford, at least, understands business and doesn't have to be prodded into understanding it, and we business men will have to go some yet before we even catch up with Mr. Ford.

Nor am I criticizing the other great pioneers of this machine civilization—Carnegie, Rockefeller, Hill and the other giants who, whatever else we may think about them, typify to us the power of individual initiative. We must remember, however, that they did what they did because they took advantage of the opportunities of their time. They were not traditional thinkers. They were not copyists. They did not hesitate to change the very face of our civilization in doing the things which America gave them the opportunity to do.

There were things, however, which they did not have the opportunity to do. Carnegie could give his millions to education, but he could not organize the steel industry to bring the most abundant life to the steel workers and to the masses who have use for steel. Rockefeller could give his millions to science; but to get those millions, he had to smash his way through competition and leave a trail of human wreckage in his wake.

Newer and greater opportunities await American business today. The time has come, to be sure, when we must work under a civilized code. The time has come when we must have order in our economic affairs, and then, therefore, we must plan on a larger scale than it was ever necessary to plan before. Doubtless, also, government will be more intimate, more understandable, less removed from the realities of our business life. But there is more need than ever for individual initiative; and as we grasp the nature of the new American setup—a setup under which we can achieve prosperity only by distributing prosperity —there is no doubt in my mind that this individual initiative will be released.

This is the American way to recovery and to a better America than we have ever had before. It is social but not socialistic. It is humane but not almsgiving, and has nothing of the ancient condescension by which masters were kind to their servants, and frequently bred in them a none-too-self-respecting loyalty. It is co-operative but still competitive—substituting competition in service for competition in exploitation. It is not even idealistic in the sense that it presupposes any basic change in human nature as a necessity. It is not even unselfish. It is the way, rather, of enlightened selfishness.

It is the American way to recovery, not for a few but for all our people.

George Washington and Financial Liberty *

MY FRIENDS:

We Americans all reverence Washington as the Father of our Country. But he is more than that. Every nation has its legendary hero, but few of them have little significance excepting to the people within that nation's borders. The name of George Washington, however, is rightly held in reverence by lovers of liberty throughout the whole world.

We may think primarily of Washington as the great patriot whose genius and devotion enabled the American colonists to throw off the British yoke. Many a nation, however, before and since the American Revolution, has thrown off a foreign yoke and still failed to achieve much liberty. For liberty, necessary as it may be to fight for it, can never be achieved by mere fighting.

To achieve national independence, it has historically been necessary to organize a war for independence; but to achieve liberty, it is necessary to *organize for liberty;* and that necessitates the use of very different tactics. Conquering heroes are not likely to understand this. Too often they have applied the tactics of war to the problems of peace. Washington made no such mistake.

It may yet be the verdict of history that George Washington's greatest contribution to his country was not the winning of the Revolutionary War. Another military genius might have arisen to accomplish that; but we may well ask whether anyone but Washington could have held these mutually jealous colonies together, and conciliated the bitter leaders of the many bitter factions which were inevitably struggling for dominance, until the

* Address before California Credit Union League, Hotel Sacramento, Sacramento, California—February 22, 1936.

American people could come to realize that they *were* one people.

Imagine a president, for instance, who could have both Alexander Hamilton and Thomas Jefferson in the same cabinet at the same time, and get results from both. I don't pretend to know how he did it; but one who makes any study of those troubled times must realize the greatness of such statesmanship.

Washington, in war, was one hundred per cent partisan, and fought the enemy with every resource at his command. But Washington, in peace, abhorred partisanship. He would not recognize those who disagreed with him as enemies to be conquered but looked upon them as fellow citizens to be given every possible consideration.

There were many American leaders in those days—some who had supported the War of the Revolution—who still did not believe in democracy. Some wanted to make Washington a monarch, after the English pattern; and while many preferred what they called a republic, they meant a republic in which only the upper classes would be permitted to vote.

And Washington himself was an aristocrat. He was a Virginia gentleman, a country squire—no hail-fellow-well-met and no professional champion of the "plain pee-pul." As an American, however, he did not ask special consideration for Virginia; and as a statesman, he did not permit his class traditions to control his thinking.

When the Constitution of the United States was eventually drawn up, Washington did not admire it overmuch. He said it had many serious flaws, but he worked for its adoption nevertheless. For under the Constitution, we could become one country, and we could work together as one country to effect any changes which might be necessary. Without a constitution, however, disagreements among the states could not be resolved. They might or might not result in actual hostilities, but efforts to settle them would be state, not national, efforts; and always in the background there would be some show of force.

Even with the Constitution, in fact, our nation did not remain united. Our people did not heed Washington's warnings; and little more than half a century after the adoption of the Constitution, partisanship had so supplanted statesmanship, and sectionalism had so triumphed over Americanism, that we were plunged into four years of terrible Civil War.

We are accustomed to refer to that war as the "irrepressible conflict." Perhaps. But conflict is regularly irrepressible, when people cannot think beyond their own special interests. When we approach our problems in such a state of mind, we cannot even effect successful compromises; for our state of mind hides the facts, and in our very efforts to compromise, we find ourselves compromising with the facts.

Oh that Washington's birthday might be set apart in America in celebration not merely of Washington's great achievements, but in celebration of a warrior who was more than a warrior, a Virginian who was more than a Virginian and a gentleman who was so much more than a mere gentleman than he *was* able to think beyond the traditions of his class!

More of his kind of thinking would have averted the Civil War; and only more of his kind of thinking in America today can save us from economic and class war. Abraham Lincoln, to be sure, displayed the same kind of thinking. Lincoln was from the backwoods, but his thinking was not bounded by the backwoods. He grew up in a small town but his thinking was not limited to his small town traditions. He was a lawyer, but his thinking was not rooted in the tradition of the law. He was a man upon whom fortune had never smiled; but just as Washington was able to think beyond his wealth, Lincoln was able to think beyond his poverty. But Washington, unfortunately, died too early to save our nation from Civil War—and Lincoln came too late.

Whether we are to have class war in America is not yet apparent. We will have it, surely, unless Americans are able to think beyond their class traditions. For a new aristocracy arose in America after the Civil War; and, like former aristocracies, it developed the tendency to think in terms of maintaining the privileges which it had gained, rather than in terms of the American problem as a whole.

I do not mean that this new aristocracy of wealth engaged in any conspiracy against the public interest. Aristocracies seldom if ever do that; for when people gain privileges, they usually come to think that the maintenance of those privileges is in the public interest.

The aristocrats of Washington's day could put up a pretty good argument against democracy—especially against the masses being given the right to vote. They did not argue merely that this would be bad for the aristocrats. They argued that it would be bad for the masses. The rabble, they said, could not possibly understand the science of government, and they would certainly enact measures which would wreck the Ship of State. History, they pointed out, was full of popular uprisings which left the people worse off than they had been before. The people, to be sure, had wreaked revenge upon their oppressors; but in the end the mob had made such a mess of things that it turned meekly to some new oppressor to straighten things out.

They could not, to be sure, point to the French Revolution as the classic example of what they feared in case the common people should ever assert the right to rule; for the French Revolution had not happened yet. But they did honestly shudder at the very thought of popular government; and so forceful was their argument that the constitution which was finally adopted provided an elaborate system of checks against its dangers.

It provided, for instance, for three co-ordinate branches in our national government,—the legislative, the executive and the judicial—and only the lower house of the legislative branch was to be selected by popular vote. As for the President, he was to be chosen by a college of electors, who were not even supposed to consider candidates for the presidency until the much-feared popular elections were all over. Then, after the electoral college had met and selected the President of the United States, the President was empowered to fill vacancies in the third branch of the government—the judicial—providing his nominations were satisfactory to the house of Congress which was *not* chosen by popular vote. The judges of the Supreme Court, however, were to be appointed for life, to guard against the possibility of the

Court's being influenced either by the Administration or by the thinking of the American people at any given time.

It is sometimes remarked that the Supreme Court is not exactly up to date. But that is precisely what the makers of our Constitution intended. They intended that this branch of the government should always be behind the times. Each succeeding Administration, to be sure, might fill one or two vacancies, and these new appointees might be sympathetic with the thinking of the day. But these new appointees, presumably, would be a small minority at any given time. Whenever the court handed down a majority decision, then, it was supposed to come from minds which *had* been up to date twenty or thirty years before. This is not a criticism of the Supreme Court. I mention it merely to point out the precautions that were taken to keep our government from becoming too responsive to the popular will.

I am not even intimating that the precautions were unwise. Democracy cannot be conferred upon the people. If they want it, they must achieve it; and even then, they cannot get it merely by seizing the reins of government. Let the people seize the reins of government *without learning how to drive,* and the result is not democracy but catastrophe.

To appreciate Washington's contribution to democracy, it is necessary to take note of two seemingly contradictory facts.

In the first place, self-government was a new idea in the world, and it was an idea which struck terror into the hearts not merely of kings and nobles, but of almost all the educated and cultured people of the day. In the second place, the American masses, long before the Revolution, had become used to self-government and had had very little experience with any other kind of government. Theoretically, they were loyal Englishmen and reverenced their king; but actually they were pioneers in a new continent and depended for their very lives not upon what the British government did but upon what they were able to do for themselves with the co-operation of their nearest neighbors.

If they wanted land, they took it. If they wanted food, they raised it. If they wanted a house, they cut down trees and built one with the logs. Each family produced its own light, heat and power. Each little community built its own roads, arranged for its own school, if any, and organized its own protection against Indian raids. Theoretically, they were protected by the King's army, and the King believed he had a right to tax the colonists to pay for this protection. But they didn't want to be taxed. They didn't care for this protection. If the King wanted to call his army home, that was all right as far as they were concerned. Almost invariably, when educated Europeans visited the colonies, they went back and reported that the colonists were very unruly.

Long after the organization of our constitutional government, in fact, it was the prevailing opinion in America that that government is best which governs least. But actually, the early Americans hardly meant that. If a village needed a sewer, for instance, the villagers demanded that the village government provide one, although *not* building one would have meant less government. What the villagers really meant was that they wanted a minimum of national government; and because each community could attend so largely to its own affairs, almost any degree of national government usually seemed to be too much.

Even in Washington's time, however, there were many things which had to be done which only the national government could do; and the conflict between the federal viewpoint and the local viewpoint became the burning political issue of the day. It was never settled; and there is reason to believe that Washington knew that it could not be settled. For if the Federalists had had their way, local government and even state government would have been largely destroyed, and the only kind of democracy with which the American people had any practical experience would have been taken from them. On the other hand, if those who bristled at the very thought of centralized government had had their way, we would have had thirteen feeble nations in America instead of one United States, and these nations, if not recaptured by England, would almost certainly have become the pawns of European intrigue.

Even on this burning issue, then, Washington refused to

become partisan; and under his administration, with all its confusions and its failures, the world learned that government by the people *is a practical possibility*.

Democracy, however, is not a formula. It is a growth. It cannot be granted by a constitution. It must be developed out of the actual conditions of life. The time came in America, in fact, when although we had greatly perfected the formulas of popular rule, the realities of democracy were almost lost.

When the Constitution was first adopted, remember, the people were privileged to elect only one house in one of the three branches of the national government; and even at that, not half of the people were entitled to vote. Within a few years, however, without waiting to amend the Constitution, the people nullified the electoral college, which was supposed to select our presidents, by insisting that the legal electors act as rubber stamps and vote for candidates named at popular conventions. Later, property qualifications for suffrage were generally repealed. Later still, our slaves were freed and enfranchised. Eventually, we gave votes to women, and arranged also for the direct election of senators. But after we had done all this and more, the American people generally had little control of their own affairs.

That control was now vested in a new aristocracy.

If Americans wanted land now, they had to buy it. If the average family needed a home, it had to rent one from a landlord; and if it could not pay the rent, it was thrown out on the street. If one needed light now, he had to apply to a public utility company which might be doing a monopoly business in many cities and states. If one needed clothes, furniture, transportation or any of the thousand and one necessities of life, one could not produce them on his own premises, after the manner of the early American family, nor even with the co-operation of his immediate neighbors after the fashion of the early American community. One had to buy all these things with money; and if one was out of money, he was out of everything.

Usually he could get money if he could get a job. But he had no *right* to a job, and he had no right to an income if he didn't have a job: that is, unless he belonged to the privileged class who were now in possession of the machines with which modern America produced the things which people need.

Understand, I am not talking socialism. I don't believe that socialism is best for our country. I am simply recounting facts; and this condition to which I have referred cannot in reason be called self-government or democracy. The masses of America had lost control of the processes by which the masses lived; and those who did control these processes did not operate them in such a way as to give everybody an adequate income, which meant that the masses could not buy enough to keep the machines going and millions therefore could not find work and were deprived of the right to earn a living.

How to achieve democracy under these new conditions is now our problem; for unless we can achieve economic democracy, our political democracy must be a sham.

But it is *not* a problem of how to overthrow the existing autocratic powers. That is the great lesson which the life of Washington has for us. Merely to throw off the English yoke, he knew, would have been worse than futile unless we could establish free government in its place.

It would be fairly easy today for the American masses to overthrow the present economic oligarchy. The masses have control of the political machinery, and they can enact almost any kind of legislation which strikes their fancy; and in the desperation of wholly unnecessary unemployment and poverty in the midst of plenty, there is always grave danger that they will enact such unsound measures as will destroy our financial and business system. But that, instead of accomplishing any good, would be the greatest calamity which could possibly befall our people.

What is needed is that the American masses shall learn the art of constructive self-government in this machine age—in this age in which life is no longer organized on a small-community pattern but in which all Americans *are* more or less dependent upon what all other Americans are doing. We must of course continue to do as little local communities the things that can best be done by little local communities; but we must learn to do by planned, co-ordinated, nation-wide action the things that can be done only by such action.

In this task, there need be no conflict of interests; for unless we are able to achieve economic liberty under law and order, the only alternative is economic collapse, as ruinous to our financial overlords as to the masses themselves. The Washington-minded, then, among our economic aristocrats, will grasp the problem. They will be as realistic as he was. They will think beyond their class tradition; and they will thus win and deserve the co-operation of the masses in the effort to solve our common problem.

It is one of the brightest signs of the times that this non-partisan, realistic, fact-finding and fact-recognizing attitude, *is* the attitude of our credit union movement. Our credit unions began as little, local units; but the same logic which caused us to organize in this little, local way is now causing us to organize also in State Leagues and in our Credit Union National Association.

One hundred individuals, saving their money individually, could not provide themselves with much protection; but let them organize a credit union and their opportunity to help themselves was multiplied. Similarly, the credit unions in California, each acting individually, could not possibly accomplish what they can now accomplish acting together in this State League; and the State Leagues, strong as they are, will multiply their strength as they learn to co-operate within the Credit Union National Association.

Just where shall we draw the line, however, between local, state and national action? That's a problem; and my notion is that it will continue to be a problem which nobody, at any time, will be wise enough to fully solve. But we know our object. It is democratic finance. It is the use of the power of money and credit by the people in their own co-operative organizations, in such a way as will serve the interests of all the people best.

But it is a movement of peace, not of antagonism, and all its tactics are the tactics of peace. It has room, therefore, for people of every mind; and if I may be permitted to use the figure, both Hamilton and Jefferson are active in our cabinet. For in this movement, both those who are fearful of mass action and those who are fearful of anything but mass action can work in harmony—temperamental conservatives as well as temperamental radicals—for we are dealing with facts, not philosophies, and the only sure and certain course is the course indicated by the facts. The most farsighted financiers of the old order, therefore, are now with us heart and soul; for what they really fear is not democracy guided by the facts of our now universal interdependence, but radical or revolutionary mass action based on the traditions of the old social order in which society *was* composed of warring interests.

Industrial evolution has brought us into a new world—as new a world in every real sense as was the American continent in the days of Washington. Washington, the aristocrat, was realist enough to recognize that *that* new world could not be governed by the traditions of old-world aristocracy. Nor can *this* new economic order be governed by the traditions of the old economic order. In the very nature of modern machinery, we have become universally interdependent, and in the very nature of this new society, the masses must have adequate buying power—that is, such money power as will enable them to buy enough to keep themselves employed. This is as necessary to employers as it is to employees. It is as necessary for business men as for farmers and wage earners. It is necessary from the standpoint of every legitimate element of the population; and our problems, therefore, have all ceased to be problems of conflicting interests and have become problems of how to achieve co-operation. The credit union movement is pioneering in the solution of those problems; and it is particularly fitting, it seems to me, that this California State Credit Union League should be meeting on the birthday of the Father of our Country, who was not only first in war but first in peace and first in the hearts of *all* our people.

Streamlining Business *

FRIENDS OF THE RADIO AUDIENCE:

I am going to speak about streamlining business—about doing some such thing to business as the motorcar manufacturers have recently been doing to their cars.

The streamline is the line of grace and beauty; and business men are not supposed to know anything about such subjects. But it is also the line of economy—the line of least resistance and the least amount of gasoline per mile.

When we get to discussing the question "What is beauty?", all of us—even our artists—seem to get bewildered.

Why do we call a lion or a tiger beautiful? And why do we think of a hippopotamus as anything but?

It isn't because we would rather meet a lion or a tiger, or because the thought of such a meeting stirs pleasant memories. I venture the guess that it is because the lion and the tiger are streamlined, while the hippopotamus is not. Anything shaped like that, we know, cannot use his power most effectively. Just one look convinces us that the hippopotamus requires too much gas per mile.

We simply cannot separate beauty from fitness. We may love the flaming red of the sunset, but we do not want to see it on our noses. Green may be our favorite color; but if the baby turned green, we'd think it awful.

Whether anything is beautiful or not depends mostly upon what it is for, and how simply, directly and economically it serves its purpose.

When we first began to manufacture automobiles, we tried to make them look like horsedrawn carriages, with only the horses

* Radio address from Station KEX, Portland, Oregon—August 24, 1934.

absent. Some of these early models actually had whipstocks, because a carriage without any place for a whip seemed to look queer.

Had one of our 1934 streamlined cars appeared on the streets in 1900, I doubt that anyone would have called it beautiful, for no human eye was then prepared for such a sight. Our cars have become beautiful, however, to the extent to which they have ceased being buggies and have become motorcars.

There is nothing essentially beautiful in mere power; for power may be used ungracefully, or even disgracefully as in ugly war.

The history of business has been the history of the use of power, but many of its manifestations have been decidedly unbeautiful. Artists have historically warred against commercialism. To them, factories have seemed ugly, machinery inhuman and the struggle for markets sordid and base.

I have no time now to review that struggle between the idealism of the artists and the so-called practicality of the business man. It is interesting to notice, however, that as business became more and more practical, more and more beauty was achieved.

There were certain architectural forms, for instance, which the world had come to recognize as beautiful; but when it became practical to build with steel instead of stone, it was no longer practical to copy those forms.

Nevertheless, we tried to do it. We tried to make modern steel buildings look like ancient stone temples. But they did not look like ancient temples. They looked like something I cannot mention over the radio and were unnecessarily expensive. Not until we broke away from traditions, and tried to discover what architectural forms were appropriate to steel construction, could we create such a work of art as the Empire State Building in New York.

Our modern streamlined cars are the result of just such a break from tradition in the direction of practical achievement. Heretofore, we have sought to get more speed only by the application of more power; and the speed which was so achieved turned out to be impractically expensive and impractically uncomfortable.

Instead of darting through the air, we smashed through it. We got through—the air couldn't stop us—but it could and did give us an awful shaking up, and made us burn a frightful lot of gas.

Then came the idea, not of overcoming air resistance, but of studying it, and dealing with it for what it actually was; and that led to the streamline, with its beauty and grace.

Business, similarly, used to smash its way ahead; and to the extent that it did so, business was powerful but ugly.

Business needed markets. It had to have them; and it went after them in what seemed to be a practical business fashion. If a competitor stood in the way, and a business was strong enough, it crushed that competitor.

If the public did not want to buy its products, and a business therefore could not sell as it wanted to sell, its only thought was to apply more selling power. High power salesmanship, it was supposed, would solve all business problems.

Well, it worked—after a fashion. It worked something in the way that the old car worked whenever we were in such a hurry to get to a gas station that we opened her up—and burned up all our gas before we got there.

If we were manufacturing something, for instance, which it cost one hundred dollars to make, we planned to sell it for two hundred; and if we couldn't persuade enough people to buy this hundred dollar article for two hundred dollars, we couldn't take in enough to cover the expenses of the business. So we hired a lot of high powered and high priced salesmen; but in order to pay their salaries and expenses, we figured that we would have to charge three hundred dollars for the article we were trying to sell, with the result that there was more sales resistance, and probably fewer sales, than before.

Only streamlining could have solved this problem. If we had had the sense which the car designers are now employing, we would have studied that sales resistance instead of trying merely to overcome it.

And if we had studied it, we would have discovered that the more we charged for the article, the harder it would be to sell; and by moving our price down, instead of up, all this high-pressure salesmanship would not be necessary.

We could make a hundred times as many sales, in all probability, if we had thought to sell the thing for one hundred dollars instead of two hundred, and one hundred times more profit.

That statement, I know, may sound strange to many persons who do not understand the secret of streamlining. Such people will say instantly that one could make no profit by selling for a hundred dollars an article which it costs a hundred dollars for him to manufacture.

But I did not speak of making one sale. I spoke of making a hundred times as many sales as the manufacturer had been making. If the manufacturer could multiply his sales a hundred times, it would no longer cost him anything like one hundred dollars to make the article.

But there are other ways of streamlining. Practical business men were always anxious to keep costs down; but until they discovered the secret of streamlining, their first thought was to smash them down.

Usually, their greatest item of cost was their labor cost; and the laborers, for some reason or other, did not like to have their wages cut. They often organized unions, in fact, for the definite purpose of compelling their employers to pay higher wages and, as the employers saw it, to bring up labor costs.

Employers, therefore, set out to smash the unions. This was an ugly use of power. The employers, however, did not want to be ugly. If they could have reduced wages by some pretty method, they would rather have done so. But they insisted upon being practical without finding out what was practical, and the result couldn't be anything but ugly.

Those who followed the course of streamlining, however, discovered *why* the workers did not like to have their wages cut. It was because they couldn't buy so many things; and since these employers were interested in selling things, they thought it might be good for business if wages were higher; that is, of course, if there was any practical way by which they could be raised.

And by studying the facts, they found out that there was. Wages could be raised, they discovered, by better management, and by the use of better methods in manufacturing. If wages were raised, in fact, it became necessary to use these better methods; and it was discovered, by Henry Ford and others, that these better methods were so much more profitable than the old methods that the higher wages sometimes resulted in lower labor costs per unit of product.

Thoroughly practical employers, then, quit antagonizing labor and became quite as interested as labor was in getting wages raised; and to the extent that this happened in America, the ugly war between labor and capital came to an end, the public was better served and both employers and employees became more prosperous.

The development in that direction, unfortunately, was not rapid enough; for the producing power of American industry increased much faster than did the buying power of the American people. The result was unemployment, which still further reduced the public's power to buy, inevitably bringing on more and more unemployment and general business stagnation.

Obviously, it wouldn't work out very well to streamline one side of a car and let the other side stand up against the wind. *All* business, it appears, must now be streamlined; and any part of it which offers too great resistance to progress must be redesigned.

That is the present job for business under the N.R.A.—streamlining the whole structure of American business—not to give business more power but so that business may operate more successfully and economically with the power which it has.

If low wages create greater sales resistance than necessary, business must see that they are raised—and not only at certain points but at every point where more buying becomes a business necessity. Prices, likewise, must be kept as low as possible, so that selling may become as easy as possible; and every item of unnecessary waste in the whole process of production and distribution must be eliminated. Such waste, we now know, destroys the streamline, for it renders it impossible to make wages as high and prices as low as they might otherwise be made.

I am told, however, that we have learned very little about streamlining yet. In the near future, it is hinted, some manufacturer will have the daring to put the engine in the back of the car and redesign the whole vehicle so that it will look and act more like an airplane than a buggy. Such a car, they tell me, will all but fly, and may make a hundred miles an hour on a single gallon of gas.

It would not astonish me if this were true. For I am sure it is true of business. For after business has raised wages, and lowered prices until the masses are enabled to purchase all its products, and after it has so shortened the hours of labor that beautiful leisure shall begin to take the place of ugly unemployment, there will still be one final, revolutionary change to make. That is to establish economic security, through universal unemployment insurance.

This, with other necessary forms of social insurance, will enable the masses always to live well, and to continue buying enough to enable them to live well, whether they are employed or unemployed. Unemployment, therefore, will not become contagious and the old familiar business depressions will cease to appear. But it will accomplish more than that. It will make it necessary for employers to become real employers. Business men must then use their business genius to discover and to organize new employment, bringing new services and new comforts to the masses, as technological progress, which has hitherto resulted in technological unemployment, releases labor to produce these new things and give these greater services.

Then, it seems to me, the streamline will be complete. It will be the line of truest economy and efficiency; but it will eliminate the old ugliness from our economic relations, and even the most critical artists, I think, must recognize it as the line of beauty and of grace.

Education for This New Time *

FRIENDS OF THE RADIO AUDIENCE:

It may seem rather presumptuous of me, a shopkeeper, to discuss problems of education. It may seem like an old bachelor discussing the principles of housekeeping.

Well, suppose it does. I *am* an old bachelor, but I know something about housekeeping which some expert housekeepers seem always to forget.

You doubtless know some housekeeper who works hard, from morning to night, to keep the house just so; and who nags the whole household from morning to night, lest some detail of her precious housekeeping routine be upset. She is never comfortable. No one in the house is ever comfortable. The children can't play for fear they will mar or disarrange the furniture; and if Dad wants to smoke, he has to go outdoors, where he will be sure not to spill any ashes on the rug. The house is so completely hypnotized, in fact, by her expert management that the house dog prefers to sleep in the garage.

Even if I *am* an old bachelor, then, I know there is something wrong with that kind of a house. A house, I maintain, should be run in the interest of its occupants, instead of the occupants being run in the interest of the house.

Schools also, I am convinced, should be run in the interest of their scholars, to help them achieve the biggest life which they can possibly achieve. I get a bit tired, then, when I hear educated business men discussing education as if schools should be run in the interest of their business routine.

I know a man who owns a coal mine; and because he owns the

* Radio address from Station W1XAL, University Club, Boston, Massachusetts, April 18, 1935.

coal mine, he practically owns the village in which the mine is located, and he is inclined to be sore because he cannot dominate the schools. It is his notion, since the children in that village are likely to become miners, that the schools should concentrate on equipping them to become the kind of miners which he would like to have them be.

I disagree. The schools in that village, as I see it, ought to go in for art and music and drama; and they ought to go in for baseball, football and swimming, as well as for such a good, practical education in history, economics and psychology that everybody in town will come to understand what makes mine owners sometimes get that way. What the youth in such a town most need is such a big, broad conception of living that they can see the coal mine in its true perspective, understanding that it is the purpose of a mine to serve human life, not the purpose of human life to serve a mine.

Business leaders frequently cry out against what they call the fads and frills of modern schooling, as if such ridicule settled the whole argument. And yet these same business men may go in strong for bridge and golf and all sorts of fads, and may even specialize in the manufacture or the sale of frills.

I believe in fads and frills. They may add little to our immediate efficiency on our jobs, but they may add much to our appreciation of life. The time seems to have come, in fact, when mere efficiency on our jobs will not do, because for one thing, it cannot give us any guarantee that we *will have jobs* on which to demonstrate our efficiency.

To make it certain now that there will be useful and profitable careers for all, the youth of America must have a fuller and broader understanding of life and its relationships than it was ever necessary to have before.

For as long as I can remember, there has been a great controversy in educational circles as to whether our young people should receive a practical or a cultural education. So far as I know, the question was never decided; possibly for the same reason that we could not decide whether the ocean is big *or* wet. Today, at any rate, the only thoroughly practical education is the broadest possible cultural education. For America has reached a crisis—a unique crisis in human history—and it is a crisis which can be successfully passed only as the American mind develops a true conception of the nature of the crisis, and of the new relations and new responsibilities which this new time has brought to all of us.

This is surely a large order, but it can be filled. In a sense, it is no more than has been required at other times; but we have been swept through such a cycle of social change that the education which was once adequate will no longer serve our purpose; and, if we do not understand the change which has come over us, the old education may even interfere with the practical action it is now so necessary to take.

In early America, for instance, there could have been no freedom unless the masses had been educated in economics and in sociology, although perhaps not one out of a hundred had ever heard the words.

But economics, roughly at least, is the study of how people make a living, and sociology is the study of human relations. People made a living, in those days, mostly by farming, and it was vitally necessary, therefore, that the average person in those days should understand the basic principles of farming.

This was not farming as farming is usually carried on today. It was not mere tilling the soil and growing a few crops, to be sent to market so that, with the money received, the farmer may buy the necessities of life and the machinery with which he does his farming. In the old days, the farm family produced not only its own food, its own shelter and its own homespun clothes, but its own light, heat and horsepower, and very largely its own household furniture. And every farm child, years before he was old enough to go to school, began to learn how all these things were done. That was basic economics; and if it had not been for this basic education, America would have been uninhabitable except for the Indian tribes or those who mastered the nomadic, *tribal* kind of economics—the study of how to make a living by hunting for it. In that case, not many could have lived in our part of North America; for getting a living by hunting was so precarious here that a great population could not be supported. It wasn't merely the superiority of their guns, then, over the bows and arrows of the Indians, which enabled the white settlers to subdue the aborigines. It was the superiority of their agrarian economy over the hunting economy.

Now we find ourselves living in a still different, and vastly more efficient, economic order. If we are to enjoy its advantages, however, we must understand the setup. It isn't a matter of the old order being bad. It was the best of all possible orders, until we got a better one. The keynote of progress, we should remember, is not merely doing away with what is bad; it is *replacing the best with something better.*

If the American colonists had had to get their living from England, it goes without saying that they could not have rebelled against English rule. It was their *actual* independence which made it possible for them to *declare* their independence and eventually to have their independence recognized. There could then have been no America as we know it, if Americans generally had not understood the workings of their economic system.

They also had to understand their system of sociology—the human relations and human responsibilities which went with such an economic order. Primarily, this meant that children must do whatever their parents told them to. The family relationship was not everything, but it was almost everything; and those who were true to their family responsibilities were generally considered good citizens. They might beat their neighbors in every horse trade, but that was expected. They might go into business and cheat their customers; but society wasn't organized on the trading principle. It was organized on the principle of the self-contained, agrarian family—and anyone who bought anything from anyone else was supposed to take his own chances.

There came a time, however, when an understanding of agrarian economics and agrarian sociology was not enough. There came a time, because of the introduction of machine industry and the expansion of trade, when the agrarian economy disappeared. Mainly, however, while our youth generally were learning machine technology, we went on teaching them the agrarian sociology, as if the new way of making a living had not made any consequential difference in human relations and human responsibilities.

It is no wonder, then, that our marvelous machine system broke down. We simply can't navigate the Atlantic with a chart of the Pacific. We can't find our way around Boston with a map of ancient Rome, and we couldn't make headway in the machine age with the traditions of the agrarian age. To live now, for instance, every American had to have money; but there was no social effort, and it even seemed contrary to American principles that there should be any social effort, to see to it that every American should have this necessary money.

What had really happened was that 120,000,000 Americans had all moved on to the same farm, without the slightest understanding that they had taken any such step. If they had known that, they would have made arrangements accordingly, and devised some plan upon which this farm, which now included all America, could be run successfully in the interest of the people who now occupied it.

That would have been a fairly simple problem, if we had only understood what the problem was. Planning production and consumption was no new idea. The early Americans were all familiar with it. Those farmers, because they knew the economics of their time, always organized farm production to meet the needs of the consuming families. If they had a surplus of anything, it might mean that they wouldn't have to do so much work in that line as they had been doing. Those who had been doing that work, however, would not become unemployed, but *released* to do any work which now most needed to be done. No one could have imagined such a thing as the children starving because there was too much food, or freezing because there was too much wood or an overabundance of clothes and blankets.

And when we now organize production and distribution in the interest of the consumer, poverty in the midst of plenty will again become unthinkable. It will, however, be no easy task; for our traditions will constantly get in the way of the all-American action which is now necessary. Our business traditions, our agricultural traditions, even our labor traditions, are still constantly blinding us to the basic facts of our human relations and human responsibilities in this machine age. That is why we must have a new education, a new outlook and a new culture; why youth must become acquainted, not only with the economic and social setup of the moment, but with those evolutionary processes which are forever transforming human society, and will, if understood, permit us to go on to greater and greater heights of human life.

Protecting the Taxpayer*

FRIENDS OF THE RADIO AUDIENCE:

It is often remarked that the American public likes to be robbed. That is absurd. Nobody likes to be robbed. Nobody likes to pay taxes without getting something in return. Yet it often looks as if we *did* like it.

Americans are noted throughout the world for their efficiency; but American city governments are notorious for their inefficiency.

Americans are famous for their scientific management. American cities are notorious for their mismanagement.

The average American citizen is honest and industrious. The average American city reeks with corruption and graft.

Then, once in every blue moon, we elect a reform administration which is often thrown out of office at the following election or, to the consternation of its supporters, remains in office accompanied by the rise of another political machine very similar in pattern to the one which has been so indignantly smashed.

I used to be a reformer—until I reformed—and I used to wonder why this was. It seemed that the forces of evil must outnumber the forces of good. Then I got to studying the facts. I met a theater owner, for instance, an honest and upright man who asked no favors from the corrupt political machine which dominated his city and was making his taxes almost unbearable; and I discovered that he was contributing regularly to the campaign fund by which that machine maintained its strangle hold upon him and upon the city.

* A broadcast in a series on YOU AND YOUR GOVERNMENT, presented by the Committee on Civic Education by Radio of the National Advisory Council on Radio in Education and the American Political Science Association, in co-operation with the National Municipal League, over a nation-wide network of the National Broadcasting Company from Station WEEI, Boston, Massachusetts—January 8, 1935.

"If I *don't* do it," he said, "they'll close my theater, and close it legally, for violation of the building code."

"I supposed," I said, "that your theater was the safest theater in town."

"It is," he told me, "but that makes no difference. That building code, which was enacted by the last reform administration, is so ideal that it could not be enforced without tearing down most of the important buildings in the city. No attempt, then, is made to enforce it. It is just held as a club over our heads. All I have to do is to cough up and keep quiet. If I do that, I could still operate my theater, even if it were a firetrap."

Business men are generally familiar with this technique of graft. Let them do something which offends the machine, and they are not mobbed or beaten up. They may simply be summoned to show cause why they should not be compelled to remove certain signs projecting over the sidewalk, or make some other very costly alterations, as per section so-and-so of some city ordinance of which they have never heard. If they make the alterations required, however, it does no good; for there are always ordinances which can be found, and cases which can be made out, against anyone who happens to be too troublesome or refuses to chip in when the hat is passed.

When the situation becomes unbearable, they may get together to clean up the city's politics. But they do not clean them up. They simply elect a lot of good men. Then each business man returns to his business and waits for taxes to come down. But taxes don't come down, and graft continues. Why?

The reform administration undoubtedly wants to please the business interests. It may not take any important steps without first feeling out the sentiment of the Chamber of Commerce; and prominent in the Chamber of Commerce are the local utility companies.

The rapid transit company, let us say, wants a higher fare; or, as in some cities, *gets* a higher fare, which only reduces the patronage and creates a deficit, and then asks the *city* to meet this deficit by taxation. What does business, organized in the Chamber of Commerce, think about such a proposal? And the Chamber, often, sees no reason why business should oppose the claim.

The Chamber of Commerce is perfectly innocent in this—innocent but asleep. When such a deal is put through, however, some politician is certain to wake up. So does every other gang which wants some special privilege.

The public doesn't like to pay higher fares; and if it is going to vote for an administration which makes this necessary, a great many voters must have some special reason for doing so. The gas company has some influence and will support the administration *on certain conditions.* So will the electric interests and real estate interests and other groups. To get enough votes to keep an administration in power, however, will usually require more than this.

What we know as a political boss is just a broker of special privileges. He doesn't have to be popular. He simply has to know what it will take to keep an administration in office, and where he is most likely to get it. So he passes the hat to the special interests who happen to be interested and proceeds to organize his ward machinery.

Special privileges, he knows, can be maintained only by distributing more special privileges. So he promises jobs to key men in every precinct. These men may be gangsters. They may simply be good fellows, or they may be men with political ambitions, willing to start at the bottom and work their way up. Good or bad, however, each has his special racket; and the price he pays for the privilege of pursuing that racket is loyal support of the machine by which the boss gets his and all the various special interests get theirs.

One curious result of all this is that almost nobody, even among the beneficiaries of the greatest privileges, is exactly pleased with what inevitably happens. The respectable rapid transit interests, engaged as they may be in holding up the city, do not like to be held up by thugs and gangsters, who maintain their position as thugs and gangsters largely through the corruption of the police and the courts. If we are to permit one kind of holdup, however, we must have votes, including the votes secured by permitting the other kind of holdup. Eventually, of course, the situation becomes unbearable and the public rebels. But it doesn't get good government. It simply begins a new cycle of misgovernment because it still imagines that it is possible to secure good government simply by electing good men.

Good government cannot be secured that way. To secure good government, we must first have some understanding of what good government is. I offer a definition. *That government is good which gives the whole public its money's worth.*

It isn't the number of dollars which we have to pay in taxes which makes taxation such a bad bargain for us taxpayers. *It is what we don't get for those taxes*—what the whole public fails to get. If the public has to pay more than it is necessary to pay, either for government itself or for public services under government regulations, it must have that much less to spend for the things which legitimate business has to sell. In the act, then, of sanctioning any special privilege, we business men injure all business, including our own.

If, on the other hand, we organize to eliminate every special privilege, we will automatically have the public with us. For the public wants its money's worth. Labor wants its money's worth. The consumer wants his money's worth. The taxpayer wants his money's worth. And the only way that all can get their money's worth is through seeing to it that no one gets more than his money's worth. Let business once organize for such a program, and the whole graft ridden public will organize to see the program through.

Even practical politicians will then provide good government, for they will want votes as much as ever, and that will be the only way to get enough votes.

We do not need new organizations. All we need is to place our present organizations, particularly our business organizations, on a true, fact-finding basis. Every Chamber of Commerce should be a real laboratory of municipal research; and if such a program should lead to the withdrawal of certain prominent members for a time, the Chamber could get along without them much more easily than it can get along without the facts.

Then, of course, it would have to plan for the organization of the government in harmony with the facts. It would have to fight, doubtless, for genuine public service, and furnish votes in support of genuine public service, with the same energy with which the grafters have been fighting and furnishing votes for graft. Right can always prevail over wrong if its army is as well equipped as the army of wrong. The army of right *is sufficiently large;* but it needs organization and well-trained shock troops who will fight as fearlessly, as determinedly, as cleverly and as *constantly* for good government as the beneficiaries and henchmen of special privilege regularly fight for misgovernment. This will furnish genuine protection to the taxpayer—protecting him not only from unnecessary direct expenses, but from the still worse phases of misrule.

Morals in Business *

There are two ways of becoming good. One is to become interested in goodness. The other is to become interested in the facts of life.

There are advantages and disadvantages in each way.

A good boy and a bad boy both grew up and became taxi drivers. The bad boy became a good taxi driver and the good boy became a bad taxi driver.

The good boy had the advantage of being considered good; and every time he became absent-minded and took the wrong side of the street, excellent character witnesses testified for him in court. The bad boy had the advantage of keeping his license. Even those character witnesses, when they needed a taxi, always seemed to patronize the evil-minded in preference to the absent-minded.

There are many good men in business. There are fewer good business men.

A good man in business will not cheat you any more than he would cheat himself. Being interested in goodness, however, rather than in the facts of business, he is all too likely to cheat himself, and the business gets bad and cannot serve you very well.

It takes a good business man to provide good service. If he doesn't give good service, he knows his customers will not come back, while the goods he has sold them will.

He may not seem the least bit moral about it. It is quite possible that he would give poor service instead of good if he could work up a bigger trade that way. But he has been interested in the facts and he found out that he can't. The other

---

* A Weinstock Lecture at the University of California, Berkeley, California—February 7, 1934.

gentleman, with a mind so lofty that it is forever soaring far above the facts, is very good. The only drawback seems to be that he is very good for nothing.

I have said it before, but it cannot be emphasized too strongly, that good men frequently do much more harm than bad men ever do.

Bad men commit more than ten thousand murders annually in the United States. But it was under the leadership of good men, not bad, that fifteen million Americans were needlessly allowed to drift into unemployment. It was good men, not bad, who let the whole world drift into war. And it is good men, not the evil-minded, who have so miserably failed to solve world problems that, although no nation and almost nobody within any nation wants another war, nobody seems to know how it can be avoided.

It is not the evil-minded but the absent-minded who constitute our Public Enemy No. 1.

When I say absent-minded, I mean that their minds are absent from the facts, and either off on some idealistic tour or else playing with some formula which, because it once played a practical part in human affairs, they still consider practical.

It is necessary in every study of morals to make this distinction between traditional morality and matter-of-fact morality.

Morals always begin with facts—mainly with the facts of human relations. Those practices which have worked well are codified, and those who obey the code are considered good people, while those who disobey are considered bad.

This is all right for a while. This is all right until the facts begin to change; for there is little deviation at first between the letter of the code and the facts of human experience.

When the facts change is when the trouble begins. And the facts are always changing more or less. It may be fortunate, then, that we have so many sinners—people who are not overenthusiastic for the formulas of goodness and feel rather free to go on experimenting.

Often, they violate the code; and if nothing too serious results, others are encouraged to violate it; and when the code eventually breaks down from all this violation, we cast about us and build a new code more in harmony with our later experiences. Thus, by and large, we achieve some progress.

In the meantime, however, something terrible is always happening. For those who are most passionately interested in goodness are likely to be least interested in improving the code. It worked, therefore it was good. It was good, therefore it became sacred. It is sacred, therefore it is not to be altered. The bulk of the moral passion of the community is often directed, not toward finding a better way of living, but toward the preservation of a code under which, because of changed conditions, it has become possible to do no end of harm.

All this is particularly applicable to morals in business. Indeed, business morals cannot be disassociated from community morals. But there are many experiments of great moral significance in business which are not generally supposed to be in the realm of morals at all.

One might think, for instance, that there is no particular moral question involved in the problem of whether a merchant or manufacturer shall employ efficient modern methods or continue practices which do not pay. But there is. If his system is bad, he cannot serve the public well, and he cannot even pay his employees as they should be paid. *Poor service is immoral.*

Moralists may not often preach about such things. They are more likely to preach about a taxi driver using bad language than about his using bad judgment; but bad judgment on the part of a taxi driver is much more immoral than any possible words in his vocabulary could be. Morals are based upon human experience. They are our *mores,* our customs, which have become our customs because they worked for the common good.

One of the great moral dogmas of the past was that thrift is a virtue. It has become a great immoral dogma now, for our modern society would fall apart if modern people were to follow the ancient moral standards of thrift. We make hoarding a sin; for it is only through buying and spending that we can keep ourselves at work and serve everybody by raising the plane of living. Eventually we shall have to recognize that many practices which were once highly moral have become highly immoral, and many practices which were once immoral have become our moral duty.

Not long ago, for instance, it was considered morally degrading for a man to permit his family to become dependent upon the community. But in present day life, we are all dependent upon the community; and if the community doesn't exactly owe us a living, it does owe us an opportunity to participate in those processes by which the people of this modern community do make a living.

Independence was a virtue in early America because, under the conditions which then existed, each citizen could take a homestead in the wilderness and, by organizing the whole family to work and save, could secure that family's independence. Today, it may be a sin against one's family, as well as against the community, for one to seek that ancient family independence. For no family can make much of a living in that way now; and to make a living at all, one may have to deprive his children of education and leisure, to say nothing of modern comforts and luxuries which the children of this new civilization have a right to have.

Independence was a virtue in those early days because it was only by this independent farming that the average man *could* support his family. When the self-contained farm was the only means by which the masses could live, we very properly cultivated the virtues of independence. Now that a far more efficient way of life has become not only practical but imperative, we must learn to cultivate the virtues of interdependence.

Rugged individualism is a constructive force if there are only a few people on a big continent and everybody can practice it. It ceases to be a constructive force in a machine age, in which everybody's work is so closely tied up with everybody else's work that few, if any, can practice it. About all that one can do with rugged, unhampered individualism in such an age is to dream about it; and while he is so dreaming, he is almost certain to neglect his actual responsibilities.

Any discussion of morals must be fruitless unless it takes full account of changing economic conditions and the resultant changes in human relations. We often hear it said of persons of doubtful mentality that "at least they know the difference between right and wrong." But they don't. None of us does.

You young men, no doubt, all love your mothers; and soon, if not yet, most of you will undertake to love, honor and cherish some other woman.

You may think you know exactly how your mother should be treated. And you may think you know exactly how wives should be treated. But the chances are that you won't know *what* to do when your wife and your mother begin to have what they call an "understanding."

Furthermore, there isn't a living person who is wise enough to tell you what to do under such circumstances. Nobody knows; and the reason why nobody knows is that times have changed so radically since we had any workable code concerning this phase of human relations, that nobody has yet been able to figure out just what the rights and duties of a mother-in-law and her daughter-in-law now are.

Until very recent years, in China, there was no such problem. That was because conditions had not changed so much and the ancient codes still held. In America, however, our economic setup has changed so greatly that our ancient codes are crumbling, not only in business but in all the relations of life.

The good life is as necessary as it ever was, but just what constitutes a good life in these changing times is still an open question.

The good life, it seems to me, is not the life which *has discovered* the difference between right and wrong. The good life is, rather, the life which *is earnestly discovering* that difference and going toward the good.

I was speaking, remember, of the good life—not necessarily of the lives of good people. The good life is not the perfect life. It is not necessarily the life which is well rounded out, or the life which has achieved all the better-known virtues. The good life may be a life full of mistakes and stumbling. It may not be a pretty life. It may not be at all acceptable as a pattern for others. It is a life, however, which is concerned with the truth of things, rather than with formulas which have become half-truths. Hence, the good life is always driving on. It is getting somewhere. It is alive.

Too often this is not true of the lives of good people. They want to be good, no doubt, and are more concerned with being good than they are with learning anything which might upset their notions of goodness. So they get nowhere. They may be impeccable but they are very dead.

Does it seem strange, I wonder, that a shopkeeper should get to moralizing like this? What does a shopkeeper know about morals anyway?

Well, I shall make no apology. I shall simply call attention to the fact that this is a business civilization; and if we want to discover its moral values, it would seem necessary to look into the facts of its business setup.

Morals are temporal and local. They are local because people live in different places, where conditions are different; and they are temporal because people live in different times and times change.

I am fully aware that the world has not habitually turned to business in its search for standards of morality. We shopkeepers have an ignoble heritage. From time immemorial, trade was deemed dishonorable and the tradesman was supposed to be a liar and a cheat.

It is all quite understandable. Business in ancient times was very largely banditry, and world trade was just another name for piracy.

The trader produced nothing; and if he rendered any service to anybody else, it was entirely unintentional. He was an alien even in his own land, for *he did not participate in the economic process of the times.*

That statement may at first seem startling. We have become so used to thinking of economics as a study of the laws of trade, that we may have some trouble in trying to correct the notion. Economics, however, is the study of the way in which the people of human societies get their living; and not until relatively recent times has trade had much to do with that.

Mainly people have got their living by hunting and foraging, by roaming over the face of the earth with their flocks and herds, or by settling upon the land in little communal groups and tilling the soil.

We do not know when trade began; but for many ages, we know, it cut very little figure in the average man's economy. The land was the source of wealth—the means of human life—and those who held titles to the land were noble. Those who lived by their wits instead—those who profited by the misfortunes of others, and who accumulated wealth outside the process under which wealth was actually produced—were ignoble.

The lords of one society, to be sure, might make war upon the lords of another society and rob and enslave their people, and that was perfectly noble. But we won't go into that. The point is that the trader everywhere was very much a social outcast.

And he knew it. He accepted the situation. He lived up to his bad reputation; and not until trade had expanded to such a point that it began to cut a real figure in the world's economic life did trade develop anything resembling morals.

The odor of dishonor, in fact, still clings to trade. With the great tradition of aristocracy behind us, it could hardly be otherwise. As trade grew, however, some practices were gradually abandoned. It was bad business, it was eventually discovered, for a trader to take everything from a customer and give him nothing. "All that the traffic will bear" became the business code, and this marked a great moral advance. It was more moral than previous codes because, if it were followed, it would not utterly stop traffic. A little trickle, at least, would continue.

I said it marked a moral advance; but the moral advance was registered by those who developed the code, not by those who stuck to it as the last word in business morals.

One day someone made an analysis of business and discovered that honesty was the best policy. That was a great day in human history. Aristocrats, of course, sneered. Their word of honor was sacred, they said, and had nothing whatever to do with profit or loss. It took the base mind of a trader, as the nobles saw it, even to think of honesty in terms of whether or not it paid.

But there is this to be said for the other side. While the nobility held to their ancient formulas, business took a step ahead. The moral problem of aristocracy was one of remaining, if possible, as good as it had ever been. Business seemed to have no moral problem. Its problem was how to do more business. To do that it had to become more honest—more moral.

When I entered business half a century ago, "Let the buyer beware" was still the accepted practice. I remember a startling innovation in my father's store—his putting up a sign which created no end of mystification.

It read: "One Price to All."

Many thought it would be a bad place to trade. They would rather take a chance in some store where they could beat the merchant down. But it worked. It resulted not only in the same price to everybody but in a lower price to everybody. Competitors generally had to adopt the plan, and business gave incalculably more service than it had ever given before.

Before the introduction of this practice, business had given relatively good service to a few customers, and might even sell certain things to certain persons below cost, making it up by overcharging others. Now, it not only refused to take this sort of advantage of anyone but so simplified business practice that all could be served to better advantage than even the expert hagglers were served before.

Here was something better—more moral—than mere honesty; but merchants did not think of it in terms of morals. When they thought in terms of goodness, instead of in terms of good business practice, they were more likely to give their money away in charity. Then the results were usually not so good.

Every employer had to hire labor, it was supposed, at the very lowest wages for which workers would work; and when people were terribly in need of work, they would work for almost anything. Employers, however, who assumed that this was a necessary business practice, often did want to be good to their employees. Sometimes they bought turkeys for them at Thanksgiving, not because working people were entitled to eat turkey, but so that they might be thankful that they were working for such good and kind employers.

But something was forever going wrong with all this charity and philanthropy. The workers often resented it outright. These good employers meant well. They were simply trying to be good according to the accepted patterns of goodness, but the results were often disastrous.

Other business men, however, were more intent upon becoming good business men. And along came Ford who hated so-called philanthropy but wanted to find out how to make and sell cars, instead of merely learning what the usual practice was.

You know his findings. One does not have to accept Mr. Ford as a profound philosopher, nor an ideal employer, and one may disagree with him in many ways. It remains true, however, that Mr. Ford, in his efforts to become a good business man instead of a good man in business, discovered and demonstrated certain basic truths which must inescapably result in the creation of a better world.

He discovered the secret of mass production—not only that mass production is more economical and more profitable than any other form of production, but that, with all its economies, it must logically become untenable unless it is accompanied by mass consumption.

He discovered that business cannot sell more than the people as a whole can buy, and that it is the function of business to provide the people with buying power.

He discovered that high wages, instead of meaning an additional expense to a business, are necessary to business success, and actually result in lower labor costs per unit of product, which is the only sane way to figure labor costs.

He did not discover a Utopia. Nor did he discover a system of society to be put into operation at such time as society may be induced to abandon the system upon which it is currently depending. He was just a business man, and proved that all these principles of his were simple and successful business principles; but the moral advance inherent in these discoveries is incalculable.

Take the case of a hardheaded, fact-finding merchant, who has the courage to follow where the business facts lead, as contrasted with some ever-so-good storekeeper, who wants like everything to raise the moral standard of his employees but is so interested in goodness that he neglects to discover the facts.

Some of you possibly know both types. One of them gives to all good causes; and to find the money with which to give, he charges the gifts to the expense of the business. In other words, he makes his customers pay his charity bills. It isn't good business; for many of his customers, finding his prices high, do not return. With less business than before, and the same overhead, he now tries to cut expenses; and not knowing much about the facts of business, he thinks of two things. He doesn't want to lay anybody off and he doesn't like to cut anybody's salary. He even explains as much to those he does lay off, and to those whom he cuts. But they don't like it very well; and neither do his remaining employees like it when it is explained that they will have to sell more of the goods which have not been going very well, if they hope to hold their jobs. Nevertheless, they do their best to sell those goods at the same old price; and if they have to lie and misrepresent the goods to do it, they excuse themselves with the thought that they'll be fired if they don't. And when they attend some store rally, and the Big Boss comes in and addresses them concerning the kind of moral lives that they should lead—somehow it doesn't go down very well.

But take the other merchant—the hardheaded fact-finder. He's in business for profit, and fact-finding has convinced him that people prefer to buy, as a rule, where they can get the most value for their money. Perhaps he doesn't think so much, then, about good causes as he does about good goods. And if he makes a mistake and buys goods which aren't so good, he tries to correct the mistake instead of organizing his business around it. He doesn't know what his customers want; and instead of guessing, and letting it go at that, he does his best to find out.

He discovers that they want their money's worth. He discovers that they want good goods at prices within their reach.

And he discovers that, if they do not get satisfactory goods, or pay more than it is necessary to pay for the goods they get, those customers are not likely to return.

He has stocked his shelves with things he *thought* his customers would like. But mere opinion does not satisfy him. He wants to *know*. The best of buyers are not infallible, he reflects. How is he to be sure as to what his customers want? And how is he to know the price which they will gladly pay? Unless he can offer his goods at such a price, he knows, there is little chance of his holding his customers.

So he proceeds to find out. The good man in business, as distinguished from the good business man, doesn't think of that. The good man in a bad fix doesn't see any way out of his difficulties except high-pressure salesmanship—forcing on his customers those goods he happens to have in stock. But the fact-finder will not do this. He will not do it because he does not want to drive his customers away—which may seem like a base motive but see how it works out.

He too talks to his sales force, and he says things which startle them. He doesn't suggest any new tricks of salesmanship. He suggests, rather, that they make no particular effort to get rid of certain goods, lest in doing so they get rid of certain customers.

"The safe plan," he explains, "is to treat every customer as you would treat your own parents if they were at your counter. Find out what they want. Remember how little money they have to spend, and how much it means to them to pay more than it is necessary to pay for anything. Then, if you have what they really want, at a price which they can afford to pay, let them have it. If you cannot fill their orders in this way, however, and you know of some place where they can get better values for the money, *send them there*."

This sounds so amazingly unselfish that the salespeople may wonder if the boss is in his right mind.

"You don't mean to send them to some other store?" they may ask.

Surely. Why not? If they buy something they do not want at his store they will go to some other store eventually. The way to keep them coming to his store, he has discovered, is to make sure that they always get their money's worth whenever they do trade with him.

And how about those goods which are still left on the shelves? The problem is easy—for the fact-finder. All he has to do is mark them down to a point where they will become desirable. To be sure, he may lose money for the moment. But he will gain business. He will gain the confidence of the public. And he will in his future purchases correct the mistake which he made when he bought those goods, instead of incorporating that mistake in his future policy.

If the goods were disposed of by high-pressure salesmanship, the shelves would be quite as empty for the moment as if they had really been in demand. The buyer will have no means of knowing how the goods were sold. He will know only that they were sold; and he will restock the shelves with that kind of goods. In other words, he will organize the whole business, not to attract customers, but to drive them away.

The fact-finder, let him be ever so hardheaded, will not fall into such a trap. He will organize the business for maximum service. He will restock with lines which his customers really want—not with lines which they have been artfully induced to buy. And the public will trade with him, more and more, not because they think of him as "such a good man," but because he can be depended upon to keep a good store.

Such a merchant, incidentally, will not have to cut wages. By fact-finding, he will come to see the necessity of raising them; for only when wages are good, and only when employees know that increased efficiency will surely be reflected in better wages to them, is it possible to keep a business at maximum efficiency.

And as to laying off employees, he will have no problem at all. Let a merchant follow fact-finding far enough, and he will soon need more employees. In his relations to his employees, then, as in his relations to the community, there will be something more than honesty and more, even, than justice. There will be friendship—a warm, human acceptance of the principle of co-operation.

In a word, there will be the Golden Rule in actual operation, not as a hazy ideal to be applied at some glamorous moment in the future, when human selfishness and human nature shall have been overcome. It will be in actual operation because *it will have been discovered* as a practical principle, instead of being accepted as a holy but impractical precept.

It is far from my intention, however, to eulogize modern business. Most of it is still very bad; but experience should teach us that we cannot look for much moral improvement until it is discovered that the things which are bad in business constitute bad business.

It was bad business when England, in her eagerness for trade expansion, forced the opium trade on China. England is still paying for that mistake.

It was bad business when our leading industrial nations, in competition for commercial supremacy, brought the whole world into war. We are all still paying for that.

Many schools of salesmanship in America today are made up largely of courses of instruction in very bad business. These schools assume to teach their students how to sell whatever they may be engaged to sell; whereas one of the primary courses in any good school of salesmanship would be the teaching of *what not to sell* and *when not to sell.*

I know one land salesman so expert in overcoming sales resistance that he sold one family enough land, on so-called easy payment terms, so that the monthly installments were larger than the family's monthly income.

I know of other land salesmen—of course this would not happen in California—who have attracted Easterners to the West with pretty pictures of fruit trees; and the Easterners have invested their life's savings in land which they were not equipped to till, at times when even those who were equipped could scarcely make a living in the process.

That's bad business. Selling anything to anybody is bad business if the transaction is not profitable to the buyer. Wall Street, I know, thought it was doing a great business in 1928 and 1929; but if I remember rightly, it did not pan out so very well for Wall Street after all.

Business men all over America today are still fearful of unemployment insurance, sickness and old-age pensions and other social legislation aiming at economic security for all. Are these men heartless? No. Can they not see how terrible unemployment is? Of course they can. They can see how terrible it is to the unemployed; but they do not yet see how expensive it is to business, and how profitable unemployment insurance would be to their own business enterprises. When they see that, they will do selfishly what their hearts have been telling them to do unselfishly, and establish adequate unemployment insurance; and they will do it better by doing it selfishly than they could possibly do it by doing it unselfishly.

The great moral significance of the present moment in American history is that we have reached a point, and have at last embarked upon an economic program, which makes it imperative that we discover these truths.

We can no longer plead that "business is business," as we could when it was possible for people to carry on outside the business order. The business order and the human order have now become one; and every violation of human good must be eliminated from the business code.

America was recently thrilled that child labor, one of the most loathsome of our social sores, passed away in a flash.* But that is only an incident in the course of fact-finding. Fraudulent advertising must soon follow. Business which does not protect the buyer must go. And in the course of time, the whole immoral, sinful wastes of production and, still worse, of distribution, must be eliminated. What I foresee as a direct result of dealing in a business way with the business facts of this business civilization, is the dedication of business to human service, and the development at last of a practical morality which, for the first time in human history, realizes our highest human ideals.

Now, I think I know what is on the minds of some of my hearers. If business morals have been improving, they may ask, and if fact-finding has been producing not only better business

---

* This of course refers to the N.R.A. codes which were later declared unconstitutional by the Supreme Court.

methods but better human relations, how do I account for its all heading up, not into a period of comparative peace and prosperity, but into the worst business and social debacle that we have ever known?

The point is well taken. Mass production, even though it led to the discovery that business, to continue successful, must serve the masses, created prosperity much more rapidly than we were prepared to handle it.

We liked the prosperity; but we viewed it through the lens of tradition, instead of finding out just what it actually was. We had created a tremendous surplus; but we viewed that surplus with the formulas of an agrarian age which had never had a surplus and couldn't possibly imagine such a thing.

Our finances, for one thing, were being directed in the main by men who were following the best traditions of finance. To a certain extent, they were even fact-finders. In a way, they even believed in service. But they failed to recognize the revolutionary character of the changes which had occurred, and the completely different basis, therefore, upon which finances must now be organized.

I insist that they were not bad men. They all had standards of goodness and morals to which, as a rule, they faithfully adhered. But these were standards of other times. The trouble was that *they were not good financiers*—at least, not for the Nineteen Twenties. They did not comprehend the financial needs of this era of mass production, which required mass consumption to make it work. If you had asked them to arrange for the financing of mass consumption, they would not have known what you were talking about; and they would not have bothered to find out. They were the ones who understood finance, they said. They were thoroughly familiar with its tried and true principles—that is, with the principles which had been applicable when conditions were altogether different; and when it was not necessary, from the business viewpoint, that the masses should have not only economic security, but greater and ever greater prosperity.

Yet that was about all that was needed to make business prosperity permanent—just an arrangement of our financial affairs so that every increase in our productivity would immediately be met by a corresponding increase in the capacity of the masses everywhere to purchase and consume the product.

Of course, this would require some co-ordinated plan of production and distribution; but all that these financiers would have had to do was to order the drawing up of such a plan and one would have been drawn up immediately.

Almost any plan would do, if it were based upon the facts of the situation. It would have to provide, of course, that factories and railroads be erected when there was a human need for their products, not whenever someone felt like selling more securities. It would have to be a plan of actual human service, not a mere Chiseler's Dream.

It must, of course, include permanent and secure employment for every employable person, and ample funds for the support of the helpless, the incompetent and those too young or too old to work; this, not as a charity, but so that the social nuisance of poverty and its accompanying evils might be abolished from our earth, and that these, too, should contribute by their buying to keep industry from being choked by its own product.

And it must have arranged, of course, for the employment of money as a medium of exchange. For our world now was based upon exchange. The old agrarian economy had gone, as far as our country was concerned. From an era in which people got almost all their living from the soil on which they lived, and to whom trade was at best a mere incident, we had evolved into an era in which all of us, including our farmers, got most of our living within the institutions of trade.

That situation gave money an entirely new character. Now it was impossible for people to live without it. Sane financing demanded then that everybody have sufficient money with which to purchase the things which it was necessary for them to purchase, if business were to sell the things it had to sell, and if the masses were to be kept employed.

This was not a difficult problem, if the mind of business had really cared to solve it. But the mind of business was not on this business problem and you know what happened. It is what always happens when, instead of dealing with the facts of any situation, we attempt to deal with it according to our traditional moral formulas.

These financiers, not being able to perceive the new responsibilities created by the new stage of business development, did not become villains. They simply became good men doing villainous things. Not understanding that finance had suddenly become a problem of getting buying power to the masses, they went on trying as usual to accumulate and control the new wealth which was now being produced on such a prodigious scale. There was no method in this madness. There was only habit—tradition. In other times, the mere accumulation of money and its investment in further productive enterprises had proven justifiable, so they continued to think of it as justifiable. And there was so much wealth waiting to be invested now that it seemed unnecessary even to wait for industries to become profitable before taking the profits.

So they discounted the expected profits of the mergers which they floated, and called the operation "finance"; and their rake-offs were so great, frequently, that the mergers were handicapped and unable to become profitable at all. For the time being, however, that did not seem to matter. Securities could be sold at higher prices; and so long as that was true, they would be bought for resale, and the prices would therefore keep going up. To accumulate money, regardless of what money was, and regardless of the fact that money would soon vanish unless it were directed toward the mass buying of the enormous and ever increasing volume of things which were now being produced—that is what these good men still looked upon as finance.

And when the bubble broke and the nation lay prostrate, they trotted out their ancient and futile goodness once more.

It cannot be said that American business leaders during that depression, were not good, kind, charitable and public spirited. Because they had not arranged for universal and secure employment, however, they now worked early and late for the relief of the unemployed. And the more they relieved the unemployed according to their good old charitable traditions, the more unemployment there was to be relieved.

It could not work out any other way. Unemployment creates no wealth. It is the negation of the exchange of services—the very principle upon which our machine-age economy is based. So we sank presently into further and further depths; until one day, a leader arose among us, and suggested that we deal with the facts.

He admitted that he did not know what to do. Therein lies the greatness of President Roosevelt. He suggested that we find out what to do—all of us—and that we work out a plan which would leave none of us out.

He did not say what that plan would be. There is no reason to believe that he knew. He did know, however, that it would surely violate tradition and precedent; and the apostles of tradition and precedent feel the violation keenly.

But at last we are on our way. The real facts and the actual human relationships of this business civilization are at last being discovered and dealt with; and the farther we go in that direction, the more beautiful the human prospect is.

No moral code of other ages can possibly serve our purpose now. No mere list of Thou-Shalt-Nots. No mere code of honesty and fair dealing. Not even a code of individual rights. All these old codes can come alive, in fact, only if we perceive them, not as final dicta concerning moral conduct, but as guideposts along the path of moral progress.

I surely do not wish to infer that business, having made such obvious moral progress through the centuries, is now entitled to a halo. I wish merely to emphasize that each true advance was brought about not so much by a great moral awakening as by a great business awakening—the perception that it was no longer good business to continue the practices of the previous era—and this awakening seems always to have occurred in connection with some definite change in the relation of trade to human economy.

Wherever the agrarian economy still lingers, and it is still possible for the masses of the people to get most of their living directly from the soil, business is still largely a matter of haggling—of taking, in each transaction, as much as one can take, and of giving as little as possible in return. This policy becomes less and less tenable wherever the machine age is in the process of development, and it has been bad business policy in America for many years.

Those who have tried to improve the situation, however, by substituting a traditional moral code for the traditional business code, have usually met with failure or with very limited success. They have gone in strong for charity, for welfare work and for the support of worthy institutions, sometimes dominating those institutions—such as our institutions of higher learning—to keep them from antagonizing what seem to be the business interests.

It is those who have discovered that it pays to give the utmost possible service who have led the way to a higher morality—that it pays to make prices as low and wages as high as they can possibly be made, that it pays to be truthful in advertising, that it pays to eliminate graft in government and all waste in human life.

This may not seem to be an idealistic approach to moral problems, but the results are great. There is a reason. For it is the way of fact-finding; and if we chase the facts far enough, we are sure to discover Truth. Our motives may not seem saintly. We simply want to *know* at any cost. But fact-finding, if carried through, can lead to but one thing; that is the law which governs the universe—the Law of God—which is good enough.

Business and Religion *

It may seem presumptuous for a mere shopkeeper—and one, at that, who finds it impossible to identify himself with any visible religious organization—to address a body of religious leaders on the subject of religion. Perhaps it is a case of where "fools rush in." In the first place, I cannot give any definition of religion with which there will be any general agreement. Most of the religious discussions to which I have listened seem not a bit lacking in either earnestness or intellectuality; what makes them confusing is that the disputants seem to be talking about altogether different things. Believe me, however, this trouble is not at all confined to the religious field. We have identically the same trouble in our business gatherings—everybody getting excited, and in a great hurry to tell everything he knows about business, but no agreement whatever as to what business *is*.

Generally speaking, we have two large factions in the business world. I have been calling these factions by a name which you may understand. I have been calling them *fundamentalists* and *modernists*.

I do not mean that the fundamentalists are necessarily fundamental. I mean that they cling to the fundamentals of an ancient business creed. It is an archaic creed. It is a creed upon which business can no longer be successfully conducted. It is the creed, in a word, that business is the process by which a business man is redeemed from the hell of poverty in which the masses of mankind are doomed to languish forever, and permitted to enjoy the good things of life which the suffering masses must go on making for them.

---

* Address delivered to a gathering of ministers and laymen from various churches invited by the Laymen's Committee (non-sectarian) for the Federal Council of Churches, at the Harvard Club, New York, N. Y.—November 15, 1929.

I wonder if you have any of this type of fundamentalist in the religious field—any, perhaps, who think that religion is primarily a matter of saving their own souls. Now, if there are any such, I am not going to quarrel with them. They may be right. But if they are right, I am wholly uninterested in their religion. I have no objection, understand, to their souls being saved; but if getting their souls saved is all there is to it, the whole thing doesn't seem to me to be worth while.

I have no objections to profits in business. I believe in them devoutly. I believe in business getting greater profits than profiteers could ever get; I do not see how on earth the public can be served by business if the business itself fails. Business must make a profit. Nevertheless, if profit making is all there is to business, I am also profoundly disinterested in that. Business, as the modernists see it, is the process of getting to the people of this world the things which the people of this world want, and should have, if they are to lead a useful happy life.

I am talking about the modernists' conception of business, understand, with no quarrel whatever with the fundamentalists' conception excepting that it is wholly out of date and not applicable to these modern times. I feel that I am on firm ground when I am saying that. I contend that the modernist definition of business is demonstrably correct. But when I speak of religion, the ground is not so firm. There, I shall have to tell you what I mean by the word "religion," and proceed to talk about that, whether you agree or disagree with my definition. Then, at any rate, we shall understand each other, and not become all tangled up in a confusion of terms.

In order to get a Christian definition of religion, I have been looking into the New Testament, and there I found something which I confess I could not understand. An ancient Jewish concept seemed to be that religion consisted of keeping a number of Commandments, most of which begin with "Thou shalt not." And let me tell you, incidentally, that that concept isn't entirely Jewish. I know a number of men today who seem to measure their religion by the number of things that they don't do. And they may be right, understand, and the only objection that I can possibly have to it is that it is all so uninteresting.

But in this Testament, He whom the Christian world calls "Master" emphasized a different note. He proclaimed a religion of Life and Love. Not quarreling with the "Thou shalt not's," He seems to have taught that they in themselves did not constitute religion, but that they were worth while only as they hung upon the principle of love. He gave two great Commandments, each beginning "Thou shalt love"; and "on these two Commandments," He said, "hang all the law and the prophets."

One of them I could not understand. It was "Thou shalt love the Lord, thy God, with all thy heart, and with all thy mind, and with all thy strength." I did not object to it. I believe in God. It seems to me to be impossible to contemplate a universe of eternal law, without becoming aware of an eternal power whose law cannot pass away. And yet, due no doubt to my own shortcomings, the contemplation of this eternal power failed to inspire me with that warm, personal, passionate interest which I would call Love, and I would have turned away cold if the teacher had stopped right there.

But He did not. He gave a second Commandment—"Thou shalt love thy neighbor as thyself"—and I have His word for it that the second means the same as the first. It is "like unto it," He said. I can understand the second. I will go so far, in fact, as to say that this Commandment embodies all the religion which I am able to comprehend. To me, then, religion is service; and if it is service to God, it is only that service which manifests itself in service to our fellow men.

But that's business. If you will accept that definition of religion, I am on firm ground once more.

When I say, however, that business is service, I trust that you will not swallow the statement too readily. Credulity is the worst form of unbelief. The true scientist, it seems to me, is the true believer; for his belief is hedged about by eternal questioning. That is what makes his belief so dynamic. If statements are accepted without questioning, it is impossible to do anything with them: the most, at least, that can be done with them is to do the thing which always has been done. That is the traditional thing. And whatever may be said in favor of keeping within the traditions, the process is not one which I can associate with faith.

What is faith? Is it blind concurrence in a formula which has been handed down to us, or is it trust in that Eternal Power which is forever pushing us onward and upward and tempting us to try new things? This power that beckons us to go beyond traditions! This power that challenges us to question the best formulas of the past. Is faith the attitude of glorious adventure which prompts us to discover this Almighty Will, so that our own wills may gladly and confidently conform to it, or is it mere acquiescence in the letter of some text because we do not dare to question it? Can such an acquiescence, I wonder, really be called belief? If we do not dare to question our formulas, can we say that we truly believe in them?

Therefore, I do not ask you to believe that business is service, until you have questioned our business system from every angle and discovered for yourself that this is so. I hope, in fact, that you suspect the statement of containing a whole lot of bunk; for if you do not approach the statement from that angle, but just believe it because you have heard it so many times, it *will be* a lot of bunk to you. We need clear thinking. We need questioning and skepticism, and genuine, instead of hand-me-down, convictions.

Let me warn you particularly against a form of bunk in which you, as religious leaders, are almost certain to become entangled, if you swallow too readily this statement that business is service. For it is one of the great embarrassments of religious leaders today that the religious institutions devoted to supposedly inspired truth have swallowed so much bunk in former times. Review your own church history, and I think you will find that, in all social crises, the church has generally lined up with the traditional thinking of the ruling classes. In states where there was slavery, to use an illustration from American history, the church generally seems to have sanctioned it and given little aid and comfort to abolitionists. Where there was feudalism, and a revolution against it, the church was not on the side of the revolutionists. Where there was royalty, and democracy raised its head, the church almost invariably rallied round the king. And where there was a bourgeois democracy, and suffering wage slaves banded in unions to fight against an almost inhuman exploitation, the church generally lined up with the exploiters.

My purpose in referring to this is neither to criticize nor discourage. If all the facts are closely observed, indeed, I think you will find them very encouraging.

So, I am not denouncing the church. Most certainly I am not denouncing religion. But we must face these facts if we are to understand the relation of the institutions of religion to the changing institutions of human life. We need not agree with Karl Marx that "religion is the opiate of the masses," but we should try to understand how an intensely sincere though very much mistaken champion of the masses could very easily arrive at such a conclusion.

I think you will admit that the ruling classes in modern America have had no little to do with outlining the policies and the programs of the church. By the ruling classes, I mean the rich and so-called successful. Mainly, they have been business men—good, well-meaning, conscientious, sincere, but with minds that had been largely organized around the idea of supreme rights of poverty, and habitually antagonistic to every movement which gave first emphasis to the needs of all mankind.

In fact, I do not see how the church could have done otherwise. The church was always an aspect of the *existing* social order, and the supporters of that order were, generally speaking, the supporters of the church. Human society, up to the present era, has always been organized in classes; and the changes which society has undergone have been due to the overthrow of ruling classes which had survived their usefulness, and the rise of some new ruling class.

In that, I think, we can all agree with Marx. But something had happened before Marx undertook his analysis, the meaning of which he was in no position to understand. Modern science had been born. It was not dominant in the world as yet, but it was destined to become dominant; *and the rule of science meant that the rule of the classes must cease.*

In an age when we were governed by tradition, it was necessary that we should have class rule. Those who were economically dominant had to become socially and politically dominant; but these ruling classes, who gained power by rebelling against established authority, could hold that power only by appealing to the tradition that established authority was sacred. That is, they made themselves the beneficiaries of all the sacred texts which upheld authority, now that they themselves were the authorities. Ruling became a matter of interpreting these texts in their favor and in the light of their own class interests. That is, the rulers ruled by opinion. If their opinions happened to hit the mark, they were tolerated as rulers, or even worshiped as great rulers. But there was no general acceptance of science in the world—no general understanding that the right way to solve a problem is not to consult the authorities, nor even to sit down and meditate about it, but to look up the facts.

The age of science did not dawn upon us in a blaze of glory. The heavens were not lit up, and there was no great thunder on the left. Science crept in, rather, like a thief in the night, and a sleeping world had no warning whatever. But science dug up truths and demonstrated them. It showed how things are done, and how things could be done; and those who adopted the scientific method of doing things, did them most efficiently. A simple fact, it was discovered, might upset the most beautiful opinion that ever was.

There was the opinion, for instance, that the earth was flat. It was a well thought out opinion, and it was bolstered up by some of the most ancient and honorable traditions in the sacred texts. But something happened to it. Science did not fight it, either. It did not organize any Round-World party, or seek to have the fact enshrined in any revision of the creeds. It simply discovered and proved the fact, and the fact did the rest.

Business, like government, had, of course, been governed by opinion, and it was a long time before science made many inroads there. But business opinions eventually had to crumble before business facts, although some of these opinions had existed from time immemorial and were shared not only by the rank and file of business men, but by the rank and file of workers.

You know, as well as I do, that a great change has recently come over all human society. You know that the old traditions are not holding. They are not holding on any front. Our attitude toward almost everything is changing; not only our attitude toward business and our attitude toward religion, but our attitude toward marriage and the family relation, toward patriotism, toward war, toward even the very ground we walk on and toward the stars that shine above. Our old opinions concerning all these things are fading, and the attempt to revive them by asserting that they ought to be revived is not seemingly having much effect.

The change, however, is something more than a change from one belief or set of beliefs to another. There is a difference in the quality of our belief. People of old believed that the earth was flat. Modern scientists believe that it is round. But if modern scientists should, by scientific methods, discover that their conclusion was erroneous, and that the earth is flat after all, they would still be as far away from the ancients as they ever were. They might believe the same thing, but they could not believe it in the same way. For their conclusions are not sacred to them. It is only the search for truth which is sacred, the eternal discovery of data, the patient attempt to weigh and measure every fact.

When I speak of business changes, then, I am anxious that you should not think of them in terms of a mere shifting of opinion. I am speaking about a complete social revolution, a revolution in all human relations, a series of happenings cosmic in their nature, which is inexorably transforming everybody's way of viewing everything.

You have heard about mass production, and you may think that it is just another business scheme, just as those who are unfamiliar with the evolution of religious thought may think of modernism as nothing more than a new religious creed demanding an acceptance of the theory of evolution in place of the traditional creeds.

If mass production were that, I assure you that I should not be here. There would be no reason, if that were the case, why you should learn about it, any more than why you should concern yourselves with some new system of cost accounting. Mass production has upset all the old theories of business. Not only that, but it is upsetting many of the old theories of life. Whether you like it or not, you are living in a mass production world, and you cannot understand that world, or become acquainted with the people who are living in it, unless you comprehend the general principles and the general nature of mass production.

Mass production is, in the first place, scientific production. That is, it is business running according to discovered facts, instead of operating according to accepted formulas. It is business based on research—not according to any mere theory of greatness, but according to demonstrated principles as to how business may *become* great.

Jesus said: "Let him who would be great among you be the servant of all." But the world could not see the point. Even the church, it seems to me, did not always see the point. If I am not mistaken, even ecclesiastical leaders have sometimes been motivated by other motives than that of universal service. But mass production is *proving the point* so that people cannot help seeing it. It is enlisting even human selfishness into this world-wide service.

For mass production means *production for the masses*. It is based, as I said, upon scientific discovery; and one of the central, guiding discoveries was that it pays better to make things for the masses than to make things for a favored class.

Business, from time immemorial, has catered particularly to the rich. It was every business man's ambition to secure customers with lots of money. That meant that high prices could be charged, and large profits made on every article. The poor, it was reasoned, could not buy much, and so the poor were neglected. Not every business man, to be sure, *could* confine his attentions to the rich, because there were a lot of business men and not many rich people anywhere. But when they did serve the poor, they gave poor service; not because they did not sympathize with the poor, but because that was the only service, as they saw it, for which the poor could pay, with their income determined as it was by the old belief that profits could be made only if wages were kept as low as possible.

So long as business was governed by tradition, nothing else could happen. Business men might wish to serve the masses, but they were not free to do so. Only when business began to operate on scientific research, was there any revolutionary change. Only when business men found the truth, did the truth make them free to concentrate upon such service.

Mass production, however, could not be contented simply with producing things which everybody wanted. Following the facts, instead of the traditions, it was discovered that these things must be produced at prices which the masses could pay. But there was tremendous competition for this business with the masses, and another ancient business tradition had to give way. When people were selling to the wealthy, they did not have to concentrate on price. They could make things as well as they could make them, discover what the process cost, and charge enough for the completed article to make a good profit. But that would never do for mass production. It cost Henry Ford many millions of dollars to make his first "Model A," but he could not hope to sell it for millions of dollars. This epoch-making producer knew that he could not sell his new Fords on the basis of what a thousand of them might cost, nor one hundred thousand. The least he could do would be to figure on what these cars would cost over a long period of mass production, when his organization had been finally geared up to produce many thousands of cars each day. But Ford did even better than that. He set a price which the masses of people could pay, and then gave his organization the almost superhuman task of *finding out how to produce cars which the masses would surely buy, and how to produce them at a profit, within that price*.

But mass production is doing more than making prices low. It is making wages high. Once again, that did not happen simply because employers felt generous. It happened because of scientific research. It happened because a fact was discovered—the fact that business cannot sell more than all the people can buy; and that a million people each with a thousand dollars to spare can and will buy more than a thousand people with a million dollars each.

Everybody believed, just a few years ago, that it paid an employer to secure his labor at the lowest wages at which he could obtain efficient workmen. A lot of people believed, perhaps, that he *should* pay more; nevertheless there was competition to be considered, and well-meaning employers were afraid to raise their wages lest some hardhearted skinflint, who didn't do so, would undersell them and put them out of business. Under mass production, however, we are learning the truth, and the truth will make us free to keep wages going up and up as new processes and better organization increase our efficiency per man. We are not only free to do so, *but the very competition which once kept us from raising wages, is now compelling us to raise them.* For we cannot go on manufacturing more than we can sell, and we are already producing much more than the classes can consume. We must increase the purchasing power of the masses. *We must set not merely a living wage, nor a cultural wage, but a MASS PRODUCTION WAGE*—a wage which will ensure the masses buying all the things which the *masses, under scientific organization, are producing.*

But this does not mean a mere surfeit of things. Conceivably we might become a human ant hill, with industry galore and nothing else. But mass production means more than security and more than material abundance. It means, first, freedom from the sordid struggle for mere existence. It means security in human life, and a security founded not upon individual thrift nor individual excellence, but upon the co-operation of the whole human family in the ways of truth. Therefore, it means more and more leisure for the masses. We are already seeing the beginning of this in the shorter workday. But it also means the consideration of the other fellow's interests as a first principle in life and, hence, the dawn of human friendship. It means the giving of first thought, even for selfish reasons, for the welfare of others, and freedom to give to others a truly loving service.

When humanity is organized on that basis, it will have a desire for something more than things; but until it is organized on that basis its spiritual aspirations will have hard sledding. If the wish for world peace, for instance, could bring world peace, we would have had it long ago. If the desire for friendship could make us friends, we could already have had a friendly world. But humanity was in chains. These spiritual aspirations were real enough, but the way was not apparent. It is not going contrary to your theology, I believe, to say that the spirit had to be made manifest in the flesh, and that we must *have* things before we can have a spiritual appreciation of them.

We had to have the family as a means of getting a living before we could learn the family virtues and the spiritual values inherent in the family relation. Now we have another way of getting a living. It is a more efficient way. It is a more profitable way. It is leading inevitably to a more abundant material life for everybody, and it is the business of the religious leaders to discover and reveal the spiritual values inherent in this system of material abundance.

I do not ask you, understand, to believe my statements about this business change. But I beg of you to find the truth about it. I beg of you not to remain neutral or uninterested as though it were a matter of no concern to our spiritual life. I don't want you to take sides; for it is the very essence of science that people shall not take sides. I do not ask you to debate the problem, for none of the old traditions which kept the human race in bondage, could ever have been upset by debate. Something more than logic is needed to help us find the answer to our problems now. Logic, without the facts, may lead anywhere—usually in the direction that the logician feels like going. By logic it was possible to prove in the Middle Ages, just how many angels might stand on the point of a pin. That is, any logician could solve the problem to his own satisfaction—arriving by perfectly logical processes at the conclusion which he wished to reach. Science could not solve the problem in that way. In fact, it could not solve that problem at all. It had to leave it to the theologians; for science, in order to solve the problem, would have had to find the angels first and take their measurements. But science did not worry over that. It simply left those problems upon which no facts could be obtained, to other agencies, and confined itself strictly to problems which had to do with facts. There was no war, then, between science and religion —not even between science and this old theology. I cannot see, at any rate, how it could be called war, for one side did all the fighting, while the other had all the victories.

No institution which expects to function in the modern world can afford to ignore fact-finding. The church can no more afford to be governed by opinion than can business. The church has suffered too much from such guidance in the past, and I am glad that it is showing a tendency to rebel against too much help, even from well-intentioned business sources. When, in the old days, you went to successful business leaders for advice, they gave you the best advice they could. Nevertheless, it was likely to be most unsafe advice, for it was founded on entrenched opinion, not upon facts. They had attained their success, and they held their position of leadership, by virtue of these opinions; for their opinions would not have been sought if these opinions had not competed successfully with other opinions current at the time. The church, however, did not do very well under such well-meant assistance. It did not do very well for the same reason that businesses which continued to run on opinion did not do very well. And the more the church listened to the supposedly wise pronouncements of the old-time business leaders, the more it got away from human life.

Human life did not listen to the church as it had seemed to listen in the good old days when the world was organized generally around the principle of authority. Human life, in fact, was not coming to church as regularly as it had been coming. Human life was at the ball game, or at the movies, or out riding in its new horseless carriages which had not any divine sanction, so far as anyone could see, but had come into existence because a number of scientists had got to asking questions about internal combustion. In a word, a world which was becoming more and more absorbed in facts, was getting away from the church, which was still trying to operate according to tradition, and the interpretation of tradition by men with an axe to grind.

This is not my indictment of the church. It is the indictment drawn up by the church leaders themselves. They were the first to point out that the church was not holding its ground in the modern world, that people were not attending church as regularly as in the good old days, and that a large percentage of those who did attend, were not taking it quite so seriously. So the church, in America particularly, went through a period of rigorous self-examination. It began to pay more attention to social problems. It began to study the aspirations and the needs of labor. It began to ponder on such all important issues as poverty and unemployment, and war. And it began, I am glad to say, to look with some suspicion upon the pronouncements of successful business men.

If these men suddenly turn around, then, and proclaim that business is service, religious leaders have every right to ask for proof. You have a right to ask what our game is, and how the church may have more confidence in business today than in business of, say, thirty years ago.

The answer is simple. Successful, opposition-conquering business today is not governed by anyone's opinion, but by facts ascertained by research often costing millions of dollars annually for a single corporation. The facts discovered may upset all the pet notions of the chief executives. They may compel the doing of things which they had least intended. The facts may necessitate their taking positions against which all their training and all the habitual motivations of their temperaments rebel. But temperament, habit, training, do not count when they are outweighed by the facts upon which real business profits depend.

Men who are succeeding through research may be just as weak and selfish mortals as the old-time business man who succeeded because his opinion happened to hit the mark a little closer than the opinions of his competitors. But these fact-finders will not be such dangerous friends; for they will carry the practice of research into their church activities, and they will be governed not by what they want to find out but by what they *do* discover.

To me, that is the great inspiration of this age of science and this much maligned machine civilization. In former times, we had to think of progress in terms of war—particularly the war between good and evil and good opinions and bad. Society was in a terrible mess. History does not record a time when society was not in a terrible mess; but the only way we could make it decent, it seemed, was to change human nature. People governed badly, we reasoned, because they were bad people. They engaged in war because they were so full of hate, and they got the best of each other at every opportunity because they were so utterly selfish and depraved. If we could only *change* human nature, if we could only tame it, if we could only turn it into a nice, mild, gentle, sweet little thing, then we might have a society which was fit to live in; but while human nature was so sinful, how in the world could there be decent human society?

Jesus said, and I think He was right, "Ye must be born again." But pardon me if I suspect that all His followers have not uniformly grasped His full meaning. I do not mean to discuss theology; I simply wish to call attention to the fact that human society is being born again. It is taking on a completely new character; but it is doing this not by the process of abolishing human nature and superimposing a sweet little ideal in its place, but by the process of seeking the truth—the process of fact-finding. We are discovering at last, by scientific research, that we are members one of another, and that these members must work in harmony if they are to attain adequate self-expression.

I have never been a Socialist, but there were times in my life when I earnestly wanted to be. Socialism was a beautiful ideal. It was ever so much more attractive than capitalism as we saw it; not merely more attractive than capitalism as the Socialists pictured it, but more attractive than capitalism as the capitalists pictured it. A society in which people would be working for each other, instead of competing with each other and fighting each other and forever trying to elbow each other out of the way—who would not prefer such a society? But human nature was what it was. And human nature is what it is. Marxian socialism did not seem to take that fact into reckoning, any more than did those who sought to establish the Kingdom of Heaven on earth by the process of making selfish folks unselfish. Even when people who had seemingly been bad suddenly became good, it did not seem to help conditions much. Good nations apparently had as many wars as bad nations, and their wars were quite as frightful. Good employers, also, had terrible conditions in their factories, and good, kind workingmen were quite as likely as brutes and bullies to find themselves unemployed.

When business got down to fact-finding, however, a new light dawned. Human relations, as ideal as the Socialists ever dreamed of, have now become a practical possibility, and with no interference whatever with the laws governing human nature.

When business was supposed to be a game of grab, there could be no social order and no all-around human love. There could be religion. There could be a desire for better things, and there could be a wish on the part of many to express themselves in loving service. But this service, for the most part, had to be exclusive. With a world full of suffering calling for relief, even the best-intentioned philanthropist had to decide whom he would relieve and whom he would neglect. Charity, it was everywhere recognized, began at home. One had to think of his immediate neighbors first. One had to think of his own; and by that token, he had to look upon the masses of mankind as not his own.

But note some of the things which happened when fact-finding began to supplant tradition in business affairs. They seemed cruel things, many of them. An employer, for instance, if he was a good employer, traditionally made it a point to give good positions to those toward whom he felt the most goodwill. Possibly his own relatives. Certainly the children of his friends and neighbors and those who were brought up in the same community. If he had foreigners working for him, it was because he could get them cheap. Their desire for better positions, even their determination to fit themselves for such positions, meant nothing to him. He had to look out for his people and let the aliens get along as best they could.

Enter the cool, hardheaded, scientific manager. In order to make the business pay, he does away with all this favoritism. Black and white, native and alien, mean nothing to him. He gives jobs to those who demonstrate that they can handle them. In other words, he establishes justice. Incidentally, he destroys provincialism and race distinctions and other illiberal notions which make human progress so difficult. But he does it, not because he himself is a great humanist, not even because he particularly intends to do it, but because he is a fact-finder trying to make the business pay.

But business did not stop with such fact-finding. It discovered in the end, or perhaps I should say it is just now discovering, that some of the very fundamentals of the business creed were fundamentally so much bunk. Business research, which led to mass production, did not alter a single principle of human nature, any more than electrical research has changed the laws of electricity: but the principle of human selfishness has been released, just as the principle of electric power has been released, for constructive, helpful, socializing service.

Business demands a profit from this service, and some of you may think that this is the great moral issue involved. You may have noticed some of the recent merger operations, and seen men drawing down millions upon millions of dollars simply for organizing the deal; and you may have said, while admitting that business is entitled to a profit, that business leaders are getting much higher profits than they should.

It happens, however, that there is no need for arguing this matter. It happens to be a problem which cannot be solved by debate. I do not know of any way by which a fair profit can be ascertained; and if one were ascertained, I cannot see that it would do the slightest bit of good. Providing these selfish men should become so unselfish as to be willing to accept a small fee in place of their million dollar splits, that, in itself, would not cure the evil which is involved. Nor would the placing of a limitation on the profits of the business organized. Such a limitation would not compel the organization to give more service than it is giving now, while a clear understanding of the principles of mass production would. The trouble is not that they are charging too much for their services, but that they are not serving the masses to the extent which they might.

There are mergers and mergers. Many of them are put over by bankers who have no conception of mass production at all. All they can see is that a dozen or a score of factories or stores cannot do business as economically as a single corporation might if all these factories were merged in one. They do not think of lowering prices; they think first of selling securities, and the exorbitant fees which they charge for transferring these securities to an optimistic public are not profits at all. Such financing interferes with profits. It handicaps the organization so that it cannot give maximum service, and thus keeps it from securing the greatest profits legitimately obtainable.

A merger which organizes strictly on the fact-finding principle will not become the victim of such financial shortsightedness, but will pay first attention to bringing prices down. The leaders who insist on this may be quite as selfish as the others, but they will have a better understanding of how the largest permanent profits can be made. They will know, for it has been amply proven, that the greatest total profit comes from giving the greatest possible service at the lowest possible cost to the people served. But this means that they must serve the masses, not only in the way to which they have become accustomed, but by giving more people better service every day.

If mergers are effected according to the old tradition, they cannot meet with permanent success; for they are bound to be undersold by mergers established on the facts. The facts do away with the issue of selfishness or unselfishness; for the facts compel selfish people to act unselfishly. The trouble with Wall Street is not greed. The trouble with Wall Street is ignorance. If the cause for our present ills lay in the depraved nature of man, I am at a loss to know what could be done about it. But ignorance is not a permanently incurable human trait. Even Wall Street is learning. It has started on the fact-finding course, and it cannot turn back. When Wall Street knows the truth, even Wall Street will be freed to think of service first.

When we are producing for the rich, we do not have to worry much about price. We may be honest and industrious, but it will not be absolutely necessary for us to give better values every day. But when we are producing for the masses—when the very first thing that we do is to set a price which the great masses can pay—we will have to move Heaven and earth to find a way to make profits at that price. In other words, instead of thinking of business in terms of an easy graft, we will find ourselves serving everybody with all our heart and with all our mind and with all our strength. Incidentally, we will find this service so successful, not merely in money but in the liberation of our creative powers, that we will love it. It is not an exaggeration to say that the world, guided by these new economic truths, is on the way toward all-around loving service.

There is nothing wrong with God, nor with His Eternal Law, not even with the laws governing human nature. If the world is suffering, it is because it does not know those laws. It is our business as human beings to find those laws and to conform to them, no matter how shocking to our existing notions each discovery may be, nor how each attempt to conform to the newly discovered law may result in our being stigmatized as Non-Conformists.

The law of business, when we understand it, will abolish war. War is the result of the assumption that the dominant interests of different nations are basically in conflict; and that it is advantageous, somehow, for one nation to get ahead at the expense of another. Mass production and distribution is teaching us the fallacy of this assumption. It is teaching us the business necessity of having prosperous neighbors; and that no nation can enjoy maximum prosperity unless all nations are prosperous. For unless people everywhere are able to buy our goods, we must slow down production and thus cheat ourselves of the supreme advantages which maximum production brings.

Class struggles will also end, for exploitation will end. Employers will take the initiative in raising wages. Men may be contented to work for a little but employers with real business vision cannot be contented to have them getting little; for, if they get low wages, they cannot buy as much as the selfish employers, dependent upon keeping up mass production, are under the necessity of selling them.

Perhaps the most inspiring ideal that has ever been held up to human life, is contained in the statement that we are all one family and all children of one Father. But this is more than an ideal today. It is becoming a reality. When it was only an ideal, we did not act upon it, for it seemed impractical to do so. But now that which seemed to be an impossible ideal is being revealed, by the hard, rigorous, fact-finding methods of modern science, to be unalterable law and undeniable, realistic, and ultra-practical fact. Those who follow fact-finding in business, then, and find it an unvaryingly dependable process, will necessarily discard their mere traditional notions and seek to learn the Eternal Will back of this unalterable law. They will necessarily become more theistic, not with a cold, merely intellectual conception of a ruling principle, but with a passionate appreciation of the Almighty Power which is working through men, to bring them into helpful and harmonious relations. They may conclude in the end, to be sure, that some of the theology and most of the sectarianism of the churches are not the result of fact-finding at all, but only the expression of traditional opinion. I am not promising, then, their support of the church. That support will depend altogether upon the church—upon whether it will cling to its traditions at any cost, or pursue the course of fact-finding which has proved so invariably satisfying, not merely to their material but to their spiritual cravings.

Religion and business, it seems to me, have not only become closely related; they are but different aspects of the same human aspiration for a more abundant life. The church, I contend, needs the fact-finding which business can bring to it, and business needs above everything the spirit of religious service.

Are we discouraged? Do we ever feel that religion has ceased to be a force in human affairs? Do we lack inspiration? Are we hungry for an opportunity to do significant things in the redemption and the glorification of human life? All I can say is to repeat the message signaled to the crew of a helpless, drifting ship, who were dying of thirst as the old hulk was tossed upon the waves. A passing boat had caught their signals and was standing by. The desperate sailors, however, could not wait for rescue. They were dying of thirst, they signaled. Nothing mattered to them except water.

"Dip up the water from the ocean," the rescuing captain signaled back. In desperation, the sailors did so and found to their amazement that the water was free from salt. But it was no miracle. The captain knew where he was, although the men on the drifting wreck did not. Although out of sight of land, they were at the mouth of the Amazon, whose mighty waters were being hurled so far out into the sea, that they had pushed the salt water out of the way.

There are oceans of opportunity all about us. There are infinite inspirations, if we refuse to think traditionally, and pull out into the center of this mighty stream of truth, which we have been calling the machine civilization. But we must become fact-finders —spiritual fact-finders. The most holy traditions of human history—even the traditions of the family—will not avail us now. We must get down to business. We must find out—we cannot evade the duty—just what makes these wheels go round. And we will find, I know, that they are running by the laws of God. We will find that the machine is holy, and that a full appreciation of its character will lead to holy living and not merely one day out of seven, as we used to think of it when business and religion were supposed to be operating on diametrically opposite sets of law, but seven enlightened days a week.

Do We Need a Leader? *

FRIENDS OF THE RADIO AUDIENCE:

I do not want to make anybody angry, but I am afraid I will.

I am afraid especially that I shall offend Republicans and Democrats. I am afraid I shall offend Republicans because I am not going to denounce the Administration; and I am afraid I shall offend the Democrats because I am not going to denounce the Republican party.

If I were to indulge in angry denunciations, both sides would take it as a matter of course. When people get angry at you, you know, they rather expect you to get angry at them; and if you don't get angry when they do, they may take it as an insult.

To keep the peace, then, may I ask a favor?

If any of my hearers are so angry at President Roosevelt that they cannot think calmly about how they are affected by the issues of this campaign, won't they please tune out now?

And if any of my hearers have made up their minds that the Republicans are all conspirators determined to defend plutocracy against the interests of the common people, won't *they* tune out?

For I am just a business man, and I am not consciously going to talk party politics. I am not a candidate and never was a candidate for any public office. Furthermore, I never expect to be a candidate; and I have never asked and never will ask for any political favors.

As a business man, however, I can't help seeing that it will make a vast difference to all of us how this campaign turns out.

For the Roosevelt Administration has led our country into new

---

* Campaign talk delivered over a nation-wide hookup of the Columbia Broadcasting System from Station WABC, New York, N. Y.—October 2, 1936.

and strange ways; and President Roosevelt has made it plain that he has no intention of turning back.

The Roosevelt Administration is committed to going forward —and forward in a direction which is disturbing, even maddening, to a great number of our erstwhile business leaders.

And the Republican party—there can be no doubt about it—is committed to stopping Roosevelt.

Further than that, it seems impossible at the present time to figure out what a Republican Administration would do.

I do not mean this as any criticism of Governor Landon. In the very nature of his nomination, however, he cannot tell us what a Republican Administration would do.

He may tell us, before the campaign is over, what he would like to have the Administration do. But Governor Landon, it must be conceded, was not nominated with any idea that he should lead the party. He was nominated, in fact, with the understanding that he wouldn't.

He was put up as a "contrast to Roosevelt." William Allen White, his close friend and supporter—and a man whom Americans generally know and respect—warned us at the very start not to expect great leadership from Landon.

One of the issues in this campaign, then, is clear. Is this a time when America needs great leadership? For whatever else has been charged against Roosevelt, none of his enemies has so far accused him of not being a great leader. They even accuse him of being a dictator in a land where free speech, a free press and complete freedom to criticise and denounce his Administration exist as strongly as ever; and one would surely have to possess superhuman power to make himself a dictator in such a land.

Personally, I cannot see that he is a dictator; for important measures have been enacted over his veto and that could scarcely happen under a dictatorship. It remains true, however, that he has induced his party, as well as many leaders of the opposition, to support legislation of a kind which was never considered practical in America before: legislation to insure higher wages to workers, decent incomes to farmers, the abolition of child labor and relief of the unemployed.

The necessary cost of these necessary things especially aroused the wrath of Mr. William Randolph Hearst, who was the first big business man to declare that Governor Landon of Kansas would be an ideal president.

Not that I would blame Governor Landon for Hearst's support. It was not a case, however, of Hearst endorsing the Republican candidate, but of the Republicans nominating the Hearst candidate whose very name was unknown to them until Hearst began to build him up; and the special interests in Big Business are now generally behind Landon.

Well, I am a business man. Some people even call me a big business man. I hardly like that, but I do want to see our government run in a true businesslike way.

But *is* the way favored by Big Business the business way? And if the Roosevelt way is so bad for business, how did business ever recover under it?

Very few Big Business men, I can't help noticing, have ever made much of a study of business in general. Each is more likely to concentrate on studying his own business, and most of them rather like to be dictators in their own businesses.

If one thinks it necessary to retrench, and to lay off a thousand employees, he doesn't want to ask the employees what they think about it. And he doesn't think it is any of the government's business either.

Up until the Roosevelt Administration, it seems, it wasn't considered *anybody's* responsibility to employ the unemployed. Everybody, of course, wished they might be employed; but in hard times, it was understood, they wouldn't be.

But when a business did lay off a thousand men, those men had to retrench. They had to quit buying things for their families.

And when these unemployed quit buying things, just what was it that they quit buying?

They quit buying the products of American farms and American industries, of course. Business and farms therefore had a thousand fewer customers; and the industries which had been producing the things which this thousand had been buying had to lay off employees, who then became nonbuyers, causing still less business, still harder times for farmers and industries and a further increase in unemployment.

No business by itself, however, could employ more people than the state of the market warranted. Only if all businesses were to act together to restore that market, could enough people be kept employed; and only if those who were employed received adequately high wages, could they buy enough to keep our industries running at capacity and therefore to *keep* themselves employed.

But men who were thinking only of their individual businesses could not be expected to see this. The only persons who would be likely to see it were those who had to think of the state of the country as a whole.

President Roosevelt was not the first to see it. President Hoover saw it and explained it all to our Big Business leaders. Then he had them promise him that they would keep wages up and employ as many employees as they could. Whereupon they went home and cut wages and laid off more employees; and the depression became worse and worse.

They didn't do this because they wanted to. We business men hate to do things like that. It was because they had to—or thought at least that they had to—for *everybody* did not stand by his agreement; and unless everybody did stand by it, it seemed that nobody could.

The main difference between President Hoover and President Roosevelt in this respect was that Hoover relied upon voluntary agreements which, under the circumstances, could not be kept, whereas Roosevelt tried to find a way to make such voluntary agreements binding.

And that would be the real issue of this campaign, if Hoover had been nominated instead of Landon.

But Hoover could not be nominated in the Republican Convention and was merely cheered instead. Everybody, in fact, who had anything to say against Roosevelt, was cheered. The claim that he was an inflationist was cheered; and Borah, who opposed him because he *wasn't* an inflationist, was cheered.

When I read the Republican platform, I was reminded of a

sign in a Chinese railway station: "Leave your baggage here and we will send it in all directions."

But that is because I am a business man; and any business man can't help seeing that the Republican party platform is not a program but a collection of mutually contradictory programs; and to stand on it, Governor Landon *has* to promise to lead us in all directions.

He has to promise to reduce expenditures without reducing any particular expenditure. He has to promise to increase our trade with foreign nations, while pledging himself not to permit those foreign nations to trade with us. He has to attack the Roosevelt Administration for not completely abolishing unemployment between 1933 and 1936, but cannot breathe one word of criticism of the administration which was in power from 1930 to 1933—as if Americans could ever forget *those* three long years of steadily increasing unemployment, resulting at last in the staggering total of 15,000,000 unemployed, which caused the people to demand a New Deal.

It isn't fair to criticize Landon too harshly for this. He is doing the best he can—in an impossible situation. To get votes from farmers and wage earners, he must promise to carry out the Roosevelt policies—only to do the job perfectly instead of in the imperfect way in which, he claims, Roosevelt has done it; and then, to get campaign funds and the support of Big Business, he must make them feel that he will put an end to all this new way of doing things.

On one point, however, the platform and the candidate are clear. They are out to stop Roosevelt; and if one does not care what happens to the country if Roosevelt is only stopped, he may consistently vote for Landon.

We haven't even a choice now between the New Deal and the Old Deal. Our choice now is between the New Deal and No Deal—between leadership and no real leadership.

The Republican platform begins with the cry that the nation is in peril. I think it is. But is a time of peril a time to turn to someone who under the circumstances cannot be a leader, and who was nominated as a contrast to a proven leader? Not as a politician, but as a business man, I am compelled to answer: No.

The coming of poverty in the midst of plenty was conclusive proof that American business could not continue longer on its customary course. There had to be a New Deal. But a great nation cannot change its course without confusion and misunderstanding; and I grant that we have had plenty of both. Under great leadership, however, we are passing the crisis; and I as a business man am forced to believe that four more years of Roosevelt will not only bring us to unprecedented prosperity, but will see business, industry and finance uniting with agriculture and labor on an all-American plan to maintain lasting prosperity for all.

But this, surely, is not a party issue. It is an American issue. It is a human issue. It is an issue which appeals to Republicans as well as Democrats. Personally, I am glad to see Democrats who want to return to the Old Deal walking out on Roosevelt, and to see Republicans who think that their party should stand for something definite, refusing to join this campaign of mere obstruction which does not promise the New Deal and dares not promise the Old Deal.

Epoch-Marking Changes in Business Today *

MR. CHAIRMAN, FRIENDS AND FELLOW STUDENTS:

When I address you as "fellow students," I am bidding for a real honor. That is, I want you to think of me as a student of business, not as an authority on business. Students must be alive. Generally accepted authorities are likely to be dead.

There can be no authority on this new epoch, because it is such a completely new epoch. I thought at first that I might talk to you about up-to-date business technique. But there isn't any up-to-date business technique. That's something we've all got to learn. I might speak about little merchandising devices which I have found very helpful; but in view of the basic changes which are occurring in the whole world of business, I could not help concluding that any such talk would be a waste of my time and yours. I am a practical business man. I make no claim to being a philosopher, and I don't want to be taken for a philosopher. But when events of revolutionary significance occur, the most practical thing that the most practical man can do is to consider the meaning of those events.

I do not mean to speak slightingly of authorities. We could scarcely get along, for instance, without an authoritative dictionary. If it suddenly became necessary, however, to speak in Chinese instead of English, an English dictionary would not help us very much; and it *is* necessary, just now, for business to learn a new language—the language of plenty—whereas our authorities seem to be authorities only in the language of scarcity.

I do not claim to have mastered this language of plenty. Nobody has. The best we can do, in view of the revolutionary

* Address before the College of Commerce and Business Administration of Tulane University, New Orleans, Louisiana—June 11, 1935.

changes which are now in progress, is to put new meanings into our old words, and try as best we can to make ourselves understood. The very word "business," however, in this Machine Age of Plenty, must mean something very different from what it has always meant. The words profit and loss must now have a different connotation. The words employer and employee cannot retain their customary meaning; while such words as thrift, credit, security, if they are to be of real use to us, must suggest to our minds the new thrift, the new credit and the new security.

Is it any wonder, when we consider the circumstances, that so many business conferences nowadays consist of about one-tenth discussion and nine-tenths headache? I don't like the recent rampage of reaction on the part of the United States Chamber of Commerce any more than you do—any more than many of its own delegates did; but give these mentally upset business men a little more time. It's a pretty serious matter—this spending all one's life in learning what we learn, and then having to unlearn it in our declining years. Difficult or not, however, we must face the facts of this new epoch—this epoch in which, for the first time in human history, we have discovered how to produce so abundantly that business cannot prosper unless the masses live abundantly.

Recently a newspaper attacked me caustically for calling this a new epoch. The writer said it couldn't be a new epoch because the Bible says that there is nothing new under the sun; and a correspondent reminded him that the Bible also says that "Old things are passed away and all things are become new."

Well, I happen to believe both statements. I do not think we can thoroughly study anything without reaching the conclusion that there are eternal principles, unaltered and unalterable; but there is no eternal principle more definitely established than the principle of constant change.

There never was a normal year which could be effectively used as a pattern for other years, hence every effort to get back to normalcy must necessarily fail. There are just Old Years and New Years; and if we do not ring out the old and ring in the new, we may be quite certain that events will ring us out. If times are good in one year and bad in another, it is not likely to be because we acted differently in one year than we did in the other. It is more likely to be because we did not see the necessity for acting differently and keeping up with the changing times.

If we would only study change, instead of studying some transient aspect of it, change would not dismay us as it does. But not many of us have learned that art. Not many of our schools, it seems to me, have yet got around to teaching it. But if we had studied business in terms of the changes which business was bringing about, we would have been prepared for what has now occurred, and the Age of Plenty might have been ushered in with unprecedented prosperity instead of with depression.

Astronomers can date coming eclipses to the very minute because they are not content to study the location of the stars and planets, but insist on finding out where they are going and at what rate of speed. When we business men studied business, however, we did not think to find out where business was going, and when, in the very nature of business events, it would be likely to arrive.

For the past fifty years American industrial genius has attracted world attention by astonishing feats of production. Our whole thought was on output. New machinery and new methods doubled, tripled, quadrupled production—and not merely production in the aggregate but production per hour and per man employed. Had we reflected on that development, we must have concluded that it would one day produce plenty; and that, in an Age of Plenty, the very logic of the Age of Scarcity would become useless. But we did not reflect. Plenty, we figured, would just bring us more of what we were enjoying. We would simply go on, it was supposed, doubling, tripling and quadrupling production; and whereas we had once counted our profits in thousands and were now counting them in millions, we would one day count them in billions—all reinvested, presumably, in expanding the machinery of production and increasing the output.

This attitude, while hardly scientific, was understandable; for business men were too busy increasing output to speculate on what would happen when the whole world became organized to produce and sell without becoming organized to buy and to consume.

Production itself, it seemed, provided a market for production. We might not be able at all times, of course, to sell all the shoes that we were manufacturing; but that was not a problem to stump the American business man. Instead of continuing to manufacture shoes, he could go into the business of manufacturing shoe factories. The whole world, it seemed, wanted factories of every kind; for factory production had proven profitable and, while the common people of the world might be largely starving, there was no end of capital available for investment in profit-making enterprises.

The Age of Plenty did not come without warning. As far back as the McKinley Administration, if you remember, Americans noticed that other nations had so much machinery that they could not sell the output profitably unless they could build up foreign trade; and there were so many nations in need of this foreign market that it seemed wise to have a big navy as a convenience in dealing with backward nations and preventing nations which were not so backward from hogging the market for themselves. It seemed wise, also, we noted, to have colonies, where machine industry had not yet been established; then to sell our machinery to those who had capital to invest in the development of those colonies. So America got into the game too. We took Cuba, Porto Rico and the Philippines. We called it "manifest destiny."

Then one backward nation after another—conspicuously Japan—bought so much machinery that they were no longer backward, but red-hot competitors in the struggle for foreign markets, whereas smaller and smaller areas remained to be developed. There were just two possible answers to such a problem as that. We could either raise the standard of living of the masses throughout the world, enabling them to buy and consume in accordance with the world's new capacity to produce, or we could engage in a War of the Nations to see which of the competing powers could, for a time, gain commercial supremacy.

A world war, to be sure, could solve none of the problems involved; for the conquering nations now could achieve their commercial ends only if they developed all the areas they could, including the countries which they had conquered; and that, in a very short time, would leave the situation as bad as it was before. But the world did not reflect on this. Our schools and colleges did not analyze the situation. Business men were too busy to give it a thought; and a young man of those days, if he entered a school of business, with the intention of preparing himself for a business career, was not given a hint as to the greatest problem with which business would surely have to deal. Business, we all supposed, consisted of the manufacture and distribution of things for profit, and had nothing to do with the world crisis which would surely come when that process had evolved to the 1914 stage.

So the world went to war, with little or no idea of what was pushing it. The masses, of course, did not fight for markets. The business men themselves did not do that. They fought, as a rule, for their nation's honor. They fought in defense of their liberties. And they went to war to end war or to make the world safe for democracy. I am not blaming them. I am not even a pacifist. It remains true, however, that the nations fought because they hadn't given sufficient thought to their real problems. It was a war brought on by business evolution, in a world which had become full of business but was minus any basic business education.

As a matter of fact, war does not belong to this Age of Plenty at all; and when we go to war, in these modern times, we do strange things. In the old days, when one nation made war upon another, it was usually for the purpose of carrying away the other nation's goods. Now each nation wants the other nations to keep their own goods, instead of sending them across her boundaries.

In the old days, the conquerors enslaved the conquered and made them do the work which the conquerors wanted done. That was cruel but understandable. The conquered people had to raise food for the conquering people to eat. They had to make clothes for the conquerors to wear. They had to build houses for the shelter of the conquerors. In other words, the first thing the conquerors thought of was to furnish employment for all the people whom they had conquered. As we approached the Age of Plenty, however, those tactics simply wouldn't work. The conquering nation of today, therefore, aims to keep its own masses working—making shoes and clothes and everything for the conquered people to consume. Of course, the conquered people, because they are not allowed to work freely, cannot actually buy many of these things, and therefore cannot furnish much employment to their conquerors. But that's the theory—not exactly fundamental thinking, but nevertheless an effort to solve the problem of what to do when modern industry made it possible to produce so much.

Nations in the Age of Scarcity reckoned their profits by the excess of their imports over their exports. In this Age of Plenty, because we have not yet learned how to distribute plenty, nations reckon their profits by the volume of their exports in excess of their imports. Their notion of ideal trade relations is to get rid of all the wealth they possibly can and take back nothing but money which, as everybody knows, is not wealth.

We all understand what is wrong with an individual who tries to hang on to all the money he takes in and never pays out more than is absolutely necessary. We call him a miser; and if he takes in a lot of money, we contemptuously call him a rich miser. Actually, of course, there are no rich misers. They are all poverty-stricken because, since they pay out no money, they take in no wealth. If they have a great deal of money, however, they suffer their poverty in the midst of plenty.

I have known chambers of commerce to indulge in campaigns to patronize home industries and "keep the money in town." If such a campaign were to succeed, of course, no one in town could possess a thing which the people of that town were unable to produce. Keeping the money in town is just a way of keeping the wealth out. Fortunately, we can't do it; but we can hurt business considerably by trying.

Hanging on to our money and getting rid of our wealth was

not, to be sure, the logic of the Age of Scarcity. Our present troubles have come, rather, from an effort to apply the logic of the Age of Scarcity to the conditions of the Age of Plenty. As machine industry developed, and trade became the universal way of life, it became difficult for us to see *exactly what was traded* when any particular sale was made. It was easy, however, for us to see that we received money for the things sold, and it was easy to jump at the conclusion that that constituted the exchange. Of course it did not. Every real exchange is an exchange of real values, not the exchange of real wealth for a mere medium of exchange. The money taken in must be used before we can know just what exchange has been effected.

Business, however, settled down to the job of taking in as much money as possible and paying out as little as possible. Fortunately, however, business couldn't keep the money it took in, any more than a single town can keep its money at home. Business had to buy materials and goods. It had to pay wages; and wherever great amounts of money were accumulated, they had to be invested somewhere; but so ignorant were we of what we were really doing that we thought of each investment merely as a scheme by which business could accumulate more money.

Actually, then, whatever business men were thinking about it, business generally paid out its money almost as rapidly as it took it in. If it had not done this, there could have been no prosperity; for business is trade, and if the medium by which trade is effected were ever hoarded, trade would certainly be strangled. Since it wasn't kept, however, but invested largely in the building of more and better industrial enterprises, the masses were generally employed for wages and kept getting back the money which they had previously paid out for goods.

From decade to decade, in fact, they seemed to be getting back more than they had previously paid out; and in America, at least, they were so pleased with the system that there was never any thought of revolt; and although there were frequent setbacks, business generally registered great progress.

But we business men did not know what we were doing. If we had known, we would have arranged definitely to pay out money *in the ways which were most needed for the facilitation of trade;* and we would have known that we could not go on forever building up machinery to multiply production without making some arrangement for multiplied consumption.

When I speak of this new epoch, then, I do not mean that one basic principle has been abolished or one natural law repealed. The same law which once caused man to capture and harness animals, so that he might use their power, eventually caused him to capture and harness other natural forces. There was nothing new, therefore, in his harnessing power; nevertheless, an automobile is not an ox team and cannot be driven as if it were.

And this age which is capable of producing and distributing plenty cannot be operated as if it were still an age of scarcity.

We need not ask for the slightest deviation, then, from any basic business principle. All that is necessary is that we apply basic business principles to the new conditions with which we must now deal; and one of the basic principles of business is that the purpose of money is to facilitate exchange.

Money cannot serve this purpose if it is kept in anyone's possession; for exchange is axiomatically a two-way process. I claim to be a fair-to-middling business man; but I was never yet able to sell any goods to myself. If I sell anything, someone else must buy it. If we business men are to sell much, our customers must buy much; and there is no way by which we can sell the output of modern mass production unless the masses can and will buy it. If the masses haven't sufficient buying power, then, business sense demands that we use our money to enable the masses to buy abundantly.

We hear it said often that we can't spend our way to prosperity, as if the very idea were utterly new and fantastic. But how did we achieve the prosperity of 1926, say, as contrasted with the relative poverty of 1906 or of 1886?

Did we do it by *keeping* the money which we took in? Positively not. We did it by investing that money where it needed to be invested, if we were ever to do business in a bigger and still more profitable way.

When the Age of Scarcity was still with us, the best business investment was an investment in something which would help relieve that scarcity. In the Age of Plenty, for identically the same reasons, the best business investment is an investment in something which will help to distribute this plenty.

I have been forced by every study which I have been able to make to conclude that the best and safest investment for business at this particular time is the payment of the highest wages which can profitably be paid; for wages constitute the buying power of the largest element of our population. Merely distributing money broadcast, I am afraid, would hardly serve our purposes; but if we make wages as high as they can profitably be made, by the most scientific planning, we may be sure that those who get the wages will not only increase their buying, thus increasing our sales and increasing employment (which in turn will cause still more buying and still more employment) but that, by being efficiently employed, they will constantly be producing more wealth than they consume.

No individual employer, however, can do much toward raising wages unless he can be certain that his competitors will do as much. We must have codes, then, and codes which can be enforced, so that wages will surely be removed from competition; and business must find a way to set up and enforce such codes, regardless of the confusion of its present leaders, regardless of what Congress does and regardless of what the Supreme Court says. This implies no criticism of the Supreme Court; but if business codes are now unconstitutional, the Constitution must be amended in accordance with the facts of this Age of Plenty, or it will be mathematically impossible to achieve any lasting recovery.

We must not only have interstate but intrastate codes, and not only industrial codes but interindustrial codes. The automobile industry, for instance, cannot be permanently prosperous unless coal miners and textile workers are able to buy cars; and if the coal and textile industries do not know how to raise wages to the necessary levels, it becomes the task of all industries and all finance, in their own selfish interest, to co-operate with such industries and enable them to do so.

We know now, most of us, that business cannot be permanently prosperous unless agriculture is prosperous. But that wasn't always so, and it is time that we learned why. In the agrarian Age of Scarcity, business men could reap fortunes out of the desperate necessity of those with whom they trafficked. But this has become no longer possible, excepting as some grafters and chiselers may achieve momentary profits by undermining and weakening our whole business structure. It becomes necessary for business then, to organize to defend itself against such economic traitors; and to do that, we must learn the technique of co-operation, not only with all legitimate business but with every legitimate element of our population. It isn't President Roosevelt who is compelling us to do this. It isn't the Brain Trust. It is eternal, immutable economic law which has brought us to a period in which business success can be achieved only through scientific business service to the mass consumer and devoted co-operation for the common good.

I know that such words seem preposterous to those who still think in terms of scarcity, and in terms of the principles which were valid in the Age of Scarcity. But we cannot reject facts because they seem preposterous; and we cannot alter them by resolutions of the United States Chamber of Commerce. That the facts are astounding, I admit. I have no language to express how astounding they have appeared to me; for they compel us selfish human beings, in our own selfish interest, to dedicate all our energies to the good of all. This discovery that we, all through these centuries, have been instruments in the carrying out of a Plan which we could not comprehend, thrilled me, at least, with awe and reverence.

We can achieve wealth now only as we distribute it. We can save only as we spend. We can be secure now only as we arrange for everybody's security; and we can have liberty only as we liberate the masses everywhere from the age-old struggle for mere physical existence, and make it possible, for the first time in human history, for them to release their energies in the ways that are indicated by human aspiration.

It may not be expected of a practical business man that he

shall speak like this. But what can one do—what other course could possibly be practical—in the face of the epoch-marking changes which are now occurring? Let us once grasp the essential meaning of this Age of Plenty, and we need not mistrust our ability to develop a technique capable of dealing with it successfully. But let us, in our confusion, strike out for the wrong goal, and any improvement in mere technique will only get us there more quickly and hasten our disaster. This *is* a new epoch. To discover the new responsibilities of this new epoch, *and to act in accordance with those new responsibilities,* is the most practical and most important problem which confronts us now.

A Merchant Surveys the New Deal*

FRIENDS OF THE RADIO AUDIENCE:

This isn't the first time that America has had a New Deal; and this isn't the first time that it has become suddenly necessary to carry on our businesses in a very different way from that to which we had become accustomed. We did a certain amount of grumbling, to be sure, every time we were compelled to do it, just as many business men are grumbling about the New Deal today. *But we did it.*

In our factories, just at the moment when we thought we had everything running smoothly, we were likely to learn that someone had made a discovery—possibly some college professor who had no reputation whatever as a business man—which made it necessary for us to throw out the system which we had spent years in perfecting and organize the factory in an entirely different way.

This was likely to happen to any business. Just about the time, for instance, that the ice business got organized, and the public and the politicians got to growling about the Ice Trust, someone discovered how to reverse the process by which electricity produces heat, and put it to work in our kitchens making hot things cold.

When the iceman heard about that, do you remember what he did?

He cursed the Brain Trust, of course. Then as now, from a certain point of view, it was a rotten shame the way these professors were always upsetting our business plans.

But was the discovery bad for business? We all know that it was not. It simply meant a New Deal in Refrigeration and the

* Radio address over N.B.C. Network—June 22, 1934.

beginning of another great new industry—the industry of air conditioning. American business, for the past fifty years, has thrived upon exactly such new deals.

To listen to some of the speeches which we hear today, it might be supposed that Americans generally are such habit bound reactionaries that any departure from their ancient customs is repugnant to them. American history proves the exact opposite. It may almost be said that the most characteristic habit of the American people is their habit of breaking their habits. I'm in the apparel business and I know. We can't even sell clothes that are out of style.

It is the American willingness to accept new deals, if they give sufficient promise of a more abundant life, which accounts for about all the business for which America has become famous.

The other day I talked with a business man who raved almost violently against the New Deal, not because it wasn't doing what it set out to do, but because it was so different from any previous deal. He was an American, he said, and believed in the good old American way of doing things.

He was in the plumbing business, and the plumbing business is surely a business of which Americans should be proud. Every American who has travelled abroad will understand what I mean. Especially if he has travelled off the beaten paths, and has got away from the big tourist hotels, he has almost certainly missed the modern bathroom which plays such an important part in American life.

So I couldn't help smiling at this distressed champion of the good old way of doing things. It had never occurred to him that his business—the business of modern plumbing—had become great because Americans, with all their sentimental attachment to the past, do not cling regardless to the old way of doing things. It was because they preferred the new way to the grand old institution of the Saturday Night wash tub that my friend had any business to worry about.

We will, to be sure, do a certain amount of grumbling before we adopt the new. There will be opposition—the very kind of opposition which we are hearing today; but if the new way answers the American longing for a larger and more enjoyable life, we can be fairly sure that Americans will adopt it.

Speaking of bathtubs, they are so typical of this American longing for a higher standard of living that I do not wonder that we think of them as an American institution, and a *good* American institution, but they are not a good *old* American institution.

There are people now living who can remember when there wasn't a regular bathtub in all America. Let me read this clipping from Collier's, quoting from a medical journal; and I surely hope that my friend in the plumbing business is listening in:—

The first regular bathtub in this country was put in a Cincinnati home in 1842. It was made of mahogany, lined with sheet lead, and its excited owner gave a party to exhibit it.

Well, that's interesting, but can it be that there was any opposition to the bathtub? Let me read on.

The next day, Cincinnati papers denounced the new device as a luxurious and undemocratic vanity. *Medical men called it a menace to health.* When introduced into Virginia, the Old Dominion taxed each such tub $30 a year. *Boston made these bathtubs unlawful, and college authorities banned them from all dormitories.*

But all this opposition, it seems, did not banish the bathtub from America. It did not even seriously set back our New Deal in Sanitation.

A large percentage of my hearers, I know, can remember another great New Deal; for at the beginning of the present century, only thirty-four years ago, very few Americans had even seen a motorcar.

There was more vociferous opposition to the automobiles, when they first appeared, than there is to any agency of progress now. Millions of devotees of the good old horse and buggy declared that the motorcar would deprive them of their liberties; and the Clarence Darrows of that time said it would keep the little fellows off the highways altogether. The automobile came, however, and we had a New Deal in Transportation, because Americans generally, in spite of their misgivings, didn't see how they could get along without it.

Now we're having another New Deal; and Americans, especially American business men, are going to see this New Deal through, for identically the same reason.

It is because we Americans, and especially we American business men, in spite of all the grumbling which we may be doing now, are beginning to realize that we cannot get along without it.

I am quite aware, of course, that there is a vast difference between a New Deal brought about by the adoption of a mechanical invention and a New Deal brought about by a new governmental policy. But if it had not been for the first kind of new deal, the kind we are now talking about would not now be necessary.

It wasn't the mere *invention* of the bathtub which built up the American plumbing industry. It was the *sale* of bathtubs and their *use* by those who bought them. It wasn't the mere *invention* of the horseless carriage which built up our automobile industry; it was the fact that masses of our people *wanted to have and were made able to purchase automobiles*.

The same principle, of course, applies to every industry, whether it is engaged in producing the bare necessities of life or whether it is producing any one of multitudinous new things which have come to be associated with the American standard of living. Whatever an industry is producing, people must be able to buy the products or the industry cannot live.

If we continue to produce and distribute the bare necessities of life, however, the masses of people can live. It may not be much of a life, to be sure, but they can stay alive. They can live without automobiles. They can live without bathrooms. They can live without modern light and power, without modern refrigeration, without moving pictures and radio and a thousand other products of modern scientific discovery. But they can't live as Americans are determined to live without all these things; and unless they can get all these things, and more, American business must die.

American business has been very sick, and for this one reason alone. It was because the American masses could not buy these things in adequate quantities. No one can dispute that. And yet every effort toward recovery before Franklin D. Roosevelt was inaugurated, consisted of some plan by which the masses at the very best might be able to get along from hand to mouth—a condition under which they would never be able to buy enough to make business good and to keep themselves employed.

If the masses live according to the old standard of living, we cannot use the new methods of producing wealth. If the new methods are to be employed, then (and *business* cannot live unless they are employed) some way must be discovered by which the masses can get and use all the things which Americans have learned to want.

President Roosevelt has proposed a way. We need not argue right here whether it is the correct way or not; no one will dispute, at least, that he has proposed a way. And the Communists have proposed another way. I don't happen to believe in their way, and I do not think that many in this radio audience do. Nevertheless, we must admit that they have proposed a way.

But how about the present critics of the New Deal—those whose criticisms we have been hearing on every hand? Have they proposed a way by which the masses can get the products of our machines and get them in sufficient abundance to keep those machines and our people employed?

Nothing of the kind. They insist that no new way is necessary. They oppose the New Deal because it is new—because it is not in harmony with the deal which was dealt before we learned how to produce so much and when the masses had to live on the verge of starvation anyway. And then, after they get tired of condemning the New Deal because it is new, they turn around, like Mr. Ogden Mills, and condemn it because it *isn't* new.

Mr. Mills says this so-called New Deal was tried in Rome and failed, which merely proves that very intelligent people can let their partisanship run away with their common sense.

The New Deal could not have been tried in Rome, or in any civilization in which the people had not yet learned how to produce an abundance. The New Deal is not a new way of solving an old problem. It is a way of solving a problem with which no civilization was ever confronted before.

There was poverty almost everywhere in the days of the Roman Empire—poverty brought about by the fact that people generally were not acquainted with any method by which they could produce much more than was necessary to keep themselves alive. There is poverty in America too; but it is poverty due to the fact that we *did* become acquainted with a method by which we could produce not only the necessities of life for everybody but innumerable comforts and luxuries as well.

I hope that some historian, sometime, will be able to tell the real story of this, the greatest revolution which ever happened to human society. Not the industrial revolution which has been well described, for that consisted mostly of our learning to do by machinery the things which we had customarily done by hand before. But this second industrial revolution in which, because we had learned to do things by machinery, we became able to do so much that never could have been done before.

We who lived through that revolution could not grasp its meaning. We could not help seeing that times were changing, but we could not grasp the nature of the change; and we could not see, therefore, that such a change would one day make it necessary to inaugurate a complete New Deal.

The masses might be employed for the time being, not in making more things to be consumed, but in the making of more machinery and the building of more factories in which, eventually, we *would* manufacture more things to be consumed. But the process could not go on forever. There would surely come a time, although we did not realize it, when there would be no market for such a deluge of things unless the masses, whom we were advising to live frugally, began to live almost luxuriously instead.

But we made no arrangements for any such luxurious standard of living. We all thought it fine for a great automobile industry to employ millions of workers manufacturing automobiles, but we still felt that it was sinfully extravagant for the poor to buy automobiles, although, if only the rich bought them, the whole automobile industry would collapse.

Business, as a rule, felt no responsibility for getting increased buying power into the hands of the people. No business man, seemingly, had got *his* buying power through any such arrangement, and he couldn't see why working people should be entitled to the privilege. The business man had got his buying power at first, he figured, by living within his income, no matter how small his income was, and saving something for future investment. Then, like my friend the plumber, he had invested in business. But he failed to see that his business was profitable only if the masses had buying power, and only if they used that buying power to buy goods, instead of investing it as the business man had done.

There was a time, to be sure, only a few years ago, when it seemed that almost everybody in America suddenly began to follow these so-called business principles and, instead of buying goods, invested their incomes in various business enterprises. But it didn't help business any. It was the worst blow that American business ever had.

That was in 1928 and 1929. The masses, for some years before then, had been buying more and more goods; and so long as they continued to buy more and more goods, business men *sold* more and more, and practically all employers were able to keep the employees fully employed. There was so much employment at such good wages that business men thought we were having wonderful prosperity.

It was a rather spotty prosperity, for the farmers did not share it, and there were already a large number of unemployed. Nevertheless, more things were produced and sold than ever before and business generally was declaring dividends. The masses, then, encouraged by business and financial advisers, decided to get in on these marvellously good pickings. Instead of spending so much for goods, then, they began to invest in stocks; and because so many people bought stocks, stocks went up, and because stocks went up, more millions of people bought stocks: *and because they quit buying goods in order to buy stocks, less goods were sold and businesses were not so prosperous.*

We all remember what happened next. The more the masses invested in stocks, up went their price and down went their value. But that also could not go on forever; and the day came when the prices crashed; then there was relatively little money anywhere to invest in goods and American business went into a tail spin. With the market gone, industries shut down and millions became unemployed, which still further restricted the market and caused more and more unemployment.

By following the good old business formula of success, millions of Americans virtually saved themselves out of a job.

I do not mean that this was the only cause of the depression. I do not mean, even, that the Bull Market was the only cause—that marvellous market in which we gave up the practice of exchanging goods and tried to get rich by exchanging bull. We would eventually have collapsed, even without that Bull Market, unless we made some orderly arrangement to provide the masses with buying power. Not with a mere living wage. Not even with a sufficient income to keep them temporarily satisfied. The business necessity—if we hoped to continue modern methods of production—was to see that the masses should always have sufficient buying power to buy the ever increasing volume of necessities and comforts which these modern methods had enabled us to produce.

That was why we had to have a New Deal. It wasn't merely that a New Deal was desirable. We miss the point if we think we can choose between the kind of setup with which we had become familiar and a different kind of setup proposed by some Brain Trust charged with the responsibility of drawing up plans for a more ideal social order.

I know that there is a lot of this sort of discussion today. People are debating the pros and cons of the old system and the new system, as if we could choose the old if we decide that it suits us better, or adopt the new if that happens to appeal to us.

We might as well debate as to what age we would like to be. Shall we be sixteen or sixty? Concededly, much could be said on both sides of the argument, only it wouldn't make any difference which we decided to be. The only thing that we can discuss, to any point, is what we are going to do under the circumstances.

And the circumstances, in this particular situation, are that we have learned how to produce an abundance; and we must learn how to distribute that abundance or business will again be ruined.

Fortunately for us business men, the masses of Americans are not satisfied with their present plane of living. Fortunately for us, they would not be satisfied even with the degree of prosperity which they enjoyed when business was at its highest peak. Fortunately for us, their wants are almost limitless. They do not, to be sure, want infinitely more wheat or infinitely more coal or infinitely more of anything which anybody is producing now. But so far from our having reached any saturation point in production, we know that Americans generally would be glad to have ten times as much as they have ever found it possible to buy, if they are permitted the liberty to say just what those things shall be.

Our basic business problem, then, is to produce the things which the masses want, and to arrange to exchange them with the masses—that is, of course, if the masses have equivalent values to offer in exchange.

And that, fortunately, is exactly what the American masses have.

To be sure, they are short of money. But money isn't wealth. Money isn't a value: it is just a measure of value and a medium of exchange. Its purpose is to facilitate the exchange of real values; and all these masses—all these millions of unemployed—have some real values which they are eager to exchange for goods and services which they want to have.

They have their skill, their ability, their training in machine methods of production; and they are not only willing but anxious to put them at the service of those who need such services. They want wages, of course—and fortunately for us, they want high wages—but that merely means that they want to exchange the services they have to offer for something approximately of equal value. Even if they might like to, they know that they cannot give their services free. We business men, surely, cannot criticize them for that. We merchants, if we once understand the setup, should be very glad that they won't work for nothing, and we should do our best to dissuade them from working for low wages because, if they work for nothing or work for a mere living, they cannot buy the things which we must sell.

Oh, I know what the average employer will say to that. It's

all right in theory, he may say; but do I, as a practical business man, practice what I preach? Do I pay twenty dollars a day to employees whom I can get for five?

No, I don't. I can't. Few if any employers ever pay wages as high as they would like to pay.

Why? *Because some competitor would undersell us.*

And that brings us to the New Deal. The first immediate object of the N. R. A. is to rescue American business by removing wages from competition; and to permit employers to pay wages which *will* be adequate.

Wages are not yet high enough by any means to furnish the market which we business men must have. But we have made a start. We are on our way. We have taken the first great step to liberate business from the tyranny which has hitherto kept us from distributing adequate buying power.

Acting as individuals, we could not do it; but under the N. R. A. codes, we can. Under those codes, we can at last effect a real exchange between what the masses of American people have to give and what they want to get.

I am not talking in any partisan way. It happens that the depression came under a Republican Administration and the great liberation is coming under a Democratic Administration. But it would serve no useful purpose to dwell on that; for five years ago, Democrats and Republicans were equally in favor of high wages on general principles and equally powerless to pay them in specific instances.

About the first thing that President Hoover did when the crash came was to urge all American employers to act in concert to maintain the wage level, and hundreds of our great industrial leaders promised him publicly that they would make no reductions. Then they returned to work and ordered wage reductions.

Why? Was it because they were liars and cheats? *No!*

It was because they couldn't help it. And why couldn't they help it?

It was because somebody cut wages and the others had to follow suit.

And yet we hear otherwise intelligent people saying today

that the New Deal means regimentation. It doesn't. It means freedom. It means freedom from the domination of the chiseler, whose power was such that he could and did compel American employers generally to cut wages at a time when only a general raise in wages could save American business from prostration.

Nothing short of nation-wide co-ordination of American industry to remove wages from competition could achieve our emancipation from this tyranny. Yes, it is something new. It's awkward. Most of us haven't got the hang of it yet; and we are acting a good deal like the first automobilists who, when they found it necessary to make a quick stop, yelled "Whoa!", instead of pulling the right gadget, and then blamed the machine for what happened next.

Nevertheless, the New Deal is here. Of course, we *can* discard it, and go back to more years of poverty and general helplessness, but we cannot return to the times when the Old Deal would work.

We cannot return to the old road because we travelled that road as far as the road went, and came to a place where we had to take another road, or stop. There may be better roads somewhere, but that isn't the point, and it is a waste of time to argue about some ideal social order—either some past Arcady or some future Utopia. The point is that we have arrived at the Machine Age and we must obey the laws of the Machine Age or take the consequences. Our machines have become so productive that the masses must have an enormous increase of buying power or the machines will choke; and to provide them with such adequate buying power necessitates the nation-wide co-ordination of all our economic forces.

Not merely co-ordination of the various units within each industry, but co-ordination of industry with industry, co-ordination of industry with agriculture and co-ordination of capital, labor and scientific management in the interest of the mass consumer and of legitimate profits to business.

This does not mean that we shall abolish competition or individual initiative. It does not mean even that they must be curbed. But it does mean a New Deal in competition and a New Deal in individual initiative; for the only competition which will now work is competition in service, and the time has come when—if we hope to continue the system of private business—we must direct our individual initiative toward the common good.

There are alternatives; and we can, by blocking the New Deal now, create such widespread desperation as to drive our country into one of them. There is socialism, for instance, in which all industry and all other business would come under the direction of political bureaus, or communism with its complete uprooting of all that Americans generally have come to reverence. Or we might be driven into Fascism, with its rule of might, and its fanatical theory that the means are justified if they promise to achieve the end which the Chief Fanatic wants.

If anyone really prefers any of these alternatives, he may honestly and consistently attack the New Deal. But American business, I am sure, does not want any of these alternatives. American labor does not want them. American farmers do not want them and American women do not want them. Nevertheless, the New Deal is under fire. While it is under fire, there is uncertainty; and while there is such uncertainty, business recovery must lag. Now is the time, then, regardless of partisanship, to end all this uncertainty. Now is the time to make it plain, however hesitant some of the old-timers may be, that America is marching with Roosevelt into the new and better day. Regardless of partisanship, then, we can support the President. And we can make it so plain that we are supporting the President that politicians will no longer hamper him, and business will no longer suffer from uncertainty and will hasten to adjust itself to that certain fact.

Speaking not as a politician—for I am nothing of the kind—but only as a business man, I can think of nothing that would do more to speed up recovery than such definite action by the masses of voters throughout the United States.

The Constitution and Economic Change *

MR. CHAIRMAN, LADIES AND GENTLEMEN:

I want it understood at the outset that I have a very deep reverence for the Constitution of the United States. One of the reasons why I hold it in such reverence is that it is capable of becoming an even better document than it is.

If it were fixed and unalterable, I could not reverence it as I do.

And may I explain, in addition, that I am not always clear as to just what the Constitution means. In this, I can heartily sympathize with the Supreme Court; for five-ninths of me often interprets the Constitution to mean one thing, while four-ninths hangs out for an almost contrary interpretation.

But there are certain things about the Constitution upon which, it seems to me, we can all agree; and if we can agree on these things, we will almost inevitably disagree in our interpretations.

We can agree, for instance, that the Constitution was drawn up by human beings—with human weaknesses and human prejudices. Among all the delegates to the first constitutional convention, there was not a single angel or archangel. They were all men, and they did not see eye to eye.

We may have been taught to think of the Constitution as a great charter of our American liberties. The majority of those delegates, however, had no such idea. They were not concerned with drawing up a charter of liberty; and the only reason that they finally were persuaded to insert a bill of rights in the Consti-

* Address before the National Conference for Clarifying the Constitution by Amendment, held under the auspices of the Michigan Committee, Hotel Statler, Detroit, Michigan—February 1, 1937.

tution was that Jefferson and the Jeffersonians refused to support the document unless they did.

But I do not say this in criticism of those delegates; for while they may not have been thinking in terms of setting up an ideal democratic government, they were thinking of things which idealistic citizens are too likely to forget, and they were things which had to be considered if democratic government were not to become powerless.

Largely, the delegates were business men, and they were thinking of a sound currency and national credit. If the young nation had been able to achieve these things under the articles of confederation, no constitutional convention would have been called. It was the state of business, not any passion for an ideal republic, which made the Constitution necessary.

Now for just one more observation as to the character and personnel of that constitutional convention. We hear it commonly stated, and there is surely truth in the statement, that the great majority of the delegates were concerned not so much with setting up a truly popular government, as they were with establishing safeguards against popular government. They were afraid, apparently, to trust the judgment of the people. They arranged, for instance, that neither the President nor the Supreme Court nor the upper house of Congress should be elected by popular vote. But when all this is admitted, and when we admit that even the Bill of Rights was inserted in the Constitution only because, if it were not inserted, the majority of the delegates could not have *their* ideas enacted into the basic law, still we shall make a great mistake if we think of those delegates as necessarily conservative.

They were not. They were New Dealers; and they were determined to change the whole political setup of America, if need be, so that it might harmonize with the economic setup.

We are not honoring such men if we look upon the Constitution in the way that many Americans, unfortunately, have been taught to look upon it.

The framers of the Constitution, while they may have been suspicious of democracy, obviously believed in change; and because they did not fear change when change had become necessary, their Constitution lived.

We are constantly warned not to tamper with the Constitution; and since tampering means ineffective meddling, we can scarcely take issue with this warning. The implication always is, however, that any change in the Constitution constitutes tampering, especially any change which would enable the Federal Government to do things reserved under the Constitution to the individual states.

Well, if advocating such changes constitutes tampering, we must admit that the framers of our Constitution were champion tamperers. They met merely to amend the articles of confederation and wound up by throwing them out the window. But the Constitution which granted these great new powers to the central government did not lessen the powers of the separate states. Each state became far more powerful than it had been.

Throughout American history, unfortunately, we have confused ourselves almost without limit upon this issue of States' rights. I promise that I shall not clear up the confusion, when the Supreme Court itself is never able to agree as to just what the Constitution meant to say. Again, however, I think there are certain principles underlying the argument upon which we can all agree. Can we not agree, for instance, that it does not strengthen the powers of the individual states to grant them the right to do things which individual states *cannot* do?

In 1787 an individual state could control agriculture to the full degree to which agriculture needed any control. No one will claim that an individual state can exercise any such control today. If agriculture does need control in these times, obviously only the national government can exercise the control.

Now, here are two problems. One is economic. The other is legal. One is the problem of whether or not agriculture needs to be controlled; or whether, if it is not adequately regulated, the welfare of all the people of all the states is seriously threatened. The other is the question of whether, under the Constitution, agriculture may be controlled by the only power which can control it.

The question came before the Supreme Court. I mean, the legal aspects of the question did. And the decision of the Supreme

Court was that the separate states, which cannot control agriculture, are the only powers which have the right to do so.

Please understand that I am not criticizing the Supreme Court. I think it is a great institution and that it is composed of great, honest, patriotic and public spirited people. The question, however, of whether the control of agriculture is necessary to the lives of the people of these United States, was not the question before the Court.

That was not a question, in fact, which could properly be settled by judges. Judges are necessarily governed by law and precedent; but law and precedent help us not at all in finding out, at any given time, whether agriculture needs to be controlled. That is an economic problem; and while judges may know something about economics too, it is not because of their economic understanding that we make them judges. We couldn't select them on any such basis, and it wouldn't solve our problems if we tried to do so. For the economic scene is always changing; and let a judge be ever so well versed in economics when he ascends the bench, and still he may be a back number, as far as economic understanding goes, within ten or fifteen years thereafter. I find myself compelled to disagree, therefore, with those who pin their faith on progressive judicial interpretation, instead of amending the Constitution as economic changes make amendments necessary. No interpretation of the articles of confederation, it seems to me, could possibly have done the work which the Constitution did.

I see no easy solution. I can think of no single amendment to the Constitution which will cover everything which needs to be covered. I think it is quite unreasonable to expect such a thing. *Our basic need in America, with relation to the Constitution, is, it seems to me, re-education; so that no young American shall reach voting age with the idea that American life must be fitted into the Constitution, and that there is something sacrilegious in the thought of fitting the Constitution into American life.*

I think we might well make the process of amendment easier. However suspicious of popular government the founders of the Republic were, the trend of American history has been toward democracy. The masses now elect their president and their senators. Women vote; and not only do more people participate in our political life than ever before, but it is becoming more and more difficult to influence their votes in favor of special economic or political interests.

That bill of rights, so grudgingly inserted in the Constitution, is now universally acclaimed; and the most conservative judges unite easily with the most liberal in protecting the obscurest citizens whose rights have been overlooked in some state or district court. That is a great democratic function which our Supreme Court is admirably fitted to perform. But it is not fitted, and we should not expect of it, to let us know when economic conditions have changed to a point where the state governments can no longer discharge the responsibilities once put up to them. *Our problem today, in fact, is much the same problem as that of 1787. Certain things must be done. The welfare of the whole nation depends on their being done. If they can be done by individuals, well and good—then, in the interest of democracy and personal liberty, government of all kinds should keep its hands off. But if they cannot be accomplished by voluntary, individual effort, and it is still necessary for the public welfare that they be accomplished, they must be accomplished through government; and if the local and state governments cannot accomplish these necessary things, they rightly become the function of national government.*

In our political history, we have argued at length, and at one time we even went to war in the effort to determine, just what functions properly belong to local and state governments and just what powers rightly reside in the government of the nation. But argument couldn't settle it. War could not settle it; and one reason why there could be no settlement was that any distribution of powers which *could* be agreed upon could *not* be agreed upon for very long. For times were always changing.

A family moving into new territory might build any kind of a house it wished. But if many families moved into the same locality, then there had to be codes. The community, however, when it set up these community codes, and used the power of taxation to provide sanitation, sidewalks and fire protection, did not thereby

THE FILENE-FINLAY SIMULTANEOUS TRANSLATOR
IN USE BY THE LEAGUE OF NATIONS, GENEVA, SWITZERLAND—SEPTEMBER 1930

(See text, page xxv. Among the world statesmen using the Translator are: 2. De Wiart, Belgium; 8. Politis, Greece; 12, 13, 14. Briand, Flandin and Poncet, France; 23. Inoue, Japan; etc.)

restrict the personal liberty of any individual concerned. These codes were necessary to protect everyone's personal liberty under the new conditions.

In 1787, every American had a right to work. The Constitution did not grant that right. It didn't have to; for it was a right inherent in the economic conditions of the time. For there was plenty of land in America for anyone who wanted to till it, and families could make a living by so tilling the soil. They didn't have to sell their products; and it didn't make any vital difference to a thrifty industrious family if other families were not so thrifty and industrious. Under the conditions of those times, success was very largely determined by individual ability and individual initiative. If that were still so, we would not now need to change the Constitution to permit us to set up adequate industrial codes. But it simply isn't so. Everybody knows it isn't so. Millions must be denied the right to work in these days unless our industries are organized in such a way that our masses, from coast to coast, will be assured of adequate buying power.

But such an organization of industry is, today, unconstitutional. To be sure, there may be a certain amount of voluntary organization, aiming to keep wages up and better working conditions. But the economic need of today is for more and more buying by the masses generally that workers in every line will have full opportunity to work. The need therefore, among other things, is for a sufficiently high wage scale and one that can be enforced throughout the whole nation.

No state can now control unemployment within its borders. Unemployment in Michigan is not necessarily caused in Michigan. It may be caused in Massachusetts or in Pennsylvania, through the inability of the people of Massachusetts or Pennsylvania to buy the automobiles they want.

In early America any farmer who neglected his farm was properly despised, and the moral disgrace which was attached to such shiftlessness was usually enough to keep anybody from yielding to the vice. But neglecting to work when things need to be done is quite as much of a vice today as ever. But it isn't an individual vice any longer. It has become a national vice. Because we, the people of the United States, fail to plan our work so that everybody may be kept profitably employed, then millions of those who are willing and eager to work cannot find employment. No one alleges that it is their fault. We all know perfectly well that whether the average American can work or not depends, not upon himself, but upon whether business throughout the nation is running smoothly.

But it is unconstitutional as yet to make business run smoothly. For four years or more, Americans generally just lolled around, not because they wanted to, for almost to a man they wanted to get busy, but simply because they couldn't get busy excepting through some kind of nation-wide agreement. If Michigan people had all gone to work, it wouldn't have helped matters appreciably. It would simply have produced millions of automobiles which could not be sold. Only if the people of all the states went to work simultaneously, and only if they received incomes high enough to enable them to purchase the resulting product, could the work which everybody was so eager for go on. But this wasn't so in 1787. It was only partially true in 1887; but the fifty years since then, with its absurd climax of a great people—ambitious, trained, expert and endowed with every natural blessing—going on one nation-wide sit-down strike against themselves and suffering actual poverty in the midst of plenty—this has made the truth so inescapably clear that even the Supreme Court must see it. But the Supreme Court has no jurisdiction over economic change. Only the American people can deal successfully with that. That they will deal successfully with it I do not doubt. But they cannot deal successfully with it so long as they regard their Constitution with superstitious fear, instead of with that real and practical reverence under which they may make of it an effective instrument of the nation's will for justice, prosperity and internal peace.

Whose Supreme Court? *

FRIENDS OF THE RADIO AUDIENCE:

Although I am not a lawyer, I am going to speak for a few minutes about our Supreme Court.

Perhaps I had better say: *Because* I am not a lawyer, I am going to talk about our Supreme Court.

We've *heard* the lawyers—on both sides. That's all right, as far as it goes. But personally, I would rather hear from the people who aren't lawyers; and these past few weeks, I believe, will live in American history as a time when our Supreme Court began to hear in a big way from the people of the United States.

Please notice that I call it *our* Supreme Court. It doesn't belong to the lawyers. It belongs to us—to you and me and every American citizen. It exists only because we, the people, want it to exist; and if it doesn't work as we want it to work, we can, if we wish, restrict its powers to any extent which we, the people, believe to be necessary to preserve our democracy.

This, I know, is not the customary way of referring to the Court. For many years, the average American citizen got to thinking of the Supreme Court not as a mere branch of our democratic government, but as a sort of sacred tribunal somehow raised above the government and endowed with some mysterious authority to tell the government what to do.

And we called that attitude reverence. It wasn't. It was superstition. It wasn't an attitude of respect for the Court, but an attitude of contempt for democracy.

If we are to have true democracy, to be sure, we must respect the courts; and we will respect their decisions, and abide by them, even when we are convinced that their decisions are wrong.

* Broadcast over a nation-wide hookup of the Columbia Broadcasting System—April 28, 1937.

Otherwise, we could not have order; and without order, the rule of the people would be impossible. But that is far different from assuming that the courts are above the people and not subject to the people's will.

I told you I wasn't a lawyer. Think of me as a man who likes good sports and good sportsmanship. As a lover of baseball, I know, we must have umpires, and we must respect and abide by the decisions of the umpire or the game could not go on. But the game, nevertheless, doesn't belong to the umpires; and if the umpires ever got to thinking that it does, we would either lose interest in the game *or, in the interest of the game,* we would demand a different kind of umpire.

In America, for many years, we seemed to lose interest in democracy. We still had our democratic forms. We still had our elections. And we still seemed to think that this constituted democracy. But I want to ask any listener over fifty years of age if the average American of his acquaintance did not seem to think of the government as something above the people, rather than thinking of the people as above the government.

But all that has been changed. In 1932, the people of these United States demanded a New Deal. We were rather hazy, doubtless, as to how it might be brought about. But we were sick of poverty in the midst of plenty, and of unemployment in the Land of Opportunity; and by the New Deal, we meant such a fair distribution of opportunity that the people generally would be guaranteed employment and their full and just share of the wealth which their work produced.

And so, taking a chance, we elected Franklin D. Roosevelt.

And two years of Roosevelt convinced the people of the United States that they had chosen well. Whereupon all the little groups of the privileged and powerful—all the groups which had come to think of themselves as rightfully above the people—began their campaign to stop Roosevelt at any cost.

Most of us, I think, remember what came of that. The answer was 46 to 2, and the largest popular majority that any President ever had. But one would think, to read some of our newspapers today, that the editors had forgotten all about it.

The American people, I am sure, have not. By 1936, surely, they knew what they wanted. They knew *whom* they were voting for. There was no hasty decision, and all the arguments against Roosevelt were given a full hearing. The opposition controlled most of the newspapers, and the special interests poured out millions for special propaganda. But the people of the United States —wage earners and farmers and housewives who had never seemed to realize their power before—declared overwhelmingly that the New Deal must go on until they, the people, could have and enjoy the good things of life in accordance with their new capacity to produce them.

I said I was a lover of sports, and you may have guessed that I believe in government by the people. But that isn't all I do. I am a business man; and for fifty years I have done my best to study our business development. If it hadn't been for those business studies, I might be as afraid of democracy in action as are some other business men. At any rate, this uprising of the people frightened most of the business men who had *not* been studying business development. They were honest and conscientious enough. They simply didn't know that this better distribution of wealth had now become as necessary for business as it was for the people generally.

So they were frightened. But they saw one bulwark between them and the New Deal. That was the Supreme Court. The Supreme Court had declared a large part of the New Deal unconstitutional; and the Supreme Court, as they saw it, was above and beyond the will of the people of the United States.

Now they and their lawyers and their other spokesmen have been telling us that President Roosevelt is trying to make himself superior to the Supreme Court. What he is really doing, of course, is keeping his pledge to the people of the United States.

He promised, in effect, to go on with the New Deal until the people of the United States would be assured of such buying power that they could purchase the products of our industries and thus keep themselves profitably employed. To achieve this, however, workers generally must have high wages, and farmers must not only be able to sell their products profitably but the very soil which they tilled must be protected from the ravages of rugged individualism which were fast wearing it out. This necessitated a nation-wide program of conservation. It necessitated checks upon grasping corporations. It necessitated the control of agriculture and of industry for the common good.

The Supreme Court, however, declared that the government could not do many of these things. I couldn't always follow its line of reasoning; and neither, in fact, could the Court itself. One day it declared that the regulation of agriculture was not a matter for the national government, which *could* regulate it, but for the individual states which, as every farmer knew, could not.

One day it said that the regulation of the labor of women and children must be left to the individual states. Then it followed with a declaration that the states couldn't do it either. Then Justice Roberts changed his mind; and in changing his mind, he changed the mind of the Supreme Court and thus changed the Constitution of the United States, for everybody had come to understand by this time that the Constitution is what the justices say it is.

Now this, undoubtedly, was all good law, the only trouble with it being that it didn't make sense. Many people began to demand amendments to the Constitution, but the Constitution was actually being amended right before our eyes. Monday was not only wash day but a day for general alteration and repairs, as far as the Constitution was concerned.

I am not blaming the Supreme Court for this. I think it is as conscientious a Court as we could hope to have. But when President Roosevelt observed that the Court needed new blood, I know that the American people could see the point.

We were interested in a fuller and fairer distribution of wealth, as promised by President Roosevelt. The President, we knew, was under oath to stay within the Constitution. So was the Supreme Court, the only difference being that the Supreme Court could and did amend the Constitution to fit the views of the judges, whereas the President could not.

He and Congress, however, could amend the Supreme Court. It was an extraordinary proposal, and it could hardly be justified if these were not extraordinary times. But they are, and everybody knows they are, extraordinary times—times as extraordinary as were the eighteen-fifties, when the famous Dred Scott decision failed to settle anything but so unsettled everything which the American people were trying to do that it became one of the chief events leading up to the War between the States.

And yet, legalistically, that Dred Scott decision was a masterpiece. If Chief Justice Taney and his colleagues, however, had only been able to look ahead, as well as back, they would not have helped to plunge the nation into war. The real issue before us today is: How can we the people of the United States be sure that our Supreme Court will possess foresight equal to its hindsight?

None of us believes in packing the Court to suit the will of the Executive; and we know for a certainty that President Roosevelt does not. In ordinary times, we know, the Court is a steadying influence, and puts a needed check upon rash legislation. But these are not ordinary times. This is an historic turning point between the Age of Scarcity and the Age of Plenty; and it is a day when the people generally must be able to buy that plenty, else the machinery of plenty cannot be kept in operation, and we are necessarily plunged into unemployment, depression, poverty and economic chaos. If, at such turning points, our Supreme Court cannot look ahead as well as back, it becomes a most unsteadying influence and may, despite the best intentions in the world, bring on national disaster.

Let me repeat: I am not blaming our Supreme Court. No one can rightly be blamed for growing old, and I am past seventy myself. It is well to remember, however, that when we aging capitalists have important new business to transact, we entrust it to people who are up and coming, not to those whose minds are too much in the past and whose decisions are fixed by the precedents of the past.

If we object to new blood in the Supreme Court, therefore, while we may hire lawyers to advance other reasons, our real reasons must be plain. It is because *we don't want this important New Deal business transacted.* It is because we don't want the people of these United States to have what they voted for. It is because we want to stop Roosevelt from effecting the fuller and fairer distribution of wealth which not only the people but these new times demand. But the American people, I am sure, will not be fooled. They, I know, are with Roosevelt in his determination to bring the Supreme Court in line with these new times and in line with the will of our American people for not only political but economic democracy.

An Open Letter

Boston, Massachusetts,
May 23, 1936.

To the President and Directors of the United States Chamber of Commerce.

Dear Sirs:

In my decision that I cannot continue to work in and through the United States Chamber of Commerce, it seems to me that I should make a definite statement. Also, I think, you would wish to have me do so.

It is not that I have lost one iota of interest in the nation-wide organization of business to advance the interest of business in general. The need for such organization is now plainer than ever.

Nor is it because I have become disgruntled over any specific stand which the Chamber has taken. For several years, as you know, I have been convinced that business has reached a stage in its development which necessitates the abandonment of an attitude which was quite applicable to a previous stage; and I have made effort after effort to induce the United States Chamber of Commerce to restudy its whole form of organization, to achieve if possible a better understanding of our new problems and discover a more effective method of solving them. That you may not think I am now making any hasty decision, may I remind you of how I tried to get this basic problem before the Washington meeting in 1934; not with the idea of committing the Chamber to any specific new course, but to have a committee appointed to make such a study and to report at some subsequent meeting. You will doubtless remember how I failed to get a hearing—how, in spite of the generally recognized new crisis in business, the very suggestion that any new tactics might even be studied was not permitted to be brought before the Chamber.

Nevertheless, I did not then withdraw my support. You will concede, I think, that my present action is most deliberate. Also, I think, my life bears testimony that I am not afraid of being in a minority and that it is not my policy to bolt from an organization because it does not see eye to eye with me.

As plainly as I can state my position, I have at last been forced to the conclusion that the United States Chamber of Commerce, as at present organized, is not an organization of *business* but rather an organization of *business men*—meeting not to study business in a business way, nor even to find out what the needs of business in general may be, but either to promote the special views of certain prominent people in the business world, or at best to discover and express the fixed opinion of the membership concerning matters which, in the most successful modern business organizations, would be referred as a matter of course to fact-finding research.

I am usually held responsible, I believe, for having originally sponsored and insisted upon the referendum policy of the United States Chamber. I make no apology for that; for in any organization it is necessary to record decisions, and I believe as strongly as ever in the democratic formula. It is the *manner of arriving at decisions,* whether autocratic or democratic, to which I am now referring.

It is well known, for instance, that the manufacturing policies of such organizations as General Electric, General Motors or the great du Pont industries are not and cannot be determined by anyone's opinion—not even by the opinions of officers and directors—but are and must be determined by the facts disclosed in their great fact-finding laboratories. I do not mean merely that they have research departments—for any organization which employs a man to keep track of timetables may be said to have a research department; and the United States Chamber has facilities for providing its members with certain statistics and routine information. But in such great, modern businesses, decisions are reached by the scientific fact-finding research method. In the United States Chamber of Commerce, decisions are reached by polling the members of the Board or general membership on the basis of their existing opinions without the presentation of data unearthed by research. There may be an effort, to be sure, to "state both sides" of a proposal submitted for referendum; but one cannot even imagine the directors of General Motors arguing as to whether some improvement submitted by Vice-President Kettering and his research staff will or will not work; for Kettering, they know, has the exact data, and although they may upset every preconceived notion of every director, none would think of maintaining his opinion in opposition to the scientifically ascertained facts.

I am convinced that the Chamber's course, so generally abandoned in the conduct of these great modern businesses, cannot be adequate to serve the needs of business generally, nor can it serve the needs of the average member. Modern business problems, general or special, cannot be solved by adding up the opinions either of board members or of the members generally, and calling that the answer.

We might as well vote as to whether some proposed treatment for typhoid or diphtheria is valid without first referring the problem to those who are in a position to find out. It may be necessary, to be sure, for a board of health composed of laymen to authorize a certain method of dealing with an epidemic; but democracy does not preclude the exercise of intelligence, and no intelligent board would in a crisis presume to set its traditional assumptions above the findings of scientific research.

When business in general became sick, however, the United States Chamber of Commerce had no independent, fact-finding body to which to refer the problem. It simply held meetings at which business leaders were asked to express their opinions, as if the opinions of business leaders were then of first importance. I am not questioning the intelligence or ability of such speakers concerning matters to which they had given special study and problems with which they had had great experience. But our problem was the problem of what to do about business in general, and these speakers were not leaders of business in general. Business in general had no such leaders; and it was the fixed opinion of our speakers, as a rule, that it should have none. Particular businesses, they knew, must have leadership, and leadership along some well-planned course; but business in general, they were certain, should not be led and should not have any planned course whatever.

They had not reached these conclusions, obviously, by fact-finding research. They made no pretense of having studied economic evolution and the successive changes which had inevitably come over business in the years of our transition from an agrarian to a machine civilization. They were simply and solely successful business men: that is, men who had been successful in their personal businesses before the times had changed and thrown all business into depression. In the case of an epidemic, by the same logic, we would not consult doctors—mere medical brain trusters—but call a mass meeting and have it addressed by those who had enjoyed the best of health before the epidemic happened.

This is not a personal criticism, nor a special criticism of the members of the program committees. The wrong attitude—the attitude which in the end proved so futile—was basic. Had any of us, in his individual business, suddenly been faced by a vanishing market, he might not know what to do but he would proceed at once to find out. That would be the business way. But when business in general was suddenly faced by a vanishing market, it was assumed that business men would know what to do, and that it would be unnecessary, therefore, to find out. That was the way of the United States Chamber of Commerce.

Eventually I was forced to the conclusion that neither the ends of business nor the ends of democracy can be served by such a policy. If business in general is to have an effective organization, it must be essentially a fact-finding organization, to which every problem of these changing times can be reasonably referred. This need not do away with the referendum. It need only do away with the practice of deciding our course by the unsupported and uninformed opinion within an organization which as yet is not equipped to find the facts of these changing times.

My studies, as you know, have forced me to conclude that there can never again be lasting, nation-wide prosperity until

American business in general is organized to pay such higher wages that the masses of wage earners will be able to buy enough of our industrial products to give our industries an adequate market and thus keep them in profitable operation. If I am wrong in that conclusion, however, I want to know it; and if I am right, I believe that business men generally will want to know it. It was not, therefore, because I found myself so hopelessly outnumbered in the United States Chamber of Commerce that I finally decided to withdraw my support, but because the Chamber had neither the facilities nor the will to find the actual answer to such an all-important business question.

I believe that this accounts not merely for my withdrawal, but for the shrinking prestige of the Chamber in our business community. By this, I do not mean merely that it is alienating progressive minds: I mean, rather, that such a policy cannot be constructive—cannot produce the results by which the members, whether liberal or conservative, may realize that they are getting their money's worth. The Chamber as at present organized may function as a successful club of business men when times are good, or as a potent center of reaction when changing times make some great new forward step necessary; but in neither role can it furnish any real help to business, either to business in general or to the particular business of the average member. The businesses, I fear, which are likely to profit most from such an organization as the United States Chamber of Commerce is today are those which have some special reason for achieving a dominant voice in the Chamber's affairs, although lacking an adequate interest in or an adequate understanding of the needs of business in general.

Until such time, then, as the United States Chamber of Commerce shall be disposed to adopt a new policy, and to substitute fact-finding research for opinion as a guide to decisions concerning the needs of business in general—even as opposed, possibly, to the ambitions of special interests—I find it necessary regretfully to withdraw my co-operation.

Yours sincerely,

(signed) EDWARD A. FILENE

The New Deal and the New Times *

FELLOW CITIZENS:

It is hardly necessary to say that I was not put on this program as any added contribution to the oratory of this campaign.

Those who asked me to speak know that I couldn't make an eloquent speech if I wanted to. Perhaps they *don't* know that I wouldn't if I could. I am a business man, and business and oratory don't mix.

Once upon a time, our notion of a good salesman was a salesman who was so persuasive and could so work upon the feelings of his customers, that he could sell them rotten eggs. Now we know that any salesman who would sell rotten eggs is a rotten salesman.

As a business man I can't help noting that there has been a lot of rotten salesmanship in this campaign.

There have been appeals to partisanship—appeals to Republicans to vote Republican to preserve the good old Democratic doctrine of States' rights, and appeals to Democrats to vote Republican in order to preserve the Democratic party. Then there have been hysterical cries that Roosevelt is a dictator and a dangerous radical; and the very newspapers that raise these cries have been doing everything in their power to get out the largest possible vote for Lemke. That is the identical strategy, by the way, which was employed by the big German industrialists and bankers, and which resulted in replacing Chancellor Bruening, a rigid Constitutionalist, with Hitler, a real dictator if there ever was one.

Then there is this cry about preserving the Constitution, al-

* Address at the Roosevelt Rally held under the auspices of the Progressive National Committee, Carnegie Hall, New York, N. Y.—October 28, 1936.

though nobody is attacking the Constitution; and if there were a dictatorship, no such hullabaloo would be permitted.

Americans rightly reverence the Constitution. But these folks who are getting so hysterical about it seem to forget how it ever came about that the Constitution of the United States won such general reverence.

It is, of course, because the Constitution was a New Deal at a time when a great New Deal was necessary.

We reverence the Constitution, also, because it worked. If it had not been practical, and if a perplexed and desperate people had not been able to recover under *that* New Deal, the Constitution would not have won the reverence it did.

New times *always* make a New Deal necessary. If we want to *think* about this campaign, therefore, instead of being swept away by mere campaign hysteria, it would be well to ask ourselves the question: "Are these new times?"

And we must know the answer. If these times had not been new times, the Old Deal would have continued to work. It *had* worked. It worked well enough, at least, so that both the Republican and Democratic parties stood for it. But the time came when it didn't work any longer, and our nation had to embark upon a very different course.

I go that far with Al Smith. It is true, as he declares, that the Democratic party never favored the New Deal, and never even heard about the New Deal, until the time came when a New Deal had to happen. My only criticism of Al Smith is that he doesn't know what time it is.

He has now come out for a horse-and-buggy candidate; whereas, if he would only look at the calendar, he might discover that this is not a horse-and-buggy age.

I do not mean that as any slur, either upon Mr. Smith or Governor Landon. I may be wrong, and I grant them the right to their opinions. Maybe this *is* a horse-and-buggy age, after all, and it is only my imagination which has made me think that it is an age of automobiles and airplanes. But we needn't argue the point; for that happens to be a question which every voter is perfectly capable of deciding for himself. But if this is *not* the horse-and-buggy age, we must all agree, horse-and-buggy government will no longer do.

And if this is an age in which the nation cannot be prosperous unless the masses of its people are assured of adequate buying power—then there must be a New Deal which will make it certain that the masses have such buying power.

But that happens to be an issue which is not discussed by the crowd which is out to stop Roosevelt.

Recall their speeches. Recall any anti-Roosevelt speech which you have heard this year. Recall everything that Governor Landon has said. Go even to headquarters and review the orations of the Honorable John D. M. Hamilton. Recall Knox and all his knock-knocks. Or, if you wish, review the scathing denunciations of that little group of serious thinkers who have walked out and talked out—and then I want to ask a question.

Has any one of them made any effort to explain the difference between these times and the times when the Old Deal still worked?

If one of them has done so, I have missed it; and I have listened to them patiently and at first hopefully, hour after hour. I longed for some inkling, from even *one* of these speakers, that he had any idea that times have changed.

It isn't any wonder, then, that they have missed fire, whenever they have tried to discuss the New Deal. They may be the most honest people in the world. They may also be brilliant, and they may be people of massive intellect. But they can get nowhere in discussing the New Deal until they first recognize that these are new times.

There is, for instance, that question of States' rights. I don't pretend to know what the rights of a state are. Neither, incidentally, does the Supreme Court, for it is always handing down contradictory opinions on this point. But I do know, and we all know, that what a state has a right to do doesn't make much difference *unless the state can do it.*

The Constitution, we all know, jealously guarded States' rights. The very essence of the Constitution, however, was that it enabled the American people to do through their national government certain things which they wanted to do, and which had to be done, but which they could not do through their separate state governments.

We voters are not really divided, then, upon any Constitutional question, despite all the learned twaddle which is intended to prove that we cannot act as a nation, no matter how much we want to nor how great the necessity for our doing so.

None of us, Republicans or Democrats, wants the national government to do anything for us which we can just as well do for ourselves or through our local governments. But there are certain things which we want—things which we must have if we are to have an equal opportunity to earn a decent living. Republicans generally want these things quite as much as do the Democrats; but they are things which we cannot achieve by individual effort nor by acting through our local and our state governments. If we are to achieve these things, then, the people of all the states must work together as a nation.

There isn't any division among us on that score—at least as far as the overwhelming majority of us are concerned. The trouble seems to be that a small minority does not want the people of the United States to have some of these things. They can't, of course, keep us from trying to get them; but if they can make us feel that we mustn't use the machinery of national government in our efforts to get them, that will suit their purposes quite as well.

I am a business man; and when I think of what people want, my mind is apt to go commercial and think of food and clothes and household goods. There are things, however, which we treasure even more than life. One of them is liberty. Most of us, however, had very little liberty under the Hoover Administration.

Millions of us, for instance, had no liberty to get a job—no liberty to earn a living.

In early America, Americans had that liberty. It wasn't guaranteed in the Constitution, to be sure, but it didn't need to be. For there was plenty of land; and one could settle on the land and rely upon his own labor, his own skill and his own individual initiative to make about as good a living as the next man.

But times have changed since then. Few Americans, if any, are free to make a living in any such way today. We must still work, most of us, but we cannot work unless there are jobs to work at; and whether there are jobs or not is no longer under the control of the man who wants one.

That old liberty wasn't taken away from the masses of the American people by any evil conspiracy. There were New Times —that's all—and there had to be a New Deal if the ancient liberty to earn a living were to be recovered.

And it remained for President Roosevelt to initiate this New Deal. I don't say that he hasn't made mistakes. I don't say, if we had the past four years to live over again, that we might not do many things much better than we did.

But we all know that the New Deal was launched. We all know that it worked. And while there are many important things which still remain to be done, if what has been gained is not to be lost, we all know that the New Deal brought with it what the overwhelming majority of the American people, Republicans and Democrats, want.

Republicans and Democrats, for instance, both want steady employment, and they both want unemployment insurance. They both want security for their old age. They both want higher wages, if they are wage earners, and higher incomes if they are toilers on our farms. All want protection for their bank deposits. All want a reasonable supervision of the security markets to avoid such calamities as that of 1929. And if people must be thrown out of work through no fault of their own, they all want adequate relief for the unemployed.

In short, the great majority of Americans in every walk of life, whether they are Republicans or Democrats, want the things which they couldn't get under the late Republican Administration, but which they have been getting under the New Deal.

And they want more of these things which are now indispensable to prosperity—not only four years more but *more and more*.

If the Republican party were to come out definitely against these demands, not one Republican out of ten would vote the

Republican ticket this year. Republican politicians all know *that*, although it took them some time to convince the heads of the National Association of Manufacturers.

A year or so ago, you must remember, that Association announced that business must go into politics; and it actually drew up a platform denouncing the demand for all these things and favoring a return to the principles which governed the Hoover Administration. But the Republican party did not adopt that platform. It adopted a platform, rather, which pretended to favor all these New Deal principles.

So what? Did the heads of the Manufacturers' Association take a walk out of the Republican party?

Nothing of the sort. They endorsed the Republican platform and began to shell out big money to elect the Republican candidate.

Governor Landon, who promises to do all the things which they denounced Roosevelt for doing, is now their ideal. Nevertheless, anyone who talks with these representatives of Big Business cannot help discovering that they have not changed their minds. That National Manufacturers' platform is still *their* platform, although the party to which they are contributing so generously pretends to stand for just the opposite.

I submit that *somebody* is being fooled. The Republican leadership is either fooling the heads of the National Association of Manufacturers and the leading lights of the United States Chamber of Commerce, or it is fooling the average Republican voter.

Everybody is entitled to guess which.

My guess is that the Republican voters were fooled a bit at the start; but that, when the returns are in, the joke will be on the heavy contributors to Landon's campaign fund.

At any rate, the situation has made it politically impossible for the Republican campaigners to discuss the New Deal on its merits. At best they have discussed nothing but the minor slips of the New Deal—a national movement which I believe will be judged by history as the greatest of all achievements of our times. At worst, they have shrieked about an orgy of spending, as if the economic liberty of one hundred and twenty million Americans were not worth even the highest money cost which they declare the New Deal has saddled upon our future generations.

It's an odd role they are playing, any way you happen to look at it.

Imagine the wreck of a ship, for instance, not to mention the wreck of a great nation. Imagine the captain organizing all hands for the twofold task of relief and recovery—some desperately working to repair the damage done by the collision and some throwing life preservers to strugglers in the water.

Then imagine an anvil chorus of those who refuse to co-operate—one group complaining because some deck hand has neglected to polish the brass while others cry out against such a waste of life preservers.

Now I ought to know something about that so-called orgy of spending; for when the income tax collectors go about their work, they never forget me. I have to give them half of my income every year. I'll admit that it hurts a bit, when I am thinking only of the taxes; but when I see what my country is getting for its money now, I consider this taxpaying the best bargain of my life.

Why shouldn't the American people take half my money from me? I took *all* of it from them.

I, for one, favor still higher income taxes in the upper brackets; and I would still feel indebted to the American people and indebted to their great President, not only for giving me the opportunities I have had, but for their determination to make America a better and ever better country by inaugurating a New Deal whenever a New Deal is necessary.

But I have moods, I may as well admit, when I just hate to cough up all those taxes; and I may as well confess what I think about at such moments. I think about this Republican campaign—the campaign of anti-New Dealers who cannot touch upon the real issues of the New Deal—and the way they are trying to convince the voters that all taxes are passed on to the consumer. Neither I nor my lawyers, I can assure you, have ever discovered a way by which I could, if I would, make the masses of consumers pay my income tax.

But honestly, I don't want to. We have no right to millions while there is still poverty in our country. Business has no right to dividends unless the workers who produce those dividends are getting a decent wage. No one has a right to champagne when children cannot get milk. And if it were not impossible to abolish poverty in America by a mere sharing of *existing* wealth, the share-the-wealth movement would be entirely justified.

Assuming, however, that taxpayers are not interested in the public welfare, and that their only concern is to bring their own expenses down, all this talk of an orgy of spending is still the veriest economic nonsense.

We haven't spent anything excepting money, and money isn't wealth. The New Deal has simply been using money for the only purpose for which money can be properly used—to facilitate the exchange of goods and services. That money, before President Roosevelt was inaugurated, had been lying idle; not because its owners wanted it to be idle, but because it was out of a job.

And because our money was out of work, millions of Americans were out of work, and millions of American families were face to face with starvation.

Our society, we must all know, lives by production for exchange. People who manufacture spark plugs don't manufacture them for their own use. They make spark plugs because they want a thousand things which other people are making; and they aim to trade these spark plugs for all these other things. America, whether we realize it or not, has become one grand, nation-wide job exchange; and if the exchange should stop, American life would have to stop.

And exchange had almost stopped; for exchange in our modern society requires a medium of exchange or money; and our money, by the billions of dollars, had got into places where it could not be used.

It couldn't be used for the buying of goods that consumers

needed, either because it was owned by rich people who didn't need enough consumer goods to keep the masses at work producing them; or it was owned by poor people who, under the circumstances, didn't dare to buy them; and it couldn't be used in any great amount for capital purposes because there was so little sale for what our machines were already turning out that any further extension of our machinery of production could result only in a loss of the capital invested.

By the expansion of government credit, however, the New Deal Administration got that money out of its hiding places and put it to work. With it, for one thing, we employed millions of the jobless. Some of them, I am told, rested on their shovels, which was a very improper thing for them to do. Nevertheless, their wages didn't rest. Their wages came directly to our retail counters. Retailers took the money, then, and sent it on to wholesalers and manufacturers; and the manufacturers, to fill their orders, had to hire workers and, with these same dollars which had previously been out of a job, they paid workers to operate the machinery of production, and prosperity set in once more.

I repeat that I am a business man, trying my best to appraise all this from a business standpoint. I believe in wise economy, and economy demands the most careful use of money.

But which Administration was extravagant—the one which spent money so that the American people might return to work and produce and distribute wealth, or the one which spent the American people in trying to save the money?

The times themselves provide the answer. I am not one who blames President Hoover for our calamities; for what Hoover did was, in the main, what American business and American political thinking in both parties had educated him to do. Mr. Hoover and Mr. Smith, to be sure, didn't exactly see eye to eye when they both wanted to be President; but now that they've both found out that they can't be President, their differences are scarcely noticeable.

While I don't blame President Hoover, then, for not seeing in 1928 certain things which Al Smith can't see yet, I must admit that the subsequent Hoover Administration was the most extravagant administration within my memory. It let our men, money and machinery lie idle, with the result that we as a nation failed to produce more than three hundred billion dollars worth of wealth which, had there been a New Deal, would have been produced and distributed among the American people.

The New Deal, to be sure, has only got well started. It won't be completed until the American people are producing at capacity and distributing to the people according to their capacity to produce. This, we may as well admit, will work havoc with a lot of things about which Americans have been traditionally sentimental, just as truly as the automobile has worked havoc with the good old livery stable and modern plumbing has all but obliterated our tender memories of the Saturday night wash tub bath.

The New Deal may even put an end to such careers as that of Al Smith or myself; for it will doubtless be impossible to rise from poverty to riches if there isn't any poverty to rise from.

Our struggle to get ahead of each other, also, must largely cease, no matter how romantic that struggle may have seemed, and we will now have to learn how to go forward *with* one another if we are to maintain prosperity.

Let us concede all this, then, to the Old Dealers. Let them live in their memories. Let them cherish the days when one class could exploit another, and then provide bread lines to show their human kindness.

But one thing we cannot concede, and that is the contention that the New Deal has been extravagant, for it has already paid for itself over and over again. To be sure, we have increased our net debt by six and a half billions; but by doing this, we have already increased our national income by twenty billions a year, which, from a business standpoint, was a most wise investment.

If people get to imagining that money is wealth, to be sure, they may be confused, and financiers have traditionally shared in that confusion. They proved to their own satisfaction, for instance, at the end of the Napoleonic wars, that Great Britain could never recover from the debt which those wars entailed. But the people of Great Britain went to work and created so much real wealth that the money debt soon ceased to be a burden.

And thanks to the New Deal, the American people are now going back to work, which is the only way to wealth and the only way, in the long run, by which budgets can be balanced.

We must, however, complete the New Deal. We must put an end to all this extravagant idleness; and we must put an end to these extravagantly low wages, which do not permit our people to buy our products and therefore cause us to cut down production and bring on unemployment.

No one doubts that that is what Roosevelt is aiming at. If it were not, he would not be hated as he is by those who do not realize how times have changed and why poverty, by destroying our markets, has now become an extravagance which America cannot tolerate.

Those of us who prefer the good old-time poverty, however, can vote for it. But the mass of Republicans don't want it any more than do the Democrats; so the New Deal is nonpartisan and can't help being so. When we vote for Roosevelt, then, we are not voting either Democrat or Republican in the old sense at all. We are simply voting for the right to work and for an abundant share of the abundant wealth which we can and will produce when, under the New Deal, this economic liberty is adequately assured to every American citizen.

Why We Must Make Higher Wages Compulsory*

When I declare that higher wages are necessary for full and lasting business recovery, I do not want anyone to run away with the idea that I am an especially kind and philanthropic employer.

Employers who believe in low wages are tenderhearted enough. Their trouble is not in their hearts, but in their heads. What they need to see is that low wages in these new days of machine abundance make it next to impossible for business generally to become prosperous; and when business generally is in the red, very few businesses have any chance of keeping out of it.

As a matter of fact, almost every employer with whom I am acquainted does believe in high wages; only he wants *other* employers to pay them. All he objects to is his having to pay them also.

Take a shoe manufacturer, for instance, selling shoes in Detroit. He knows very well that if the automobile industry should reduce wages fifty per cent, it would just about ruin his market in Detroit; so he wants Ford and General Motors and the others to keep wages up.

The chances are, however, that he himself is not paying more than half as high a wage as the motorcar manufacturers are paying. If that is so, his employees will not be able to buy many automobiles.

The automobile industry, you see, furnishes a good market for this low-wage employer; and he in return furnishes a very poor market for the automobile industry.

---

* Statement issued during the 1936 campaign to re-elect President Franklin D. Roosevelt.

So what? We don't have to guess. The thing happened just a few years ago; and it will happen again unless American low-wage industries can be transformed into high-wage industries. That is, even the high-wage industries will have to slow down.

If coal miners, for instance, do not get wages high enough to enable them to buy automobiles, a great number of automobile workers must be kept out of the job of making those automobiles; and being out of a job, their incomes won't be high enough to enable them to buy enough coal.

We need not be unselfish, then, in advocating high wages in all American industries. All we need is intelligent selfishness—self-interest guided by common sense.

But advocating high wages won't make wages high. Every time I speak on this subject, I get letters from angry employers telling me that they are already paying wages as high as they can afford to pay, and that any increase in their operating expenses would mean their ruin.

And the chances are that what they say is correct. But it doesn't do away with the problem, nor with the fact that all business must head generally for ruin if wages generally are not high enough.

I have something of a reputation, I believe, as a high-wage employer; but I am perfectly aware that the wages I pay are not nearly high enough. And they would still not be high enough, even though they were as high as we could make them without giving our competitors such an advantage over us as to endanger our business.

But what does that mean? If the time has come when business generally cannot be prosperous unless wages generally provide enough buying power to keep it prosperous; and if it is true, as I believe it is, that individual employers, trying to solve the problem individually, cannot pay wages which are nearly high enough to keep business prosperous—then what?

Then it necessarily follows that this problem of wages can no longer be safely referred to individual employers for solution. Some way must be found, instead, to make high wages compulsory for all employers. In other words, wages must be taken out of competition.

I know, of course, what a great many business men will say to that. They will cry "Regimentation!" But let's see.

What is the exact difference between my stand and theirs? I maintain that high wages must be made compulsory; and the traditional business mind replies that that is regimentation. These same business minds, however, insist that wages, although not high enough to provide an adequate market for our industries, are already as high as they can pay.

But if that is true, surely, these employers are already regimented. If that is true, the wage rate is compulsory anyway; only, in the kind of regimentation of which they are now the victims, it is low and utterly inadequate wages which are made compulsory—wages inadequate to permit the people to buy, and therefore inadequate to permit employers to sell their products in quantities necessary for their prosperity. Wages, therefore, which cause shutdowns. Wages which produce unemployment and create poverty in the midst of plenty. Low wages—wages which do not permit the wage-earning population to buy the abundance which they are now able to produce—are as bad for employers as they are for employees. And yet we cannot pay adequately high wages until high wages are made compulsory on all employers.

The reason must be plain to all. If I pay wages greatly above what my competitor pays, he may undersell me. Even if most of us get together and agree upon a high wage scale, the competitor who will not agree may undersell us all. We employers, then, are not only regimented in this matter, but we are regimented by the meanest chiselers in our line, and made to do things which no decent employer wants to do.

The problem, therefore, is not one of regimentation or individual initiative. It is a problem, rather, of who shall say how high wages shall be. Shall *he* make *us* pay low wages in order to compete with him; or shall we, by securing government co-operation, make *him* pay high wages if he is going to compete with us?

I know that many Americans shrink from that word "compulsory." They don't want even prosperity forced upon them. I can appreciate the attitude, for I am just as cantankerous as the next man, and in theory I don't want other people telling me what to do.

But wait a minute. It isn't a question of whether prosperity shall be compulsory or optional. It is a question, rather, of *what* is to be compulsory. Compulsory high wages or compulsory low wages? Compulsory high buying power or compulsory low and utterly inadequate buying power? Compulsory prosperity or compulsory poverty?

Now, this is not a political argument. It is strictly a business discussion; but there are ideas abroad in our politics today which, if they were to dominate, would strangle business and make it impossible for the masses of Americans, with all their marvelous resources and capacity, to achieve a decent standard of living. I refer especially to the idea that making high wages compulsory would in some way tend to curb our personal liberties.

We will all agree, I am sure, that the New Deal Administration was the first administration in our peace-time history to attempt to make high wages compulsory. The effort has not yet succeeded. Organized business itself was so confused, apparently, that it did not co-operate in the effort. Later the Supreme Court declared that such an effort on the part of the national government was a violation of States' rights; and later still, that the states didn't have any such rights either. Whether we are for or against the Administration, however, and whether we agree or disagree with its policies, we will admit, I think—all of us—that the aim of the New Deal has been to raise the buying power of the whole people, especially wage earners and farmers, and that one means to this end was the attempt of the N.R.A., the Guffey Law and other legislation to make higher wages compulsory, so that even would-be chiselers would have to pay them.

And we will admit, also, that much of the opposition to all this has been based on the theory that such compulsory high wages constitute a violation of our ancient American liberties.

Now, I am not going to take issue with the Supreme Court,

which has virtually declared that enforced high wages are at present unconstitutional, even though such enforcement be the only way by which wages can become adequately high. I don't know what is constitutional and what isn't; and neither does the Supreme Court regularly know, as its many disagreements prove. But I do know that wages cannot be high enough to achieve full and lasting prosperity until higher wages are made compulsory; and not assuming to say that such compulsion is constitutional, I do assert that it is necessary—and quite as necessary for business as it is for the wage earners themselves.

And I also assert that early Americans, confronted by much the same problem, decided that it was *not* a violation of personal liberty to make certain good things compulsory.

Education, for instance.

The Liberty Leaguers of those days were all against compulsory education. They said that it was up to each family to say whether its children should go to school or not; and, if a family did send its children to school, the family, whether rich or poor, should pay for their schooling. This all sounded sweetly logical to them; for they were rich, just like our modern Liberty Leaguers, and if education were kept a purely private matter, there was no danger of *their* children being left uneducated.

Early Americans, however, did not fall for that. The people believed in liberty, but not in this Liberty League conception of liberty. If education were not made compulsory, they noted, the average family could not afford to send its children to school. Their choice, then, was not between compulsory education and personal liberty, but between compulsory education and compulsory ignorance.

And they chose compulsory education.

Today, if wages are left in competition, and each employer is free to pay his employees only what their need may compel them to accept, there can be no real freedom for any of us. For such employees cannot be free to buy enough to keep our industries in operation, and neither farmers nor business men will be free to sell. Masses, therefore, must remain unemployed—not even free to earn a living. Employers, meanwhile, cannot be free to pay the wages they would like to pay, or wages that are adequate to maintain prosperity.

When my critics write me, therefore, and tell me that they just can't pay higher wages than they are paying, I sympathize with them far more fully than they know. For they are victims of their own system—the system which keeps wages in competition and therefore makes a commodity of human life.

The New Deal, if carried through, would liberate such employers, quite as much as it would liberate the farmers and wage earners; for it would substitute high wages and a capacity market for the low wages and the limited market which now make the paying of even those low wages so difficult.

Paying high wages, if everybody had to pay them, would be no hardship whatever. For money is not wealth. It is the things which we produce and distribute which constitute our wealth; and unless we make adequately high wages compulsory, we must drag along, producing and distributing at a small fraction of our capacity.

The alternative is to stand behind President Roosevelt in his determination to carry the New Deal through.

Education in This New Age *

LADIES AND GENTLEMEN:

I cannot speak to professional educators upon the theory and technique of education. When business men assume to educate our educators, the results are not always satisfactory. They may even educate the educators into an understanding of what a lot of things there are in life which business men do not know.

But educators also are not free from unwarranted assumptions. That has recently become obvious. No matter how big a fool a Big Business Man may make of himself before an audience of educators, those educators have usually assumed that he *did* understand business. And we know now that that is not so.

Great financiers wrecked our finances. Power kings turned out to be weaklings. Captains of industry fled from the battle at the first smell of danger and, by cutting wages and curtailing the public buying power, led the grand stampede away from industry and toward unemployment.

It is time, surely, that we business men should be very humble, and begin to question our assumption of a divine prerogative to give advice to everybody else. And yet I do not see how business could, if it were in a mood to do so, keep its hands off our problems of education. Nor can I see how educators can longer leave the field of business to business men.

Business problems are your problems quite as definitely as they are ours. And uneducated as we may be to cope with it, the problem of education is our problem quite as much as it is yours. The time has come when we must think these things through together.

---

* Address before the Department of Superintendence of the National Education Association, Cleveland, Ohio—February 28, 1934.

Fifty years' study of the problem of business, and of the social and political problems which have arisen from the evolution of business, has compelled me to see that there is no basic solution for them except in education.

On the other hand—and I say it with full knowledge that I am unqualified to tell professional educators what to do—I have been forced to conclude that there is no solution merely in *more* education of the traditional and customary kind.

No student of business during the past fifty years could fail to note how the whole world was being brought closer and closer together by the advance of trade. But there was no general education in accordance with this great world fact, with the result that the world was torn to pieces in war.

No student of business evolution in America could fail to note the inescapable tendency within our economic mechanism toward greater and greater co-operation. But our education was not in co-operation. Our education was in hotter and hotter competition and in rugged individualism.

It was evident everywhere that we were living in a new order, but it was equally evident that we were experiencing a new and increasing disorder, and we were not being educated to discover what the trouble was.

We said, for instance, that parents should bring up their children in the way that parents used to bring them up, not troubling ourselves very much to find out why they were not doing so or even if such a thing were longer possible. We said there should be stricter laws and swifter justice, and thousands of committees and commissions busied themselves promoting this and that reform. But we were dealing everywhere with effects, not causes. Everybody was engaged in repair work, not in reconstruction in accordance with the revolutionary changes through which our world was passing.

In the so-called exact sciences, to be sure, amazing progress was being made; and a new discovery in a chemical laboratory might suddenly result in the total scrapping of huge industrial plants, and the inauguration not only of new methods, but also of a new science and a new approach to the whole fundamental problem. In our social, political and educational experimenting, however, we have had no such luck.

We never exchange a going social order for a better one if we can help it. We wait invariably until the old order is completely wrecked, and then our tendency is to keep as much of the old pattern in the new design as possible.

We suffer from corrupt and inefficient government in our cities; but if it is not too utterly corrupt, it is next to impossible to get our citizens to do anything about it. And when they are aroused to elect a reform administration, the reforms are usually so ineffective that there is always imminent danger of the majority voting in the forces of evil again.

It is true that we have experimental schools; and after years and years of discouraging effort, some of these experiments are gradually given an opportunity to make limited demonstrations here and there; but you educators know how slow the process is.

Now, why is this process slow? Is it because we have so much time that there is no need for haste? Is it because we are producing such a satisfactory brand of citizenship now that we can afford to let well enough alone? Or is it, perchance, that Americans are naturally so conservative that great changes are not to be expected?

We all know that it is none of these. We have little time. Staggering problems are pressing upon us, requiring a degree of understanding that we have not developed. Our citizens are not only unequipped to cope with these new problems, but are pitifully unable, often, to maintain standards of ordinary honesty and decency in their municipal and state, and sometimes even in their national, governments.

As for conservatism, the average American is not in the least averse to change. Millions of Americans turn in fine, serviceable and efficient automobiles annually because each insists upon having a car with a few new ideas in it.

You may criticise that attitude. You may call it flashy. You may call it extravagant. The point is that you cannot call it conservative.

But how about the matter of human relations in America,

and the American's attitude toward them? Our educators will agree, I think, that there can be no more important problem. All morality, all character, all so-called spiritual development can be measured only in terms of human relations and the responsibilities which they entail. But how many Americans, up to March 4, 1933, evinced any particular eagerness for new ideas in that direction?

Have our American schools so advanced in their understanding of human relations as to be able to sell us a better code of human conduct year after year? Have they kept pace, say, with the motorcar industry?

Some may think these questions unfair. We cannot draw an analogy, they will say, between the development of human character and the development of a machine. The schools, they will protest, do teach good citizenship. They uphold the moral code. They exalt virtue and warn against vice. And if it happens that crime and corruption fill the land, the responsibility lies with the criminal and the corrupt, not with an educational system which has consistently upheld the opposite ideal.

In other words, we should judge our educational system by its intentions—not by its results. Well, we will not argue the point. Let us ask, rather, why do we get such great and such rapid results in the field of chemistry and physics, and why are results so slow and so disappointing in the matter of human conduct and of human character?

Is it because we understand the laws of chemistry and of physics, and can therefore teach them accurately and exactly, whereas we do not know the laws of moral and spiritual development and cannot be certain as to just what we *should* teach?

No. *The exact opposite is the case.*

We do not know the laws of chemistry and physics. We *know* we do not—*therefore we have to find out what they are,* and therefore we do make appreciable progress.

As to moral conduct, however, we are sure that we know it all to start with. Therefore, we don't have to learn anything. Therefore, no matter how human relations may change, we make little change in our teaching—at least until conditions get so terrible that no one takes the old teachings seriously any longer, and we don't even believe them ourselves.

Therefore, we do not make appreciable progress.

One result of this sort of moral education is that many students do not see the point and eventually become bad men, while others readily accept it and become good men. And the result upon society, as a rule, is that many of the good do more harm than the bad.

It has been good men, not bad, who have given us our worst government. It was good men, not bad, who have led us into wars. It was good men who exploited labor most abominably. It was good men, as a rule, who recently wrecked our financial system and brought millions to the verge of starvation.

These were men of character. If they had been mere self-indulgent weaklings, they would never have been exalted to such places of power. They were educated, according to our existing concept of education, both intellectually and morally. You could trust them absolutely not to pick your pocket or to hit you over the head with a lead pipe. They were fine husbands and fathers. They fairly doted on their families, and they denied themselves leisure, often, preferring to toil and scheme early and late to make it possible for those families to live like royalty. That is, like royalty used to live.

No, they were not immoral. Some of them did not even break the law. But they broke the country. They were educated but they didn't know any better. For they were not educated in human relations as they are and had no conception of their responsibilities. They were educated in the code of human relations as they used to be; and their conduct was conduct which used to be all right.

They understood the necessity for sweeping changes in industry; for production had become a matter of fact-finding, and when they found a way to produce more goods with less overhead, they did not hesitate to scrap their obsolescent machinery. But they saw no necessity for any change in man's attitude toward man. That subject had never been presented in terms of fact-finding at all. Those who proposed sweeping changes in this field—that is, changes in keeping with the sweep of events—were looked upon as extremists. It seemed normal, and Americans generally were educated to think of it as normal, that in a world where human relations were changing with dazzling rapidity, our attitude toward human problems should change only by imperceptible degrees.

We called this attitude conservatism although, as we must now perceive, nothing whatever was conserved by it.

We cannot conserve the values of the past by trying to conserve the formulas of the past. A course of conduct which is normal and constructive in an agrarian age may become abnormal and destructive in a machine age.

"The letter killeth. Only the spirit giveth life." Orthodoxy in morals is the end of true morality; for by overemphasizing those virtues which were once successfully developed, it neglects to call attention to the virtues which most need to be developed now.

Similarly, orthodoxy in teaching is the death of education. Teaching our children *what* to think cannot possibly fit them for life in these changing times. *We do not know* what they should think; for they must deal with things which we know nothing about. We must teach them *how* to think—how to find out about those things, so that they may apply this new knowledge to the new problems with which they will inevitably be faced.

That way, I am convinced, lies education. With the old approach, much of our education becomes a lie. Naive ignorance is dangerous enough, but confident knowledge of things that have ceased to be true is more dangerous. The toughest task before the business man today is not the learning of business. It is the unlearning of what he was taught was business—what he is positively sure is business because it used to be business.

We may even learn a lot of new truths; but if we simply add them to our ancient superstitions, we are very likely to be sunk. That is how business was so recently sunk. American business men generally had come to see that high wages meant high buying power; and in the early days of the depression they made more or less effort to keep wages up. That was a wonderful new thing in history, but it didn't work. It didn't work because we tried to combine that idea with a lot of fatal knowledge which we had not yet unlearned.

We tried to keep wages at a certain level, for instance, when if we had studied all the facts, we would have seen that that level was still not high enough to provide a market for the enormous and constantly increasing output of our machine age. So we couldn't sell and we had to slow production down; and we laid off men and created unemployment and put still further crimps in the public's buying power. And when the public inevitably bought still less, we dropped the high-wage theory as impractical and brought on conditions of panic and paralysis.

Now, we did that because we didn't know any better; and we didn't know any better, not because of any natural stupidity, but because we had not been properly educated.

Oh, I know what educators can say. They can say that we business men would not permit the schools to tackle the problem of human relations in the same bold, experimental, fact-finding way in which they tackle the problems of chemistry and physics.

That's true. The schools have turned out graduates so densely ignorant of the things which most needed to be known that these graduates would not permit the schools to turn out a better product. There is no need, then, of the pot calling the kettle black. Traditional thinking was our common enemy. Neither the best type of business nor the best type of education could, in the very nature of things, result from it. And so, in the course of time, we had a nation with more graduates per square foot than had ever been known before, utterly baffled by the problem of how to keep a people with great surpluses of all of life's necessities from suffering individually for the want of them.

I think I can say without even being accused of partisanship, that had it not been for the extraordinary leadership of President Roosevelt, America would very likely have been thrown into some such social convulsion as has occurred in several European countries. And had there been such a convulsion, it would not have been the fault of radical tendencies in America, but of a fixed and firm American tradition which would not permit us to consider and to deal with fundamental changes when those fundamental changes were actually taking place. We had to wait for a collapse.

What, I wonder, would any of us think of a system of physical education, if its graduates uniformly waited for a physical collapse before taking any measures to guard their health? We know that many individuals are thus neglectful, but the course is not advocated and not accepted as normal. It is chiefly in the matter of human relations—of the actual structure of society—that we have learned not to expect results from our educational efforts.

This structure is basically economic. It changes as our economic mechanism changes; and if in this period of the greatest and most rapid changes in human history, we do not find out what these changes are, and how they relate us to other human beings, we shall be powerless to deal with the human problems which arise.

If these changes were a great mystery and beyond the province of human investigations, perhaps the only hope for society would be to keep its members regimented as far as possible, under high-pressure policing, according to some code of conduct handed down to us from Heaven knows where. But our economic structure, complicated as it may be, is no more mysterious than the human body; and the human relations which are determined by it can be and would be understood and dealt with, if it were our educational practice to approach the problem in an objective, fact-finding way.

Now, I do not presume to give you the formula for this new and necessary kind of teaching. You *have* the formula already and are using it constantly. In the scientific courses—that is, the courses which aim not merely at the handing down of old knowledge but the digging up of knowledge which has never been known before—students are encouraged to experiment and to make a note of everything that happens. And when they complete an experiment successfully, they are encouraged to apply the principles which they have learned to the perfection of chemical, mechanical and electrical apparatus which, if perfected, will still further change human relations.

But are they encouraged to employ this method in solving the problems of these new human relations? You educators know, better than I can tell you.

Is it suggested that they clean up their cities by this method? Or are they not exhorted, rather, to stick to the traditional method —the method by which we periodically throw bad men out of office and elect good men to do the bad things thereafter?

Is it suggested that, having learned the scientific method, they try their hands at creating an up-to-date Constitution for America, in place of one which divides us into now meaningless geographical districts and makes it next to impossible for our so-called representatives to achieve a national view?

Is it suggested that they find out what are the moral principles governing human conduct in this machine age and that they employ fact-finding for the purpose of constructing a practical moral code? Or are they not urged, rather, to follow the codes which were practical in societies where human relations were altogether different?

We cannot make good citizens of those who cannot see their actual relation to society, and cannot therefore become conscious of their actual responsibilities. We may make them obedient and law-abiding, and they may even be well intentioned and kind. But good citizenship demands a positive, constructive attitude toward society, and an understanding of the relationships involved. We cannot develop this by telling children to be good, or even by priming them with the formulas of goodness which actually were effective and constructive in the days when human society was put together in very different ways.

What we do get from this attempt to fasten ancient formulas upon modern minds—and calling the process education—is not even the conservatism which seems to be our aim. When we try to teach people what to think, instead of how to think, we get such extremes of conduct as to threaten our social stability.

I refer to the law of pendulum thinking.

Now it is possible that you never heard of any law by that particular name. I do not care about that. I do not care what you call it, and if you can give it a better name, I shall not be offended. But the law is obvious and it works like this.

Whenever a society hangs on to a formula as long as it can, and does not change it when, as, and if the facts disclose that it needs changing, it eventually lets go of that formula with a violent reaction. It does not go back to some moderate, more rational position. It swings definitely to the opposite extreme; and when this position becomes no longer tenable, back it goes again, away past the point of equilibrium, toward the first or a similar extreme once more.

America has seemingly been saved in the nick of time from such a catastrophe by the sudden introduction of experiment and fact-finding government and business relations, before the point of desperation had quite been reached. The secret of President Roosevelt's leadership cannot be found either in his charming personality or in his exceptional political acumen. Fortunately, he is well equipped with both; and considering the seriousness of the national crisis, we may well rejoice that he is so endowed. Nevertheless, the essential greatness of the President lies in the fact that he has not appealed to tradition or to prejudice. He has not even appealed to "public opinion," for the crisis was one in which government by opinion would not do. He did not say: "This is my platform, and I shall abide by it," or "This is my creed and I shall remain loyal."

What he said in effect was: "This is the trouble; and *this* is one of the things which we are going to try in seeking to effect a cure. If the experiment is successful, we shall go on with it. If it fails, we shall abandon it and try something else."

The nation is not out of danger yet by any means. Already the voice of the Tory is heard in the land, not with any contention that the President is ignoring the facts, but that he is violating the sacred traditions of Pioneer Times, when everybody of necessity did business according to his individual hunches and protected his profits with his individual six-shooter.

There is great promise, however, that America will now turn

permanently to fact-finding in the arrangement of its economic affairs, and this promise must be of peculiar interest to educators. For with fact-finding accepted as the normal approach to the study of human relations, the schools will be freed to educate in a sense in which they have not been able to educate before.

Education, I understand, means drawing out—the drawing out of the individual mind into a greater and greater awareness—especially awareness of one's relations to the community and the acceptance of the responsibilities which they suggest. But heretofore our schools, even if the business interests had permitted it, could scarcely have initiated their students into an understanding of America with any certainty that the understanding would make for effective loyalty and devotion.

For America, with all its prosperity, was chaotic; and drawing out the mind of youth into an awareness of this chaos, while it might lead some to seek the way of law and order, was quite likely to result in the acceptance of chaos as a fundamental condition of life. Millions at least were so educated—in and outside the schools. The result was cynicism, individualism, irresponsibility—the negation of any purpose and plan, and therefore of any real faith, in life.

At last, however, we have the beginnings of an ordered society in this machine age. By fact-finding, we have discovered that it did have a human purpose after all. The function of business, we have discovered, is to get goods to people—not merely to offer goods for sale, but to enable the masses to buy. This, of course, will necessitate a plan; and the plan is being worked out, not according to anybody's Utopian dreams but with a direct and scientific approach to the social facts.

Under this plan, whatever its eventual details may prove to be, we know that the masses must have a more adequate share of the wealth that is produced. We know also that they must have leisure, else they cannot consume the masses of things which, under science, have become available now.

But they must have more than that. They must have responsibility—an awareness of their relation to the whole plan and consequent interest in its success.

All this could not be taught before, because it was never true before. Earnest critics of our social planlessness could proclaim their theories; but so could self-seeking demagogues, while dreary traditionalists chanted their outworn formulas of the past. There might be endless debate, but the economic struggle was so strenuous that few could give attention to the merits of the debate. Under the circumstances, we can hardly wonder that education failed.

But that era, it appears, is over. The day of economic order and of social understanding has dawned. Our opinions may differ widely still, but now it doesn't matter. We are through, I hope, with following opinions. We are now after the facts of everybody's relation to everybody else.

Nor will the intense struggle for individual existence divert us now from considering these facts. For that struggle has now become collective, and it is to everybody's individual interest to see to it that everybody else's interest is considered.

That is the meaning of the New Deal. That is the meaning of all these business codes; and those who are viewing the event in terms of particular criticism are missing the point entirely. It may be that this Administration, which I have considered so wise, is doing wrong and foolish things. But if so, in the very nature of this fact-finding program, errors will be corrected as they are proven to be errors. Some plan which will take everybody into consideration must eventuate; and it must provide for consumption by the masses of the tremendous volume of wealth which the masses, under science and scientific management, are now able to produce.

Fascism does not provide for that. Hitlerism, based on the archaic theory that might makes right and the end justifies the means, can have no enduring social plan. Nor does communism provide for it; although, to be fair to the great Russian experimenters, we must recognize that it is their ultimate intention to provide for everybody when in the course of time everybody shall have been made over into an unquestioning Communist.

In America, however, regardless of our conflicting theories, we may all unite in finding out just what plan will make such ample provision for everybody. Our machine has become so productive that capitalism cannot continue unless adequate consumption is provided for; and if, as some contend, capitalism cannot continue if there *is* such adequate consumption, none of us need worry. So long as everybody is provided with wealth, leisure, security and culture, and in the nature of this provision, becomes so definitely and understandably related to the whole scheme that social responsibility may normally be expected, it will make little difference whether we call it capitalism or something else.

Education in this new age will be effective because it will be dealing not with the worn-out axioms of former ages, nor with the other-worldly dreams of those who can find no place in their Utopias for the facts of human nature. It will be effective because it will be dealing with actualities. And there is no reason why it should not be as effective in the development of social and spiritual values as it now is in the development of material achievements.

Mass Prosperity and Medical Care—A Business Man's Viewpoint *

FRIENDS OF THE RADIO AUDIENCE:

All too often, the worst thing about sickness is not the sickness itself. Thousands of people recover from severe illnesses or accidents, only to find themselves unable to recover from the financial ruin which their illness has brought about. It is not the sickness which ruined them, but the *cost* of the sickness and the *cost* of medical care.

This is, perhaps, our most typical American tragedy.

I am not thinking of the mere loss in dollars and cents. I am thinking also of the loss in morale—the spiritual defeat involved in such experiences.

The real value of systematic saving cannot be measured merely by the amount saved; and the havoc created by the melting away of the results of years and years of prudent living cannot be measured by the number of dollars lost.

One may win a fortune in the sweepstakes, but it is not likely to do him much good. The good life is the life which accepts and discharges its responsibilities; and the family which, by careful planning, and the careful budgeting of outgo with relation to income, succeeds in saving even a very modest amount, achieves something far more important than the amount saved.

Such a family achieves a constructive character and a constructive social relationship. It achieves confidence, also, and a technique of competence, even though the amount saved can hardly be called a competence. The drifter who is the mere

* A broadcast in a series on DOCTORS, DOLLARS, and DISEASE, presented by the National Advisory Council on Radio in Education, over a nation-wide network of the Columbia Broadcasting System—December 3, 1934.

recipient of good fortune will almost certainly continue to drift until not only the fortune, but he himself is on the rocks.

It has generally been impossible, however, to budget the cost of medical care. Savings of a lifetime, then, may easily be swept away. People who had been competent and confident then become uncertain and discouraged. Often the injustice rankles and one's whole outlook becomes sour and destructive, unfitting him to deal rationally with any of his problems. This is an ideal breeding ground for the most dangerous kind of radicalism.

I am not speaking of real radicalism—radicalism founded upon reasonable social criticism. I am speaking of radicalism founded upon that sense of injuries endured which often makes reasonable thinking impossible.

Thousands of American families have been reduced to despair by the as yet unbudgetable costs of sickness and of medical service. After their savings have gone, they have borrowed money—often from loan sharks because they could not get it from any other source—and have *never* been able to get out of the clutches of the sharks.

Other thousands, to be sure, secure medical attention without paying for it. Every doctor in the country is sadly aware of that. There is probably no business on earth which has such a high percentage of utterly uncollectible bills. And *that* means, as a rule, that those who *do* pay their doctor's bills pay not only for the medical attention which they receive but for the medical attention received by those who do not pay.

This, of course, is tough on the doctors. With fees necessarily so high, people as a rule do not consult their doctors when they should. They put it off until the condition becomes serious—when the chance of a cure will be greatly lessened and the bill necessarily much higher than it would be otherwise.

Each doctor, of course, hopes to get a sufficient number of rich patients so that he can afford to give his services freely to those who cannot pay. But there is a catch in that. For there are more doctors than there are millionaires; and if the average doctor is to get a good living, he must get it somehow from people of limited means.

Doctors, of course, aim to give the same conscientious service to rich and poor. Regardless of such good intentions, however, most of those patients whose income is extremely limited *cannot get the same service* which the more fortunate can get. If the doctor, for instance, should advise them to consult this and that high priced specialist, he knows very well that they can't go. The average patient, therefore, is limited to the service which one family doctor, working alone, can give him; and he finds even this service so expensive that he usually postpones seeing the doctor until disease has made such inroads on his system that the doctor's chances of helping him are greatly reduced.

Cancer, for instance, is curable in its earliest stages; and if one goes to a competent physician at the first sign of cancer, the chances of his being saved from cancer are excellent. But one does not go to a competent physician at the first sign of anything. He does not, as a rule, go to a doctor until he is too sick to go to work. And because he can't work, his income stops and he therefore either uses up his savings or does not pay his bill. This situation is so bad for both doctors and patients that it makes a new deal in medical care absolutely necessary.

Imagine our treating our automobiles in the way in which we customarily treat our bodies. Imagine our never having our cars examined and serviced before they break down. This would not only be mighty expensive to car owners, but, because so few people could pay such bills, the repair men themselves would largely be out of work.

Many of us today, if we have an ache or a pain, trot over to the drugstore to get some pain killer. By the same logic, if we hear our engine making some abnormal noise, we would buy some cotton with which to plug our ears.

We know better than to treat our cars that way; and we should know better than to treat our bodies that way. Since this is our custom, however, the medical profession has generally organized in the past to undertake the very expensive job of trying to cure the sick, rather than the relatively inexpensive job of keeping well folks well.

As a result of this the average doctor makes such a poor living that doctors often remark to each other that the profession is overcrowded. It isn't. In the new way that the doctors and the public are now at last beginning to organize, there will soon be far less sickness, far lower costs for medical care, yet far greater incomes for physicians, and a demand for more physicians than our medical colleges, with their present facilities, will be able to supply.

This is a matter upon which a business man has a right to speak. I can suggest nothing in the way of medical science or medical technique; but I can speak of business problems, and this problem of making any human service profitable is a business problem.

Henry Ford was told that the automobile business was overcrowded. (And may I say to any doctor who may be listening in, that I am not suggesting that he start an operation factory, with patients coming in on moving belts, according to the technique of automobile production. I simply say that there are business principles which apply to every business, and there is something which the medical business can learn from Ford's experience.)

Ford was told that so few people were able to pay for such expensive things as automobiles that altogether too many people were engaged in manufacturing them. But Ford had another idea. These car producers, he noted, were providing cars for the rich. He set out to provide cars for the masses instead, at a price which the masses could afford to pay.

We know what happened. He was ridiculed of course. But the masses, who had never had this kind of transportation before, now got cars. And because the masses got cars, Ford got profits, and the whole automobile industry soon followed Ford's example. In a little while, the masses were not only buying cars but buying *better* cars than the rich had ever been able to buy before; and there was highly profitable work for many thousands of experts and professionals, and many hundreds of thousands of nonprofessional assistants, in a line which was supposed to be overcrowded when a few hundred at most had been engaged in it.

The traditional, official, ultraregular type of business mind was appalled and baffled by this demonstration, just as some doctors are now confused by recent developments in medical practice.

In Los Angeles, for instance, a group of leading physicians—diagnosticians and specialists—undertook to give the most scientific medical care to their patients at a low, fixed, monthly rate—about two dollars a month. They were soon swamped with patients. To be exact, they now have 45,000 patients who are each paying two dollars a month for this medical service. Obviously, they could not treat 45,000 very sick persons, nor could 45,000 very sick persons procure adequate treatment from their family doctors for $90,000 a month. As it is, this Los Angeles clinic, under the administration of Dr. H. Clifford Loos, pays first attention to the prevention of disease—to keeping people well. And because it concentrates on preventive medicine and brings the 45,000 under periodical examination, it is able to provide all who *do* become sick with the more expensive attention which the sick require, including hospital care—all for a regular charge of two dollars a month.

I am sorry to report that the answer of the County Medical Society to this great and beneficent effort to keep the masses well, was an attempt to exclude Dr. Loos and his associates from the Society.

That, however, cannot stop the movement, for Los Angeles is but one of a number of cities where similar enterprises are being launched. Doctors everywhere are divided. Some medical societies have come out enthusiastically for the movement and some are issuing warnings against it. Some even who have hitherto been objecting are now beginning to understand and are entering the experimental field themselves.

We laymen must let the doctors fight that out. The point is that the masses want health; and that they can secure health, with adequate, scientific medical attention, *for a fixed charge which can be budgeted*—that is, a charge which can be known in advance as definitely as rent is known—and a charge so low that it can readily be paid by a large majority of our people. That has been demonstrated in Los Angeles. It is being demonstrated in some other cities; and the Committee on the Cost of Medical Care, after studying the problem in all its phases, for more than five years, was forced to conclude that this form of medical practice is practical throughout the nation. That means that such low-cost medical care can be organized in every town where you and your friends and neighbors demand this solution of their most tragic problem.

It solves their problem because health is wealth. *Health,* which enables us to keep on earning, *can pay for itself,* whereas sickness, which destroys our earning power, can not. The health of the masses is the most important of all factors creating individual buying power and mass prosperity; and its importance is now recognized by our national Administration. I suggest that those interested write to President Roosevelt or to the Secretary of Labor, Miss Frances Perkins, who has been charged with the responsibility of working out such a legislative program as will best promote mass health.

The New Deal and American Democracy *

History seems to have no parallel to that amazing month of March, 1933, following the inauguration of Franklin D. Roosevelt as President of the United States.

The world has become used in recent years to political upheavals, but the election of Mr. Roosevelt was not a political upheaval.

Mr. Roosevelt was never a radical. He had not been a pioneer in the cause of social planning. He had been an able Governor of New York State, but there was nothing spectacular in his Administration. He was not nominated for the Presidency because of his political record, nor because of any great popular clamor for his nomination. He owed his nomination very largely to the support of delegates who were not particularly interested in him but who, after the manner of politicians generally, were particularly interested in their own political advancement; and he owed his election to the fact that the nation was in the depths of economic depression.

In European countries, a severe economic depression seems always to be a signal for the rise of some great radical movement; but no such movement had yet appeared in America in the fall of 1932 when the presidential elections took place. Unquestionably, I think, some such movement would have appeared if President Hoover had been re-elected. But American voters, instead of turning to radicalism in politics, had tended rather to become cynical concerning politics; and in the 1932 elections, the Socialist and Communist votes were politically negligible.

It is hardly correct to say that a large majority of the voters voted for Mr. Roosevelt. He was elected by a large majority,

* Address before the Board of Trade and Rotary Club at a joint meeting in Vancouver, British Columbia—August 28, 1934.

but I think it will be generally conceded in America that the vote which elected Roosevelt was not so much a vote for him as an expression of lack of confidence in the Republican Administration.

In the United States, it must be remembered, the two political parties did not stand for two distinct political philosophies. No one could seriously say that one party was conservative, for instance, and the other liberal. Each party had its reactionaries and its radicals, with all the various shades of political opinion in between; but elections, it must be confessed, were usually contests for the spoils of office and had little to do with political convictions.

Not that the average American was without political convictions. In the American political setup, however, the voter with convictions usually battled for them within his party; and even if he lost the battle, he did not as a rule desert his party. The other party, he told himself, was equally bad or worse; and to vote for it by way of punishing his own party would merely result in his losing prestige in his own party where, if he remained loyal, he might continue to fight for his convictions.

In its appeal to the voters, of course, each party claimed to stand for all that was good and true, but relatively few were fooled by this appeal. The average American, even though a party member, was quite willing to admit between campaigns that one party was as bad as the other; but the Republican party had one distinct advantage. For several decades America had generally been prosperous, and this prosperity had happened under Republican administrations. The Republicans, therefore, never failed to capitalize this coincidence and always referred to prosperity as Republican prosperity.

But the Republicans worked this trick once too often. If, in 1928, they had foreseen the depression, and proposed some measures for defending the nation against it, their future history might have been much different. But instead of that, they raised the old battle cry once more. They called on the voters to continue this Republican prosperity by electing Hoover; and the voters elected Hoover. The following October, the depression for which Mr. Hoover was in nowise responsible, struck.

The American public, however, was not so politically gullible as it might seem. Many laughed, to be sure, at the embarrassment of the Republican leaders, but there was no tendency, during the first year of the depression, to hold the Republican party responsible for it. President Hoover acted, it was generally felt, much as any American president would have acted under the circumstances. No financial measures were adopted without consulting the great financial leaders; and the great industrial and business executives of America, regardless of their party affiliations, were frequently called into conference. No one questioned the President's integrity; and America felt itself rather fortunate, on the whole, that a great engineer and business man with such a firsthand knowledge of world conditions, was now at the helm.

Only as the years dragged on, and the depression deepened, did any considerable change of sentiment appear. But when, in 1932, the Administration policies had so signally failed that unemployment reached the staggering total of fifteen million, it seemed that any candidate nominated by the Democratic party would probably be elected.

This made things easy for Candidate Roosevelt, if he were only careful not to alienate any considerable section of the electorate. And he was careful. He talked of a "New Deal," but he talked vaguely; and there is no reason to believe that even he was thinking of the sort of deal which eventually was dealt.

He was an excellent candidate. Personally, he was charming. His voice over the radio was easy to listen to, whereas President Hoover's seemed somewhat distant and official. And when his political record was examined, it more than passed inspection. That record not only showed that he had fought consistently for clean politics, against the most corrupt elements within his own party, but that he was essentially conservative, with no leanings toward socialism or the overthrow of American political institutions.

Unless this peculiar political setup is understood, it will be very difficult for Europeans or even Canadians to grasp the meaning of America's New Deal.

The New Deal was not the result of a political victory on the part of those who favored it. It was not the result of any nationwide swing toward radicalism or Fascism during the presidential campaign of 1932. The American New Deal is the very antithesis of Fascism. It is not only democratic, in harmony with the deep-seated American desire for democracy, but America under the New Deal is much more democratic than America ever was before.

The New Deal marks the end of an economic era in America. Instead of marking the end of American democracy, however, it marks the realization of American democracy.

Mr. Roosevelt was elected in November, 1932, but did not take office until the following March. In the meantime, an economic situation which, for three years, had steadily gone from bad to worse, came to a head. Thousands of small banks throughout the country had closed their doors. Now, some of the supposedly strongest institutions in the larger cities were unable to pay off their depositors and moratoriums were being declared in state after state. On the day of President Roosevelt's inauguration, banking was temporarily suspended almost everywhere, and the first act of the new President was to order every bank in the nation closed.

One might have supposed that this would have thrown the nation into panic, but it had the opposite effect; for it was in that moment that the New Deal was really born.

In that moment, all America seemed to realize that a chapter of American history had ended. There was no suggestion that we had tried the Republican way of doing things and were now going to try the Democratic party's way. The feeling was, rather, that we were through with the old way, which Republicans and Democrats had both supported, and were now entering upon a wholly new course.

What the course would be few were prepared to guess; but the fact that we were off the old road and must now go somewhere appealed to the American spirit. Other nations have had this same experience when a new leader has suddenly appeared; and if, in that moment, President Roosevelt had declared himself a dictator, he would doubtless have achieved a great and enthusiastic following.

But he did something far wiser and far more effective. He took the whole nation into his confidence and admitted, over the radio, that he did not know what to do. The time had come, he said in effect, for the American people to *find out what to do,* instead of blindly following political and economic precedents. His counsellors, it became apparent, were not politicians. Americans generally were disgusted with politicians and longed for an opportunity to escape from a system under which government had largely become a matter of political manipulation. Nor were they the great heads of corporations to whom the nation had formerly looked for economic wisdom. They were scientists, rather—men of research recruited largely from the faculties of our universities—to whom the journalists referred as the President's "Brain Trust."

And Americans generally—Republicans and Democrats—rather liked that. They liked the idea of having brains in their government, in place of oratory and political ambition, especially if the brains did not know everything to start with but were willing to find out what remedies to apply.

And they liked it especially when the President, instead of trying to usurp authority, asked the American people to decide whether, in this emergency, they wanted him or Congress to become their leader.

Officially, he asked Congress to delegate certain emergency powers to him. But he did not stop with that. He could not order Congress to do any such thing. In some countries, to be sure, dictators have done just that; and if a dictator can control the army and navy, it can be done. The New Deal in America, however, cannot be accounted for in any such way. In America, there was no political revolution. It was a scientific revolution. It was a revolution made possible very largely by that recent scientific development—radio.

There was a power in America before which all congressmen quailed. That was the power of the voters in their respective districts. In ordinary times, however, the politicians in each district, who played politics the year around, were usually able to control the voters who took up politics, as a rule, only for a short period before election. Even though a congressman knew nothing about national issues, that did not disqualify him for Congress. It might *qualify* him; for he could secure his election, often, by special promises to certain constituents to get them special favors, whereas a congressman who was principally interested in the welfare of the whole nation would not have the time to play the kind of politics by which these special favors could be secured.

But these were not ordinary times, and the voters of every district knew that they were not ordinary times. Unemployment was not a local issue. The financial collapse was not basically local; and these district minded politicans were hardly the leaders which the voters of those districts wanted now. In former days, to be sure, they might have looked to their congressmen for information as to what was really happening in Washington. With the radio in their homes, however, and with President Roosevelt talking intimately to them, they often knew more about what was happening in Washington than their own congressmen seemed to know.

When President Roosevelt asked Congress for this emergency authority, then, he did not depend upon how the congressmen might feel. He asked the American people how they felt about it; and it was the American people, not the President, who really told their congressmen what to do.

To refer to President Roosevelt as a dictator is to misunderstand the whole story; for not only has he followed the Constitution literally but he has enabled the people to dictate to their politicians in a way which never seemed quite possible before. Before Roosevelt's election, millions of Americans were becoming quite discouraged with democracy. They did not wish to give it up; but it had become a matter of common observation that the politicians, not the people, really ruled. The only alternative, however, had seemed to be to hold mass meetings and to arouse the citizens to action against the course of their elected leaders; and there were two reasons why such a course did not seem feasible. In the first place, people cannot think their problems through in a mass meeting. The best they can do is to elect some leader to be their representative, and the leaders so elected in the excitement of a mass meeting are quite likely to be the same type of self-seeking politicians against whose rule the masses have become aroused.

Nor have they ever dared before to delegate extraordinary powers to their Chief Executive, excepting in war. Their whole theory of government has been opposed to this; and while the emergency of 1933 was such that they might temporarily have endorsed any course which the President might suggest, an ever growing minority would surely have viewed the course of any dictator with suspicion.

When President Roosevelt suggested a course of government-by-fact-finding, however, to replace the old habit of government-by-opinion, he won the confidence of the rank and file of both the Republican and Democratic parties. What the masses really wanted, obviously, was not some particular answer, but the *correct answer* to their present problem. They didn't know the answer; but if the problem were studied in a fact-finding way, instead of being debated by opinionated orators, there was a promise at least that a solution might be found.

That was the spirit in which Americans began to follow Roosevelt. They have not followed him blindly. They have not followed him as they might follow a popular hero, only to turn against him at his first misstep. He appealed not merely to their idealism but to their realism. He was a leader who admitted that he could make mistakes, but promised to abandon any experiment, and try something else, whenever it became apparent that the experiment would not work. Instead of setting up a censorship, then, he invited criticism; and never in American history have we had more free speech.

But the movement toward democracy did not end with that. Democracy under fact-finding has come to mean more than political democracy. Under fact-finding, democracy is at last becoming a fact, not merely in American politics, but in American life.

This does not mean socialism. There is nothing socialistic in the New Deal. It does not mean bureaucracy or the administration of industry by the political state. It does mean the recognition, however, of everybody's right to live, and of everybody's right to participate in the economic system upon which everybody must depend for a living.

The most typical and most dramatic feature of the Rooseveltian New Deal has been the National Recovery Administration, usually known as the N. R. A.

The N. R. A. is so utterly contrary to a certain fixed American tradition that, had it been proposed by Mr. Roosevelt during his campaign for the Presidency, Mr. Roosevelt could not possibly have been elected.

This tradition, however, which was so generally accepted by Americans both rich and poor, was not a tradition of democracy. It was a tradition, in fact, which had done more than anything else to keep democracy from being realized. It was the tradition of rugged individualism—the mental picture of human society not as a human society but as an arena in which it was everybody's individual business to fight his way to the top, and somehow get ahead of everybody else.

Of course, there never was any such human society. Even our first settlers were not and could not be ruggedly individualistic. They were colonists and each had to act with regard to the welfare of the colony. Later we became a nation and had to act with reference to the nation's welfare. Otherwise we could never have had any liberty or any democracy.

Even as farmers, we could not be ruggedly individualistic; for farms were operated not by individuals but by families, and each member of the family had to act with reference to the welfare of every other member. In the development of our factories, however, there seemed to be no social order to which it was necessary to acknowledge responsibility. In our private business adventures, we could not visualize any social scheme; and as long as the masses made their living by independent farming, and industries were being launched rapidly enough to keep the ever increasing population of wage workers regularly employed, there was no imperative necessity that we should.

When we had built up the factory system, however, to a point where the masses everywhere became dependent upon its being kept in operation, it did become imperative to achieve some social vision, and Americans paid a great penalty for their failure to achieve it. To be sure, we achieved prosperity; but at best it was prosperity without security. It was a tense, nervous, speculating prosperity; and it crashed at last, as it was inevitable that it must, into the great depression.

Incidentally, the social irresponsibility which we fondly called rugged individualism all but robbed us of the democracy which we had once enjoyed. There can be no real democracy where the masses are denied access to the means of production of wealth; and while our political institutions still survived, and we still went through the motions of democracy, it became more and more apparent that the business speculators, not the people, were the real rulers of America, and that our so-called democracy was largely an empty shell.

This was not and could not be good government; for it was lacking in the first essential of good government, which is social responsibility. In the end, moreover, it turned out that it was not good business. America had sunk into poverty, and was sinking year by year into deeper poverty, not because of any scarcity of the good things of life but because these things could now be produced so efficiently and so abundantly.

Only fact-finding, however, could solve the problem; and the President, working with his so-called Brain Trust, worked out a plan to get buying power into the hands of the masses, so that they could purchase enough to satisfy their wants, to keep the wheels of industry going and to keep themselves employed at sufficiently high wages so that they would continue to have sufficient buying power.

If this were to be done, however, business and industry would have to desert the path of social irresponsibility. That was the elemental principle of the National Industrial Recovery Act which authorized the N.R.A. It was a principle which the average congressman was in no position to understand, and which the average American voter could not understand; and if democracy had continued to be merely an expression of traditional opinions, the N.R.A. could not have happened without a political revolution.

Democracy under fact-finding, however, pointed the way—the recognition by the masses that the problem was a problem which could be solved only by fact-finding, and their notifying their congressmen to give the President authority to act upon his findings.

Not that they understood the Industrial Recovery Act. They did not even know what its provisions were, and neither did many of the congressmen who voted for its passage. They did not even know that the act, instead of limiting democracy, would extend democracy into the affairs with which they were most concerned.

If there had not been such a complete financial collapse, such a revolutionary change could not have happened excepting by political revolution. American business, however, had about reached the end of its rope. It had nothing to suggest as an alternative measure, and fell in with the President's program.

The first necessity was that every industry in the nation be brought under a code; and the first necessity in each code was the raising of wages and the shortening of the workday for all employees. This, however, was not a mere Presidential decree. It was decreed by economic law—now that machine industry had become the economic system upon which everybody depended for his very life. In no other way than by the shortening of the workday could more millions be immediately employed, and thus receive the buying power which it was necessary that they should have if business hoped to increase its sales and industry its production. And by no other way than by the raising of wages could the employed be enabled to increase their buying and thus provide the greater market which industry had to have.

At this point, however, there was considerable confusion. The avowed purpose of the N.R.A. was to "increase prices"; and, in one sense, an increased price was probably necessary for certain industries. With the collapse of the market through unemployment and the practical withdrawal of fifteen million breadwinners and their dependents from the role of regular customers, some industries and many farms were offering their products for less than the cost of production. Obviously, this could not continue indefinitely. Such business men must necessarily go out of business; and if such farmers continued to farm, they must quit trying to raise food for the market and resort to the ancient system of self-contained farming, raising what they could for their own consumption and going without whatever they could not produce.

Many business men, therefore, thought of the N.R.A. as an opportunity for them to raise prices to some level which would insure profits without price competition. With their competitors all bound to the same code, they reasoned, they would not be undersold, and their business troubles would about be over.

Nothing in their business training enabled them to see the fundamental fallacy of such a course. Raising prices on such a basis would not increase mass buying power and could not result in a larger market; whereas a larger market would reduce their overhead and might make their present prices profitable. Raising prices, moreover, would offset any advantages which might be secured from raising wages; for the wage workers with their higher wages could buy no more than before.

In spite of the fact, then, that one object of the N.R.A. was to guarantee profitable prices to business, in place of the existing unprofitable prices, it soon became obvious that these profitable prices could not be arrived at by any agreement to abolish competition and fix a monopoly price. Nor could anything but harm come to business from such a course; for the price so fixed must be a price which the most inefficient units of each industry would find profitable; and with inefficiency setting the pace for industry, the mass consumer could not possibly be well served.

Largely due to the Administration's gold policy, higher commodity prices were achieved. They were higher, however, only when reckoned in dollars. When reckoned in terms of human life, as real prices must be reckoned, they were generally lower than before. When the masses had little or no buying power, even those prices which were below the cost of production, and therefore wholly unprofitable to the producer, were still high enough to be beyond the mass consumer's reach. In spite of the confusing terminology, then, the real object of the N.R.A. was and must have been to bring the products of industry within the reach of the masses; and if prices were raised as wages were raised, this could not have been achieved.

To the extent that American business men began to understand this principle, the N.R.A. became immediately successful. To the extent that they failed to understand it, recovery lagged. The codes, however, were rushed. It was necessary, as someone put it, to harness the industrial horse before it could be driven to market; and even if American business did not entirely understand what it was doing when it consented to the harnessing, the harness was nevertheless on.

As to what wages should be paid, no one could say. Obviously, however, they had to be higher than they had been, even though the industries paying them were not yet profitable; for only sufficient mass buying could make them profitable. Lacking any other way of discovering how high a wage would meet the economic needs of business, as well as the economic needs of the country at large, it was arranged in every code that wages should be agreed upon by collective bargaining.

Here was an extension of democracy for which a great many American business men were not prepared, and it marks one of the striking differences between the American New Deal and Fascism. Under Fascist dictatorship, all democratic institutions must fall, but the first marked for slaughter are usually the labor unions. Under the American New Deal, the labor unions were called to play a most important part in the industrial government of the nation.

Yes, there were misunderstandings and strikes. Many of the labor unions had been organized to fight the employers, just as many employers had organized to fight the unions. The traditions of the old class struggle hung to both types of organization; and to expect them now to co-operate for the common good, without a great deal of suspicion and a great deal of misunderstanding on both sides, would be to indulge in unreasonable expectations. But democracy, after all, is an adventure rather than a formula. It is something to be achieved by practice; and one of the greatest victories of the New Deal was in the relatively little labor trouble which was not amicably adjusted before strikes were called.

The New Deal, of course, included many other things besides the N.R.A., and it must include many adventures which have not yet been launched. It included the setting up of an Agricultural Administration, a task more difficult in many ways than the harnessing of industry. It also included a gigantic program for Public Works, an emergency employment program in co-operation with states and municipalities, a program for relief of home-owners who could not meet their mortgage payments, and a long list of financial reforms which required congressional action along the lines indicated, whether the congressmen could comprehend the necessity for each specific bill or not.

Heretofore, so-called strong executives have sometimes managed to hold a whip hand over Congress by an adroit use of the power of patronage—permitting loyal senators and representatives to nominate their friends and partisans for Federal offices within their states and congressional districts, while refusing to give such political assistance to members of Congress who refused to co-operate with the Administration. But although Mr. Roosevelt is unsurpassed as a political strategist, he could scarcely rely upon such a slight weapon in this emergency. Direct appeals to the people, especially over the radio, proved more effective than any other political strategy could possibly have been; but there was not the slightest hint of demagoguery in any of these appeals.

Not once did he pose as the People's Champion against the conspiracies of Special Privilege. Not once did he interject a note of class prejudice. Always he spoke of the task before the nation—particularly the task of distributing buying power in proportion to our new ability to produce the necessities and comforts of life. There were no villains in his picture of the situation. There was just misunderstanding. Not once did he guarantee that his proposals would surely solve the problem; but the Old Deal had failed, and it was necessary, with all the intelligence and with all the facts which we could muster, to try a new course.

That was the spirit in which the New Deal was launched. That is what made it possible for America to achieve a revolution without any of the outward signs of revolution. The revolution has not only been peaceful; it has been *happy*. It has demonstrated that a social revolution can be not only bloodless but positively good-natured; for although the revolution has not yet been completed, and although millions of Americans are still unemployed, there is a hope and faith and buoyancy throughout the nation, and a confidence not merely that prosperity will return but that the whole problem of poverty amidst plenty is being solved.

The greatest opposition to the New Deal, in fact, comes not from those who have lost faith in it but from those who have found it very successful. For a degree of prosperity has already returned to America; and to some business men, this would seem to be an excellent time for unrestricted unplanned economic action. The restrictions of the industrial codes, however, scarcely permit this. Under the codes, business is not free to exploit either labor or the consumer, as it could and did in the days before this machine civilization had reached its full development. In many ways, business is now freer than it ever was before; but this freedom is freedom to serve, and business men who hope to accumulate without serving will find the codes annoying.

As emergency measures, applied at a time when there were no business opportunities, they considered them all right. Like drunkards recovering from delirium tremens, however, some of them now want to discharge the doctor who brought them back to life and start out on another spree.

It was not for such business men, however, that the New Deal was evolved. It was for business, and for all American business, but for American business which cannot be permanently prosperous unless it does serve all America. I do not think, then, that this rising impatience with the New Deal on the part of business men and industrialists who still seem to be leaders, will result in turning back the clock. There may be temporary setbacks. There may be missteps which will have to be retraced; and the hastily thrown together organizations under which the New Deal made its bow may all be changed. In one way or another, however, business must be co-ordinated in the interest of the mass consumer. Poverty in the midst of plenty must go; and to that end, unemployment, low wages, unnecessarily high prices and inefficiency and waste throughout the whole process of production and distribution must be abolished. The great significance of the American New Deal to date is the promise that all this can happen, and happen quickly, under democracy when democracy is guided by fact-finding research.

How to Make the Most of Life *

FRIENDS OF THE RADIO AUDIENCE—PARTICULARLY THE HIGH SCHOOL STUDENTS THROUGHOUT AMERICA WHO ARE NOW LISTENING IN:

I have been asked to answer the all important question as to how a high school graduate, in this great year of 1937, may make the most of life.

My answer, in three words, is: *I don't know.*

Let's be honest about it. In such changing times as these, we of the older generation are not equipped to tell the younger generation how to live.

For the world in which *we* got our experience has passed away; and it is up to you to learn how to live in a very different kind of world.

That's the fun of being human. Animals and insects do not have to learn much of anything that their ancestors did not know. With human beings, however, all the wisdom that can be handed down to them is not enough.

I might tell you, for instance,—and it would surely be true—that if young people wish to make the most of life, they must be honest and industrious, and they must be temperate and clean minded.

Such virtues are as good as they ever were, but *they are not enough for you.*

For your world is threatened by world war. If you cannot achieve world peace, you can't make much of anything out of life;

---

* Address over a nation-wide hookup of the National Broadcasting Company in co-operation with the Office of Education of the United States Department of the Interior on the occasion of the First National School Assembly Program—May 14, 1937.

and yet, if you are to have peace, you must have what it takes to make peace. Our world in 1914 did not.

We were good, as a rule, in the ways in which our ancestors had told us to be good, but we weren't good enough. The great majority of us were honest, industrious, temperate and clean minded. Also, we were kind, peace loving folks and did not as a rule wish anybody ill.

But world peace was a problem in co-operation on a scale which had never been necessary before, and we were not sufficiently co-operative.

We thought of social problems in terms of our own special interests, and the result could not be anything but war.

You of this generation must learn to think of your special interests in terms of social interest; for there is no other way to peace. You must not only develop the will to co-operate, but you must develop the science and the art of co-operation; and these happen to be things which you cannot learn from us.

You may know me, perhaps, as a business man. They say I made a success in business, along with some thousands of other business men of my time, and perhaps you expect me to lay down certain rules for success.

But wait a minute! Did our generation make a success in business?

It is true that we developed the greatest and most productive machinery which civilization ever knew—machinery capable of producing so much wealth that, for the first time in human history, it became physically possible for every family to have a decent living.

And then, believe it or not, we were so lacking in a social viewpoint that we couldn't run the machines which we had set up. We couldn't keep them going, so we shut them down and threw millions of honest, industrious and competent workers into unemployment; and instead of security and plenty, we had poverty, misery and fear.

Is there anything in that business record of ours to furnish an inspiration to you young men and women?

Some of us, to be sure, got rich; and with our riches, we were able to do a lot of things which other people couldn't do.

We might drink champagne, for instance, when children all over America were crying for milk which they couldn't get. Do you earnest and sincere young people want to do anything like that? I just don't think so. I don't think you would call that sort of thing success. At any rate, that game is about over now; and if we could tell you how we succeeded in what we called business, it wouldn't do you any good.

For the people of these United States have recently made it plain that they aren't going to tolerate that kind of business success much longer. If we are to succeed in business from now on, the people have decreed that we must do it in a way which will serve the common good; and these are days, we must remember, when power has passed into the hands of the people; and when they speak, therefore, we business men must obey.

Some of us business men are still quite angry over this; but you who are choosing a career in life will, I am sure, take note of it. In our day, we might simply ask: "In which line do people seem to be making the most money?" But you, I am sure, in entering a business or profession, will want to know whether it is coming or going; and if it does not promise to serve the people, and to serve them better and better as the years go by, you may make up your minds that there is no future in it.

And you will not only think of service individually, but you will of necessity think of it collectively. As employers or employees or as citizens and voters, you will not be asking merely the question which *we* customarily asked: "How will this proposal affect me and my work?", but also the question: "How much will the people generally profit by it?" And if the people generally do profit by it, you will find that your share of the profits will not only inevitably be adequate but also that it will be *yours* more safely than it can be in any other way in these new times of the rapidly rising power of the masses.

Now, think for a moment of what all this means:

Always, from time immemorial, the masses have had to work

hard and long on the definite job of keeping themselves alive. Prophets and teachers were forever calling their attention to higher things; but they had no resources, no time and no energy to devote to these higher things. Because of our industrial development, however, all that is passing; and the stage is now being set, not merely for a new kind of economic setup, but for a new kind of human life.

Liberty is humanity's most cherished ideal, but the people of the world have never had such liberty as your generation may enjoy.

America means opportunity today in a thousand times greater sense than it ever did before. In our America, at best, there was freedom to make a living. In yours, if you will have it so, there will be freedom for every American to make the most of life.

But freedom, of course, imposes responsibility; and this liberty, greater than humanity has ever known, must carry with it the greatest responsibility. Once it was necessary to consider only ourselves, our families and our immediate neighbors. Now our design for living must consider every family, every community, every state and every nation—must not leave anybody out.

Let me say in defense of our generation that, by developing the machinery of plenty, we did at least lay the foundation for the social and spiritual order which therefore it is now practically possible for you to build. In a sense, then, although we did not know it, we were co-operating with you. It is not with regret, therefore, but with a deep sense of gratitude, that I recall the humble part which I was privileged to play. But yours is the greater task; and in the very nature of the task, you cannot expect much worth-while advice from us, who assumed when we were toiling that we were toiling merely for ourselves.

We have been disciplined by work. *You* must school yourselves to rise beyond mere work. *We* have been disciplined by scarcity. *You* must school yourselves to solve the problems of abundance. *We* have been disciplined by the struggle to get ahead of others. *You* must learn how to get ahead *with* others. *We* have been disciplined by the conflict which we thought would never end—the conflict of man against man. We have now reached a time, however, when that war must end, else the machinery we have developed will become machinery of destruction—used to halt the upward march of the human race. It is up to you, therefore, to learn a way of life—a way of human peace, of human co-operation and of human kinship—which we of the older generations can scarcely comprehend.

We who are about to die salute you! Long live the onward-marching human race!

What Religion Means to Me *

To me, religion is first of all *belief*—not a list of beliefs. It is a *drive toward* ultimate good—not a *conclusion concerning* ultimate good.

It is not a thing to get. It is a force to use; and like other forces, to use as wisely as we can.

I like the word *belief* or *faith* to describe the nature of this force, but if faith is thought of as a force, not as a formula, the opposite of faith is not skepticism or agnosticism or even atheism, but fear.

I believe, intellectually, in God, but I see no particular religious value in such an intellectual conclusion; and if further study should induce me to amend this conclusion, I cannot see that it would particularly affect my religion. I would have the same faith as before—the same confidence in going on and in continuing the search for truth and good.

On the other hand, as I see it, if I were to pin my faith to my present concept of God, it would cease to be faith and become fear. I would become dominated by fear—fear of going any farther in my search for truth, fear of discarding my fixed formula—which seems to me to be about as religious an attitude as fear of walking under a ladder or of meeting a black cat.

The scientist may not know intellectually that the disease which he is studying is curable. But he believes it is; or at any rate, he believes in the great adventure of finding out all that he can find out about the matter; and his faith is so intense that it overcomes even his fear of death or failure. And that, to me, is an excellent religious attitude and the only kind of faith, incidentally, which actually conquers disease. It was men motivated by

* Contribution to widely-syndicated symposium on "Religion—Today and Tomorrow," published May 26, 1934.

such faith who conquered yellow fever. They were true religious leaders. Those who sought to end these plagues by burning witches, and by similar approved concessions to a supposedly angry God, do not seem to me to be true exponents of the religious life.

The great irreligious forces in the world today are fear of growing up; fear especially of intellectual maturity, a fear which causes seeming grownups to cling childishly and superstitiously to the most ancient fairy tales; fear of leaving the beaten track; fear of disobeying the rules handed down to us from former civilizations, even when they obviously do not apply to ours, and fear of any New Deal in politics, economics or theology.

I do not mean by this, that faith is any safeguard or that religion, in the sense I use the term, can be relied upon to make our lives either happy or successful. Religion is the motive power of human progress, not the steering gear. New Deals, unless they are based upon fact-finding, are pretty sure to be disastrous deals. Religion to be effective, then, must be combined with a reverent search for truth; with a reverent effort to know the law—whether we call it God's law or natural law makes little difference if it is the law which actually governs the universe. Since man is essentially social and human life cannot exist apart from human society, the essential facts to be considered in the achievement of the most abundant human life are the facts of human relations. The person whose religious experience consists largely of working himself up into some particular state of mind is undoubtedly religious, but what of it? An automobile running wild is undoubtedly an automobile, but it is only the car which is under scientific control which is of any human use.

On the other hand, religion is all important; for the most expert driver can get nowhere if he is out of gas—without that urge to go. Religion is that urge to live a larger life—to experience, if you will, a life beyond any life which man has experienced. In the childhood of civilization, this usually suggested a picture of individual life beyond the grave; and it also suggested ghosts and hells and all sorts of supernatural terrors. Today, when we are not so sure that human life can be individual, religion is prompting us to help create a better world than man has ever known before. That is why, it seems to me, the modern world has come to say that religion is service. It is, perhaps, more accurate to say that religion under scientific direction will inevitably manifest itself in service. Under another kind of direction, it may manifest itself in persecution and holy war.

Edward A. Filene died in Paris

on September 25, 1937, of complications

following an attack of pneumonia.

His work goes on under the auspices of

TWENTIETH CENTURY FUND, INC.

EDWARD A. FILENE GOOD WILL FUND, INC.

CREDIT UNION NATIONAL ASSOCIATION

CONSUMER DISTRIBUTION CORPORATION

FILENE, Edward A., merchant; pres., chmn. finance com. Wm. Filene's Sons Co.; *b.* Salem, Mass.; *s.* William and Clara (Ballin) F.; pub. and high sch. edn.; LL.D., Lehigh U., 1931, Rollins Coll., 1932, Tulane U., 1935; planner and co-organizer Boston Chamber of Commerce, Chamber of Commerce of U.S. and Internat. Chamber of Commerce; pioneer in applying scientific methods and efficient organization in retail distribution; active in promotion of better organization of production and distribution in U.S. and Europe, "in order to lower costs, eliminate waste, increase wages and profits and raise the general standard of living"; founder and pres. Twentieth Century Fund, organized to study and advance the next steps forward in the social and economic life of the people; organizer of credit union movement in U.S., 1909; founder Credit Union Nat. Extension Bur., 1921, directing organization of coöperative credit assns. through U.S.; founder and past pres. and now mem. exec. com. Credit Union Nat. Assn.; founder and pres. Consumer Distribution Corpn., the central organization for a nat. league of coöperative dept. stores, 1935; founder and pres. Good Will Fund, Inc., 1936; ex-chmn. Metropolitan Planning Commn. of Boston; coörganizer and ex-pres. Pub. Franchise League of Boston; chmn. Mass. State Recovery Bd., 1933-34; was chmn. War Shipping Com. and mem. U.S. Chamber of Commerce Com. for Financing War; served as vice-chmn. exec. com. and chmn. finance com. League to Enforce Peace, organized and financed European Peace awards in Gt. Britain, France, Germany and Italy. Officer Legion of Honor (France); le Cavaliere, Order of the Crown (Italy); Comdr. Order of the White Lion (Czechoslovakia); Great Gold Cross of Merit (Austria). Mem. Advisory Council of Am. Acad. Polit. and Social Science, Acad. Polit. Science; vice pres. Am. Assn. for Labor Legislation; mem. Am. Chamber of Commerce (London), Am. Civic Assn., Am. Economic Assn., Am. Statis. Soc., Beacon Hill Assn., Bostonian Soc., Council on Foreign Relations, Foreign Policy Assn., Nat. Econ. League (exec. council), Nat. Inst. Pub. Affairs (advisory council), Nat. Student Federation (nat. bd. of adv.), Netherland-America Foundation (patron), Nat. Council U.S. Ednl. Assn., Nat. Child Labor Com., Soc. for Advancement of Management, Am. Com. Internat. Chamber of Commerce (vice chmn. distribution commn.), Am. Soc. of French Legion of Honor; life mem. Austro-Am. Inst. of Edn. *Clubs:* Advertising (Boston), Boston City (a founder); Cosmos (Washington); Town Hall (New York); American (Paris). *Author:* The Way Out, 1924; More Profits from Merchandising, 1925; The Model Stock Plan, 1930 (all in Am. and foreign edits.); Successful Living in this Machine Age (Am., British, French, German, Italian, Dutch, Czech. edits.); Next Steps Forward in Retailing, 1937; and very many business and economic articles. *Address:* 426 Washington St., Boston, Mass.

Reproduced (by permission) from "Who's Who in America."